EAST MEADOW PUBLIC LIBRARY

3 1299 00762 7806

D1301170

CIRC STAFF CHECK FOR
...MPANYING DISC

Cutting Edge PowerP...
2007 For Dum...

Maximum Text Contrast

For a dark background

- Dark text provides the worst contrast.
- Text of a similar color provides a better contrast but still isn't legible.
- Light text provides the best contrast.

For a light background

- Light text provides the worst contrast.
- Text of a similar color provides a better contrast but still isn't legible.
- Dark text provides the best contrast.

...B Color Model

RGB is a *color model* that computers understand. Each color has a numeric value that ranges from 0 to 255.

- When all three RGB values are 0, you get black.
- When all three RGB values are 255, you get white.

You can use different combinations of any three integers between 0 and 255 to create about 16 million shades of color. These are some color values:

- **Blue:** R:0; G:0; B:255
- **Green:** R:0; G:255; B:0
- **Red:** R:255; G:0; B:0
- **Yellow:** R:255; G:255; B:0
- **Orange:** R:255; G:153; B:0

Safe Background Colors

Color	Denotes
Blue	Endurance, capability, and vastness
White	Peace and blank space
Black	Sophistication
Violet and purple	Luxury, opulence, spirituality
Gray	Balance and stability

Audio Formats

PowerPoint can accept and play almost all the standard audio formats, including the ones listed here:

- **WAV:** This is the most common sound file format for Microsoft Windows. PowerPoint works well with this format.
- **MP3:** You can insert and play MP3s in PowerPoint — but they're a no-no for slide transition sounds.
- **WMA and ASF:** The same concepts for MP3 apply to WMA, but because it's a proprietary Microsoft format, stay away from it if your presentations need to be shown on a Mac.
- **MID or MIDI:** These are actual music notations that your computer's sound card interprets and plays in real time. To enjoy this type of sound, you should have a high-fidelity sound card. Anything less than that will still do a good job unless you start comparing the sound outputs!
- **AIFF and AU:** These are the other sound formats that PowerPoint accepts. However, it's best you leave them alone — and they'll probably leave you alone too!

For Dummies: Bestselling Book Series for Beginners

Cutting Edge PowerPoint® 2007 For Dummies®

Cheat Sheet

Video Formats

PowerPoint can cope with a plethora of video formats. Here's a rundown:

- **AVI:** AVI has been around for the longest time, and PowerPoint is usually happy with this format unless it has been rendered using a non-standard codec.

- **MOV:** These are Apple QuickTime files that you can play easily on Windows-based machines using the free QuickTime Player application. Alas, PowerPoint is not so benevolent — it can play only really old QuickTime content rendered using obsolete codecs from a decade ago.

- **MPG and MPEG:** Conventional MPEG movies, also called MPEG 1 movies, play well in PowerPoint — and they're the best option if you need to create a presentation to be played on both the Windows and Mac versions of PowerPoint.

  MPEG 2 movies are DVD quality and aren't too PowerPoint friendly — they're more reliant on both hardware and software and might not play in PowerPoint even if they play well in Windows Media Player.

- **WMV and ASF:** When Microsoft first introduced the Windows Media format, both audio and video files used the ASF extension. Later, Microsoft started using the WMV and WMA extensions for video and audio respectively. For all practical purposes, WMV and ASF are identical.

- **Flash:** Flash isn't actually a video format — rather, it's a vector format that supports animation. Not surprisingly, PowerPoint, or for that matter Windows itself, doesn't consider Flash as a native video format. However, you can successfully play Flash movies within PowerPoint.

- **VCD:** VCD (Video CD) files usually have the DAT extension — for all practical purposes, they are MPEG-1 videos. Several tools, including freeware applications, can convert VCD DAT movies to MPEG files without any problem. An online search for VCD to MPEG converter should result in several hits.

- **DVD:** DVD is more of a problem area because it isn't too easy to convert (or decrypt) DVD VOB files to MPEG-2. Even if it were easy, several copyright issues are involved. However, some third-party tools allow you to play DVD movies right inside PowerPoint.

Wiley, the Wiley Publishing logo, For Dummies, the Dummies Man logo, the For Dummies Bestselling Book Series logo and all related trade dress are trademarks or registered trademarks of John Wiley & Sons, Inc. and/or its affiliates. All other trademarks are property of their respective owners.

Copyright © 2007 Wiley Publishing, Inc. All rights reserved. Item 9565-2.

For more information about Wiley Publishing, call 1-800-762-2974.

For Dummies: Bestselling Book Series for Beginners

by **Geetesh Bajaj**

Wiley Publishing, Inc.

Cutting Edge PowerPoint® 2007 For Dummies®

Published by
Wiley Publishing, Inc.
111 River Street
Hoboken, NJ 07030-5774
www.wiley.com

Copyright © 2007 by Wiley Publishing, Inc., Indianapolis, Indiana

Published by Wiley Publishing, Inc., Indianapolis, Indiana

Published simultaneously in Canada

No part of this publication may be reproduced, stored in a retrieval system or transmitted in any form or by any means, electronic, mechanical, photocopying, recording, scanning or otherwise, except as permitted under Sections 107 or 108 of the 1976 United States Copyright Act, without either the prior written permission of the Publisher, or authorization through payment of the appropriate per-copy fee to the Copyright Clearance Center, 222 Rosewood Drive, Danvers, MA 01923, (978) 750-8400, fax (978) 646-8600. Requests to the Publisher for permission should be addressed to the Legal Department, Wiley Publishing, Inc., 10475 Crosspoint Blvd., Indianapolis, IN 46256, (317) 572-3447, fax (317) 572-4355, or online at http://www.wiley.com/go/permissions.

Trademarks: Wiley, the Wiley Publishing logo, For Dummies, the Dummies Man logo, A Reference for the Rest of Us!, The Dummies Way, Dummies Daily, The Fun and Easy Way, Dummies.com, and related trade dress are trademarks or registered trademarks of John Wiley & Sons, Inc. and/or its affiliates in the United States and other countries, and may not be used without written permission. Microsoft and PowerPoint are trademarks or registered trademarks of Microsoft Corporation in the United States and other countries. All other trademarks are the property of their respective owners. Wiley Publishing, Inc., is not associated with any product or vendor mentioned in this book.

LIMIT OF LIABILITY/DISCLAIMER OF WARRANTY: THE PUBLISHER AND THE AUTHOR MAKE NO REPRESENTATIONS OR WARRANTIES WITH RESPECT TO THE ACCURACY OR COMPLETENESS OF THE CONTENTS OF THIS WORK AND SPECIFICALLY DISCLAIM ALL WARRANTIES, INCLUDING WITHOUT LIMITATION WARRANTIES OF FITNESS FOR A PARTICULAR PURPOSE. NO WARRANTY MAY BE CREATED OR EXTENDED BY SALES OR PROMOTIONAL MATERIALS. THE ADVICE AND STRATEGIES CONTAINED HEREIN MAY NOT BE SUITABLE FOR EVERY SITUATION. THIS WORK IS SOLD WITH THE UNDERSTANDING THAT THE PUBLISHER IS NOT ENGAGED IN RENDERING LEGAL, ACCOUNTING, OR OTHER PROFESSIONAL SERVICES. IF PROFESSIONAL ASSISTANCE IS REQUIRED, THE SERVICES OF A COMPETENT PROFESSIONAL PERSON SHOULD BE SOUGHT. NEITHER THE PUBLISHER NOR THE AUTHOR SHALL BE LIABLE FOR DAMAGES ARISING HEREFROM. THE FACT THAT AN ORGANIZATION OR WEBSITE IS REFERRED TO IN THIS WORK AS A CITATION AND/OR A POTENTIAL SOURCE OF FURTHER INFORMATION DOES NOT MEAN THAT THE AUTHOR OR THE PUBLISHER ENDORSES THE INFORMATION THE ORGANIZATION OR WEBSITE MAY PROVIDE OR RECOMMENDATIONS IT MAY MAKE. FURTHER, READERS SHOULD BE AWARE THAT INTERNET WEBSITES LISTED IN THIS WORK MAY HAVE CHANGED OR DISAPPEARED BETWEEN WHEN THIS WORK WAS WRITTEN AND WHEN IT IS READ. FULFILLMENT OF EACH COUPON OFFER IS THE SOLE RESPONSIBILITY OF THE OFFEROR.

For general information on our other products and services, please contact our Customer Care Department within the U.S. at 800-762-2974, outside the U.S. at 317-572-3993, or fax 317-572-4002.

For technical support, please visit www.wiley.com/techsupport.

Wiley also publishes its books in a variety of electronic formats. Some content that appears in print may not be available in electronic books.

Library of Congress Control Number: 2006939599

ISBN: 978-0-470-09565-2

Manufactured in the United States of America

10 9 8 7 6 5 4 3 2 1

WILEY

About the Author

Geetesh Bajaj is based in Hyderabad, India, and he got started with his first PowerPoint presentation more than a decade ago. He has been working with PowerPoint ever since.

Geetesh believes that any presentation is a sum of its elements. Everything in a presentation can be broken down to this element level, and PowerPoint's real power lies in its ability to act as glue for all such elements.

Geetesh contributes regularly to journals and Web sites, and has authored two other PowerPoint books. He's also a Microsoft PowerPoint MVP (Most Valuable Professional) and a regular on Microsoft's PowerPoint newsgroups. Geetesh's own Web site at indezine.com has thousands of pages on PowerPoint usage. It also has a blog, an e-zine, product reviews, free templates and interviews.

Geetesh welcomes comments and suggestions about his books. He can be reached at geetesh@geetesh.com.

Dedication

This book is dedicated to my family.

Author's Acknowledgments

I knew I wanted to write a book like this for a long, long time. Yet, when I actually started on this book, it dawned on me that this would not have been possible without the involvement, encouragement, and existence of so many others.

To begin with, I wish to thank God.

And now for the lesser mortals who make miracles happen . . .

Heading this list is my family: my wife Anu, my parents, and my children.

And thanks to Ellen Finkelstein, who encouraged me to get here. And to Echo Swinford, the amazing tech editor of this book.

Thanks to April Spence, who is my MVP lead at Microsoft. She also helped me go ahead with this whole book concept.

Thanks to acquisitions editor Greg Croy, who probably is the best of his kind on this planet. I couldn't have asked for someone better!

And then this sequence of thanks heads to project editor, Jean Rogers. Thank you, Jean, for all your patience and confidence levels — I needed them both! You are amazing! And to Eric Holmgrem, Jennifer Webb, Virginia Sanders, Mary Lagu, and Laura Moss.

Thank you to all the wonderful folks at Microsoft. I know I won't be able to put all those names here, but here are some of them, in alphabetical order — Richard Bretschneider, Howard Cooperstein, Abhishek Kant, Shu-Fen Cally Ko, John Langhans, Sean O'Driscoll, John Schilling, Jan Shanahan, and Amber Ushka.

Thanks to so many others, including Rick Altman, Joye Argo, Nicole Ha, and Betsy Weber.

Thanks also to the PowerPoint MVP team of whom I am privileged to be a part — others include Bill Dilworth, Troy Chollar, Jim Gordon, Kathy Jacobs, Michael Koerner, Glen Millar, Austin Myers, Shyam Pillai, Brian Reilly, Steve Rindsberg, Glenna Shaw, TAJ Simmons, Mickey Stevens, Julie Terberg, and Shawn Toh. And to Sonia Coleman, who is no longer with us.

Finally, a big thank you to all whose names I have missed here!

Publisher's Acknowledgments

We're proud of this book; please send us your comments through our online registration form located at www.dummies.com/register/.

Some of the people who helped bring this book to market include the following:

Acquisitions, Editorial, and Media Development

Associate Project Editor: Jean Rogers

(Previous Edition: Pat O'Brien)

Executive Editor: Greg Croy

Copy Editors: Virginia Sanders, Mary Lagu

Technical Editor: Echo Swinford

Editorial Manager: Kevin Kirschner

Media Development Specialists: Angela Denny, Kate Jenkins, Steven Kudirka, Kit Malone

Media Development Coordinator: Laura Atkinson

Media Project Supervisor: Laura Moss

Media Development Manager: Laura VanWinkle

Media Development Associate Producer: Richard Graves

Editorial Assistant: Amanda Foxworth

Sr. Editorial Assistant: Cherie Case

Cartoons: Rich Tennant (www.the5thwave.com)

Composition Services

Project Coordinator: Adrienne Martinez

Layout and Graphics: Carl Byers, Joyce Haughey, Stephanie D. Jumper, Laura Pence

Proofreaders: John Greenough, Christine Pingleton, Aptara

Indexer: Aptara

Anniversary Logo Design: Richard Pacifico

Special Help: Andy Hollandbeck

Publishing and Editorial for Technology Dummies

Richard Swadley, Vice President and Executive Group Publisher

Andy Cummings, Vice President and Publisher

Mary Bednarek, Executive Acquisitions Director

Mary C. Corder, Editorial Director

Publishing for Consumer Dummies

Diane Graves Steele, Vice President and Publisher

Joyce Pepple, Acquisitions Director

Composition Services

Gerry Fahey, Vice President of Production Services

Debbie Stailey, Director of Composition Services

Contents at a Glance

Table of Contents

Introduction

··

Welcome to *Cutting Edge PowerPoint 2007 For Dummies,* a book that will show you how to create PowerPoint presentations that will dance and sing.

Millions of PowerPoint presentations are created each day. Some of those poor things are never presented! Probably half of those remaining are presented just once. And an average presentation takes more than two hours to create. That brings forth two questions:

- ✔ Why are so many presentations created?
- ✔ Why are so few reused?

This book gives you the answers to these questions. In the process, you create presentations that are truly cutting edge. Even better, these jaw-dropping presentations will take you less time to create!

By *cutting edge,* I don't mean space age graphics and bouncing animations — rather in this book, *cutting edge* means using PowerPoint's amazing features to create aesthetic presentations that contain the right balance between visual content and text on one hand, and animations and multimedia on the other so that your message can get through to the audience. In short, *cutting edge* in this book translates to creating presentations that will bring you success.

About This Book

If you use PowerPoint, this book is for you.

Cutting Edge PowerPoint 2007 For Dummies contains a treasure trove of tips, ideas, and information. The entire book has been completely updated for Microsoft's latest version of PowerPoint. Best of all, I present it in a way that helps you get results immediately. You're truly on your way to PowerPoint nirvana.

If you want to be known as the PowerPoint wizard in your office, society, or home, you can't do better than to read this book.

All the information contained within these covers comes from my years of experience gained from working with PowerPoint users. This experience has provided me with an opportunity to realize the type of information that PowerPoint users need.

If you thought this book was going to be fun, you hit the target spot on! I believe nothing can be learned without bringing fun into the experience, and I brought that philosophy to the writing of this book.

In addition to the tips, trick, and hints on the pages of this book, I provide you with tons of goodies on the CD, plus many more you can download from the book's companion Web site:

www.cuttingedgeppt.com

How to Use This Book

This book shows you quick ways to create effective design and content — and save you and your audience from a ho-hum presentation. Fortunately, you don't need to read this book from cover to cover. You can read each chapter individually — in fact, I encourage you to use this as a reference book. Just explore the problem areas that you need to tame:

- ✔ If you have just one day or a few hours to create that critical presentation, explore the areas where you need help. Get ideas to instantly make over your presentation. Watch it metamorphose from an ugly duckling into a beautiful swan.

- ✔ Read Chapters 3 and 4 for help with color, masters, templates, and themes that will save you so much time.

- ✔ If you have more time, read this book from cover to cover. Explore all the samples and goodies on the CD.

- ✔ If you have all the time in the world, explore all possibilities. Perform all the tutorials. Walk 16 miles each day.

- ✔ If you still have time, send me some feedback at www.cuttingedgeppt. com/feedback. I'll try to send you some tips and pointers.

What You Don't Need to Read

Most of the chapters and sections are self-contained. This book is designed to save you time — so just read the sections that you need help with. Later, when you need help with something else, read that section or chapter.

Foolish Assumptions

I make just one assumption — that you're currently a PowerPoint user.

This means I can save some trees by not discussing the buttons and commands inside PowerPoint. Also, there's no tutorial in this book that shows you everyday PowerPoint tasks, like how to cut and paste, save presentations, and insert a new slide:

- ✔ If you already know how to do these tasks, *Cutting Edge PowerPoint 2007 For Dummies* is for you. I'm so happy you found this book.

- ✔ If you still want to know about the basics or refresh your skills, check out the small section in the Chapter 1 that gets you familiar with the new interface that Microsoft introduced in PowerPoint 2007. This section introduces you to the Ribbon tabs, galleries, and the Mini Toolbar.

How This Book Is Organized

Cutting Edge PowerPoint 2007 For Dummies is divided into five main parts. Each part is further divided into chapters that contain sections. All chapters are self-contained volumes of inspiration and creativity. In addition, some chapters contain design guidelines that explore hidden design facets to help you make even better PowerPoint presentations.

When required, the book is cross-referenced so that you can move immediately to the topic that interests you. You can also find references to the CD and companion Web site throughout the book so that all three sources (book, CD, and Web site) provide a unified experience.

Each part of this book represents a specific area of PowerPoint usage.

Part 1: Powering Up PowerPoint

This part begins by looking at what PowerPoint is and isn't. You discover timesaving housekeeping tricks that prevent your presentations from becoming bloated or corrupted. You also streamline the new PowerPoint interface and find out more about PowerPoint's many file formats.

Part I also covers color and how colors relate to each other in contrast and combinations. Use it to your advantage in PowerPoint's amazing Color Schemes feature. And if consistency and time matter to you, you'll love the expert tricks on PowerPoint's masters, templates, and themes. Truly powerful stuff.

Part II: Achieving Visual Appeal

This part looks at adding and enhancing visuals and text. You begin the magic with shapes. Using them as individual building blocks, you watch, mesmerized, as they create amazing compositions that will blow away effects you thought were possible by using only expensive drawing programs. You also find out more about PowerPoint's sophisticated fill, line, and effect technology.

Discover PowerPoint's drawing abilities with lines and curves — and keep them in control with grids and guides. Discover more about PowerPoint's smart connectors and add pizzazz with effects.

This part also has a full chapter that explores the font factor. You see how to make text look attractive and polished — and how you can convert your Word outlines into instant PowerPoint presentations.

Get ready to parade your photos in slide shows and get the whole skinny on resolution and compression. Find out how to combine Photoshop with PowerPoint and create visuals that evoke *oohs* and *aahs*. And then create fancy charts and graphs that dance to the tune of figures. If that doesn't work for you, get more charts from programs like Visio and SmartDraw right inside PowerPoint. And yes, you also become familiar with the SmartArt graphics that are new for this version of PowerPoint.

Part III: Adding Motion, Sounds, and Effects

This is the part where PowerPoint dances and sings for you and your audience.

Find out everything about sound and video formats and their codecs. Add narration to PowerPoint and play back your CD tracks inside a presentation. And then export your presentation to a movie by using Camtasia, which you can use to create a DVD of your presentation! And if you're geeky, you can take the movie online.

Animation adds interest to all PowerPoint elements — discover more about PowerPoint's amazing entry, exit, and emphasis animations. Get more accolades with trigger and motion path animations and make sure you play with the transitions. Anything for a little fun!

Part IV: Communicating beyond the PowerPoint Program

If you think this book is only about PowerPoint, think again — or even better, go straight to Part IV and find out the cool tricks of working with Flash, Acrobat, Word, and Excel and making them move in concert with PowerPoint.

Take your presentation on the Web and discover awesome distribution and repurposing tricks. Use custom shows and password protect your presentation. Print your handouts and slides.

You also see how to do so much more inside PowerPoint — create a quiz, add interactivity between slides, and overcome your linking problems.

Part V: The Part of Tens

If you thought there was still something left to discover after what you read about the other parts, you were absolutely right! I saved the absolute eye-popping, jaw-dropping stuff for Part V of the book.

In this part, you find my ten favorite PowerPoint tips and tricks, and I'm not even going to give you an inkling about that now. Just turn to these pages and discover. I also show you how to overcome the ten worst problems and bugs in PowerPoint-land. You even find out about accessibility issues.

Icons Used in This Book

Throughout this book, I mark certain paragraphs with the following icons to alert you to specific types of information:

This icon is for nerds and geeks. Read this if you want to get to know more about the intricate details or need information that you can use to impress your boss.

Make sure you read these — they contain important information that can help you create the cool, cutting-edge, wow look.

Did you blow a fuse somewhere? Or did lightning strike? Or does your PowerPoint presentation have some problem areas? The text marked by this icon tells you how to step gingerly through the technical minefield, or better yet, avoid potential problems altogether.

If you ever tied a string on your finger to remember something, this icon is for you. If you set your morning alarm, this is for you, too — and surprise, this one is also for everyone else!

If a feature or tool is very different from how a feature worked in earlier versions of PowerPoint, you find it mentioned by this icon.

If something on the CD works with the example or technique being discussed, this icon tells you that the CD has some goodies or source files that you should take a look at.

Where to Go from Here

Flip the pages and get into an amazing world where cool presentations help you influence your audiences and get ahead in life.

I wish you all the best with your presentations. Feel free to send me feedback through this book's companion site:

```
www.cuttingedgeppt.com/feedback
```

Get ready to go on a fantastic journey into the colorful, musical world of PowerPoint. This book is your ticket. *Bon voyage!*

Part I

Powering Up
PowerPoint

In this part . . .

In this part, I show you how you can smooth all the rough edges you might encounter, and start you thinking about PowerPoint as a collection of elements. Each element can enrich your overall presentation experience.

Chapter 1

PowerPointing with the Best of Them

*U*nlike many other applications, PowerPoint is easy to figure out and to use. And although PowerPoint 2007 is even more amazingly simple to use than previous versions, this also means that creating terrible presentations is even easier! Although anyone can create a PowerPoint presentation with a few words and visuals, you can use PowerPoint to its complete potential only if you understand the composition of its *elements*.

All these elements come together to form the *structure* of a presentation — but there's more to a PowerPoint presentation than just structure and the elements. One of the most important ingredients is the *workflow* that makes up the order in which you create and add elements to your presentation.

This chapter first looks at the new PowerPoint 2007 interface. Then it discusses PowerPoint's elements, a presentation's structure, your workflow for creating a presentation, and more. Although these topics cover theory more than practical application, spending a little time internalizing these concepts will take you a long way toward making your finished presentations more effective and cutting edge.

And that brings me to what I mean by the term *cutting edge.* After all, that term is part of the title of this book. By *cutting edge,* I mean using simple concepts to create presentations that will work in all situations. The cutting-edge part here is the results — not that I expect you to create presentations in a space satellite somewhere outside the earth's atmosphere! And those types of results mean that you have to be element-savvy. Later in this chapter, I discuss these elements — and each of these elements is also discussed in separate chapters within this book.

Taking a Look at PowerPoint 2007

Maybe you've worked with PowerPoint for the last several versions of the program, or you might have just started with the program. Either way, you'll find that PowerPoint 2007 has a new interface. Gone are the menus and the toolbars. In their place, you see the Ribbon with all its tabs and galleries. And yes, you have the Mini Toolbar, as well.

Cut the Ribbon and get started

Figure 1-1 shows you the new PowerPoint interface. It's actually the embodiment of simplicity, but I still explain its components because I refer to the interface all through this book!

- ✔ **Office Button:** The Office Button (see Figure 1-1) is a round button placed on the top left of the interface that works almost the same way as the File menu in earlier versions of PowerPoint.

- ✔ **Quick Access toolbar:** The Quick Access toolbar is a customizable toolbar that can store your often-used commands.

- ✔ **Ribbon:** The Ribbon comprises the area above the actual slide. It replaces the menus and toolbars in earlier versions of PowerPoint.

- ✔ **Tabs:** The Ribbon is tabbed. You can access each tab by clicking the tab header or selecting a particular slide element, which automatically activates one of the tabs. In addition to the tabs normally visible on the Ribbon, contextual tabs appear when a particular slide object is selected. In Figure 1-1, you can see the Drawing Tools Format tab of the Ribbon — that's a contextual tab.

- ✔ **Buttons:** Each of the tabs has several buttons that do something when clicked — they launch a dialog box, reveal a gallery, change the tab itself, or just do something on the slide.

✔ **Groups:** Buttons are arranged logically into groups. For example, all the paragraph formatting options are located within the Paragraph group of the Home tab of the Ribbon.

✔ **Galleries:** Galleries are collections of preset choices. Most of these choices are in the form of small thumbnail previews that show you how the final effects will look. Many galleries can also be seen as drop-down galleries so that you can see even more thumbnail previews.

✔ **Dialog box launcher:** Dialog box launchers are small arrows below some groups that launch a related dialog box.

✔ **Status bar:** The status bar provides information and viewing options.

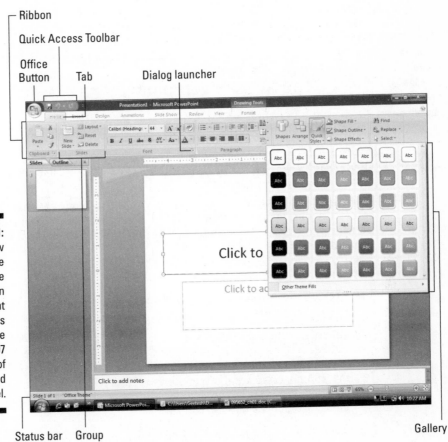

Ribbon

Quick Access Toolbar

Office Button

Tab

Dialog launcher

Figure 1-1: The new interface works the same way in PowerPoint as it does in the Office 2007 versions of Word and Excel.

Status bar   Group

Gallery

The Mini Toolbar

So what is a Mini Toolbar? As much as you might like that mini bar in your hotel room, I promise you this one is more helpful! If you select some text in PowerPoint, you'll see a semitransparent floating toolbar that provides all the text formatting options you need without having to make a trip to the Home tab of the Ribbon. That's the Mini Toolbar.

Figure 1-2 shows you the Mini Toolbar in all its resplendent glory. Just move the cursor away or deselect the text, and the Mini Toolbar gets sad and goes away. If you want to get it back again and it's in no mood to come back, you can always right-click the selected text to order it back into your esteemed presence.

Figure 1-2:
Here comes
the Mini
Toolbar.

The Elements of PowerPoint

When you open PowerPoint, it presents you with a blank canvas that you color with your ideas and your message. The brushes and paints used to transform this blank canvas into an amazing interactive medium are its elements of composition:

- ✔ Text
- ✔ Background, images, and info-graphics
- ✔ Shapes
- ✔ Fills, lines, and effects
- ✔ Sound and video
- ✔ Animations and transitions
- ✔ Interactivity, flow, and navigation

If you've heard or read any of those "Death by PowerPoint" cries in the media these days that bemoan the lack of aesthetics in PowerPoint presentations shown all over the world, you need to make friends with all the elements of PowerPoint so that you can use these elements more effectively to create more aesthetic PowerPoint presentations.

In the following sections, I explain more about these individual elements and then follow it up with how they team together to form an entire presentation workflow. I discuss each of these elements in greater depth in separate chapters throughout this book.

Text

Text is the soul of a presentation — it relates to content like nothing else. Your text could be in the form of titles, subtitles, bullets, phrases, captions, and even sentences.

A barrage of visual content might not be able to achieve what a single effective word can say — sometimes, a word is worth a thousand pictures. Text is significant because it means you have something to say. Without explicit text, what you're trying to say might not come through as strongly as you want.

Too much text is like too much of any good thing — it can be harmful. For example, a slide with 20 lines of teeny-weeny text just doesn't work. The audience can't read it, and the presenter doesn't have time to explain that much content! Anyway, if you're cramming so much text on a slide, you've already lost the focus of your presentation.

Backgrounds, images, and info-graphics

PowerPoint uses three types of graphical elements:

- ✔ **Backgrounds:** The backdrop for your slides. Backgrounds need to be understated.

  You can create a great presentation with a plain white background. On the other hand, artistic backgrounds are a great way to bring a presentation to life.

  The new *themes* in PowerPoint 2007 also let you recolor background graphics by applying new *Theme Colors*. These are explained in more detail in Chapter 3.

- ✔ **Pictures:** Images that you insert in slides. Pictures share the stage with text.

- ✔ **Info-graphics:** Images that combine visuals and text to make complex information and statistics easier to understand. Info-graphics include charts, tables, maps, graphs, diagrams, organization charts, timelines, and flowcharts. You can also create info-graphics in a separate program, such as SmartDraw or Visio, and bring them into PowerPoint later.

Images and text always work together — collectively, they achieve more than the sum of each other's potential. However, images need to be relevant to the subject and focused; using an unsuitable visual is worse than using no visual at all. The same rules apply to info-graphics, as well.

PowerPoint provides many ways to present images — from recolored styles, effects, and outlines to animations and builds.

Shapes

Simple objects such as circles, rectangles, and squares can help you explain concepts so much better. PowerPoint looks at the entire shape concept in a different way through its Shapes gallery. The shapes within the Shapes gallery seem like regular lines and polygons, but that's where the similarity ends; they are very adaptable in editing and creation. Shapes can also function as building blocks and form the basis of complex diagrams and illustrations.

Fills, lines, and effects

Shapes, pictures, and even info-graphics in PowerPoint can stand out from the slide by using as assortment of fill, line, and effect styles. Most styles are found in galleries on the Ribbon tabs.

Sound and video

PowerPoint provides many ways to incorporate sound: *inserted sounds, event sounds, transition sounds, background scores,* and *narrations.*

PowerPoint was perhaps never intended to become a multimedia tool — nor were presentations ever imagined to reach the sophisticated levels they have attained. Microsoft has tried to keep PowerPoint contemporary by adding more sound capabilities with every release. This version finally makes it easier to work with sound in PowerPoint by adding a whole new Ribbon tab containing sound options.

As computers get more powerful and play smooth full-screen video, viewers expect PowerPoint to work with all sorts of video formats. But that's a far cry from reality. In Chapter 11, I look at workarounds that keep PowerPoint happy with all sorts of video types.

Animations and transitions

Animations and transitions fulfill an important objective: introducing several elements one at a time in a logical fashion to make it easier for the audience to understand a concept. Keep these guidelines in mind when using animations and transitions:

✔ Animation is best used for a purpose. An example would be using animation to illustrate a process or a result of an action.

If you use animation without a purpose, your presentation might end up looking like an assortment of objects that appear and exit without any relevance.

✔ Transitions can be either subdued or flashy depending on the flow of ideas being presented. In either case, they need to aid the *flow* of the presentation rather than disrupt it.

Animations and transitions are covered in Chapter 12.

Interactivity, flow, and navigation

Amazingly, interactivity, flow, and navigation are the most neglected parts of many PowerPoint presentations. These concepts are easy to overlook because, unlike a picture, they aren't visible:

✔ **Interactivity,** in its basic form, is the use of hyperlinks within a presentation to link to

  • Other slides in a presentation

  • Other documents outside a presentation (such as Word files)

✔ **Flow** is the spread of ideas that evolves from one slide to the next. Flows can be smooth or abrupt.

✔ **Navigation** aids interactivity. It is the way your presentation is set up to provide one-click access for the user to view other slides in the correct order.

Navigation is mostly taken care of by using the PowerPoint Action Buttons, but you can link from any PowerPoint object to move from one slide to the next.

Interactivity and linking are covered in Chapter 13. Good flow concepts are influenced by proper use of consistency and animation. Consistency is covered in Chapter 4, and animation is covered in Chapter 12.

Going Outside PowerPoint to Create Presentation Elements

Although you might believe that all the elements of a cutting-edge presentation are accessible from within PowerPoint, that's not entirely true. Professional presentation design houses don't want you to know the secret of using non-PowerPoint elements in your presentation — this knowledge is often the difference between a cutting-edge presentation and an ordinary one!

Examples of non-PowerPoint elements include the following:

- Images retouched and enhanced in an image editor, such as Adobe Photoshop
- Charts created in a dedicated charting application
- Music and narration fine-tuned, amplified, and normalized in a sound editor
- Video clips rendered in a custom size and time in a video-editing application
- Animations created in a separate application, such as Macromedia Flash

When these non-PowerPoint elements are inserted inside PowerPoint, most of them can be made to behave like normal PowerPoint elements.

Structure and Workflow

The words *structure* and *workflow* might sound a little intimidating, but they are merely a way of ensuring that your presentation elements are working together.

Presentation structure

A typical presentation structure combines the elements I mention at the beginning of this chapter into something like what you see in Figure 1-3.

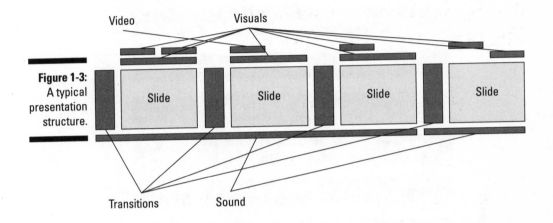

Figure 1-3: A typical presentation structure.

Figure 1-3 is just an example — almost every presentation has a unique structure depending on the content of the presentation and the audience. On the other hand, the presentation *workflow* for most presentations remains unchanged, which is what I explain next.

Presentation workflow

The presentation workflow decides the sequence of the elements that I explain earlier in this chapter. In addition, it includes some more abstract elements such as *delivery* and *repurposing*. Chapters 14 and 15 discuss these vital concepts.

Figure 1-4 shows a typical presentation workflow.

As you can see, the workflow begins with concept and visualization and ends with delivery and repurposing. But that's not entirely true — repurposing can often be the same as the concept and visualization of another presentation! That's food for thought — and the stimulus for thoughts on another interesting subject. . . .

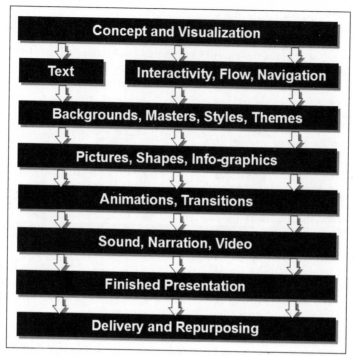

Figure 1-4:
A typical
presentation
workflow.

What Can You Use PowerPoint For?

You can use PowerPoint to create all sorts of presentations:

- **Business presentations:** More than anything else, people use PowerPoint to create presentations intended for the boardrooms and conference halls of the corporate world, where people of all sorts come to see and hear content. And as those in corporate corridors have discovered, the most important thing is to have a PowerPoint presentation ready for every proposal and product — and I should add sales and service to that list!

- **Homework projects:** Don't be flabbergasted if your kid asks you to help create a presentation for school. Or maybe you are a kid reading this and can't understand what's so great about creating a PowerPoint presentation for a project. Schools all over the world are discovering the virtues of PowerPoint — the program lets you assemble all sorts of media, such as images, text, and sound, in one document. And think about the amount of paper and ink you save by replacing that project poster with a PowerPoint presentation!

- ✔ **Educational content:** Colleges and universities commonly have their own banks of presentations for every conceivable subject. Some of these presentations are sold for very high prices as "talks" by specialized vendors — and the high prices are because these talk presentations were created by highly renowned professionals. Even at the high cost, these talk presentations are a steal because they're the next best thing to inviting those professors to speak to your students.

- ✔ **Kiosks:** Kiosks can display anything and everything nowadays — from travel information at airports to the playlist at the coffee shop jukebox. And many of those kiosk displays are actually PowerPoint presentations.

- ✔ **Religious presentations:** And now for the godly frontiers — that projection of the hymn lyrics in church was likely created in PowerPoint. So was that fancy slide show that displayed pictures from the missionary trip to South America.

- ✔ **Government presentations:** PowerPoint is used everywhere in the administrative sphere. Be it presidents or prime ministers — or even organizations like the United Nations and its various agencies all over the world — so much these days happens on a PowerPoint slide. And yes, when something goes wrong, such as space shuttle disasters, PowerPoint often is given some of that blame!

- ✔ **Multimedia demos:** This is probably the most controversial use because PowerPoint was never intended to be used as a tool to create multimedia demos that run from CD-ROM. Nevertheless, PowerPoint allows interactivity and navigation between slides — and because so many people already have PowerPoint, all those bosses decided that they might as well ask untrained office staff to put it to good use!

Of course, you can use PowerPoint for so much more — electronic greeting cards, quizzes, posters, and even multiplication tables. You're limited only by your imagination. PowerPoint is a great tool to present your ideas.

Giving People What They Like to See

The simplest secret of creating great presentations is to give audiences what they like to see. If you give them anything else, they're bound to complain with bouts of loud-mouthed vengeance and stupidity. Okay — I admit that was an exaggeration. They're more likely to doze off and snore loudly while you're presenting!

So what do audiences like to see? That's what I discuss next.

Truth and sincerity

More than anything else, audiences want sincerity and truth. Just because you put that sentence in a 48-point bold font in a contrasting color doesn't mean that your audience will believe what it says. If there's something in common among audiences of any place, age, and sex, it's that they want something they can believe — and if there's even a hint that something mentioned in your presentation is gobbledygook, you can wave goodbye to the remaining 999 slides in that presentation! (And please don't make such long presentations.)

Of course, there are rare exceptions to that rule. A few centuries ago, audiences didn't believe that the earth was round — or that people could find a way to fly. If what you're presenting is similarly groundbreaking, I'll let you put that in your next PowerPoint presentation. And I'm so proud that you are reading this book.

Never use any content that can be thought of as discriminatory toward race, gender, age, religious beliefs, weight, and so on. Not only will discriminatory phrases or even images reflect badly on you, they'll also hijack the entire focus of your presentation.

Style and design

To enliven your message, use as many of these style and design guidelines as you can balance on a single PowerPoint slide:

✔ **Choose an uncluttered background for your presentation.**

  • Plain color backgrounds get around that clutter problem just by being plain!

  • Other background types, such as textures, gradients, and photographs, have to be more carefully chosen.

Test your background choice by inserting enough placeholder text in an 18-point font size to fill the entire slide area in two slides. Use black text on one slide and white text on the other. If you can read text on both the slides clearly, your background really works! If just one color works, you can use that background if you make sure that you use the right colors for all other slide objects. See Chapter 3 to find out more about picking the right colors.

✔ **Make sure your text is large enough that it can be read even by the audience members in the last row.** You don't want to make anyone in the audience squint to read your slides!

✔ **Make sure that you use just the right amount of visual content to get your message across.** Don't use too little and certainly don't use too much.

  • Don't add 16 pictures when a few are enough.

  • Use only relevant content; don't waste your audience's time and energy (or yours, for that matter) on images that have nothing to do with the topic of discussion.

✔ **Make sure that any sounds you insert in your presentation all play at the same volume.** You don't want the sound on one slide to be low and then follow that with a sound that's loud enough to wake up your ancestors.

Correct spelling, accurate grammar, and good word choice

Nothing is as embarrassing and shameful as a misspelling on a slide — especially considering that PowerPoint includes an excellent spell checker. But even beyond the spell checker, make sure that the spellings work for the country and audience you are presenting to. Thus, *color* is perfectly fine in the United States, but make that *colour* if you're presenting in the United Kingdom or in India.

Avoid repeating the same word on a slide when possible. For example, if you see a phrase like "report results in weekly reports," you need to do some editing! You can use PowerPoint's thesaurus (accessible on the Review tab of the Ribbon) to find alternatives if you find yourself repeating certain words.

Don't read the slide aloud to your audience while you're giving your presentation. Slight differences in language and wording can make all the difference. Audiences want you to take the content further by sharing your experiences, opinions, and ideas on the subject.

Chapter 2

Empowering Your PowerPoint Program

You can't learn to swim without getting into the water. That's a good thought if you're jumping into a 3-foot-deep pool, but not the middle of the Pacific Ocean. Diving into PowerPoint is as easy as jumping into the ocean — but you won't drown or become shark food. Yet, it's a perfectly good idea to take precautions before you wade into the PowerPoint sea. Luckily, you bought this book. I safeguard you with this chapter, which contains all the before-you-begin tips.

First, I show you how to set up PowerPoint with one-time tweaks that will increase your productivity and also reduce your chances of causing crashes and creating corrupted presentations. I also show you how you can keep your PowerPoint program updated with some help from Microsoft — and how the folder method of working works so much better than working with a mere presentation. Finally, I give you an introduction to PowerPoint's file formats, followed by bite-sized chunks about all the bits and pieces that make up a PowerPoint presentation. Dive right in!

Housekeeping with One-Time Tweaks

How do you tell PowerPoint that you're the boss? If you adapt the application to your working style, PowerPoint realizes that you're the no-nonsense type, and it works exactly as you want. A few minutes of housekeeping now can save you tons of time later.

Moving and customizing your QAT

Do you miss all the toolbars that Microsoft trashed for the 2007 version of PowerPoint? Or do you just want a toolbar where you can place some command icons that you use more often than others? Either way, you will love the Quick Access toolbar (QAT), which lets you do some customization.

The QAT is a small toolbar that normally stays right next to the Office Button with three or four icons, as you can see in Figure 2-1.

Figure 2-1:
Look! That's
the QAT!

You can place the QAT right below the Ribbon so that you have more space on the QAT to add more icons. To do that, follow these steps:

1. **Choose Office⇨PowerPoint Options to bring up the dialog box of the same name, and then select the Customize tab to see the options shown in Figure 2-2.**

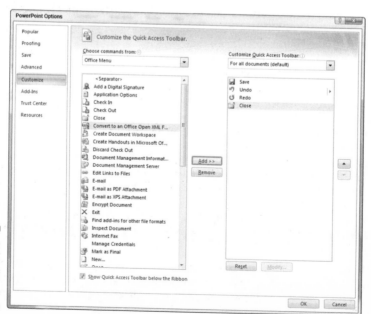

Figure 2-2:
Change the
location of
the QAT.

2. Select the Show Quick Access Toolbar below the Ribbon check box.

3. Click OK to close the dialog box and get back to PowerPoint.

You now see the QAT below the Ribbon, as shown in Figure 2-3.

You can also click the tiny downward-pointing arrow at the right end of the QAT and choose Show Below the Ribbon.

Figure 2-3:
The QAT is
now right
below the
Ribbon.

After you change the location of the QAT, you can populate it with icons for the commands you use more often than others so that they're all accessible with one click.

Imagine you want to add a Close icon to the QAT so that you can close your open presentations with one click. To do that, follow these steps:

1. Choose Office⇨PowerPoint Options and then click the Customize tab.

2. Select any of the Command categories within the Commands list box.

For example, I chose the Office Menu category (refer to Figure 2-2).

3. Select a command within this category and click the Add button to place the command on the QAT.

I clicked Close on the left and then clicked Add; it popped over to the right.

4. Click OK to get back to the PowerPoint interface and see your chosen icon on the QAT.

You can use the same procedure to add more commands to the QAT. You can also add galleries, such as the Shape gallery, to the QAT in the same way.

To quickly add any command to the QAT, right-click a command button on any of the Ribbon tabs and choose the Add to Quick Access Toolbar option.

Turning on AutoRecover

AutoRecover is a very useful option that creates a recovery presentation at a predetermined interval. Having the recovery presentation can be a boon if your computer crashes or if the power shuts down without warning.

The next time PowerPoint launches after a crash or power failure, it starts with the recovered file open and prompts you to save the file.

Follow these steps to access the AutoRecover options:

1. **Choose Office⟹PowerPoint Options and click the Save tab to bring up the dialog box shown in Figure 2-4.**

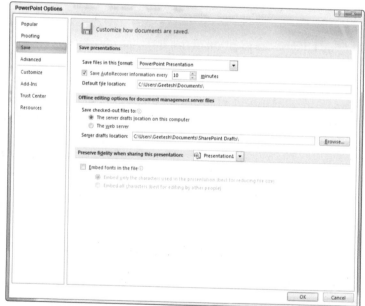

Figure 2-4:
Power
Point's
Save
Options.

2. **Make sure the Save AutoRecover Info Every *xx* Minutes check box is selected.**

3. **Change the timing (minutes) to something like 10 minutes.**

4. **Click OK to exit the dialog box.**

If you're already in the habit of pressing Ctrl+S every other minute, you won't find much benefit with AutoRecover. In that case, consider increasing the 10-minute AutoRecover period to something longer.

The AutoRecover option is not a substitute for the Save command or a periodic backup save option — you still should save your presentation often.

Changing the save location

By default, PowerPoint saves all your new presentations in your My Documents folder — also, if you choose Office⇨Open, you'll end up in the same folder.

You can change this default location, which can be helpful if you're working on a particular project and want to choose the project folder as the default save location. After you move on to a new project, you can change the save location to another folder or back to the My Documents folder.

Follow these steps to change the default save location:

1. **Choose Office⇨PowerPoint Options and then click the Save tab (refer to Figure 2-4).**

2. **Type the path to your folder in the Default File Location text box.**

   You don't get a Browse button to navigate to and select your chosen folder. This means you have to make sure that you type the path and folder names correctly!

   A quick way to do this is by copying the path from the folder address bar and pasting it into this text box.

3. **Click OK to exit the dialog box.**

Installing a local printer driver

If you already have a local printer installed, you can skip this section.

For everyone else, I know it's sort of funny asking you to install a local printer if you have no physical printer attached to your computer. Maybe you use a network printer or perhaps you just don't need a printer. But if you use PowerPoint, a local printer driver is necessary so that PowerPoint can find all the fonts installed on your system and show you print previews.

You don't need to buy a printer to keep PowerPoint happy. Instead, simply install a printer driver so that PowerPoint is fooled into believing that you have a printer! If you don't know how to install a local printer driver, follow the steps at this book's Web site, www.cuttingedgeppt.com/localprinter.

Undoing levels

PowerPoint's Undo options are great. They let you go back to a previous stage in your presentation. By default, PowerPoint allows 20 undos, but you can change it to as high as 150.

Don't use the maximum number of undos. That translates into sluggish performance and a drain on system memory.

Your best bet is to set your number of undos to something between 10 and 40, depending on how powerful your system is. Even then, you might want to change the number again per the requirements and needs of each individual presentation.

Follow these steps to change the number of undos:

1. **Choose Office➪PowerPoint Options to summon the PowerPoint Options dialog box.**

2. **Click the Advanced tab to bring up the options shown in Figure 2-5.**

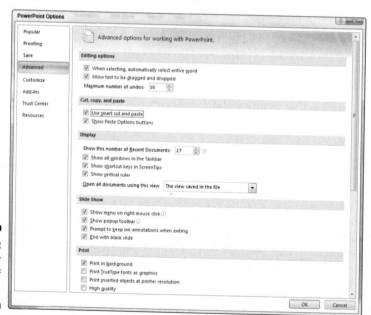

Figure 2-5: Set your number of undos.

3. **In the Editing options section, set the Maximum Number of Undos option to a number you've chosen.**

4. **Click OK to accept.**

Other advanced options

While you are in the Advanced tab of the PowerPoint Options dialog box to tweak your undo levels, you might want to tweak some more options:

✔ If you select part of a word, does PowerPoint automatically select the entire word for you? If you want to turn off this behavior, uncheck the When Selecting, Automatically Select Entire Word option.

✔ You can ask PowerPoint to show you a greater number of recent documents in the Office Button now than you could in previous versions. Change the number in the Show This Number of Recent Documents box to tell PowerPoint how many recent documents to keep track of. Although you can show up to 50 recent documents now, 20 or fewer is a more practical figure unless you're using an extra-high-resolution monitor that can display that many recent documents!

✔ If your PowerPoint program becomes sluggish and unresponsive as you multitask by printing slides at the same time, turn off the option called Print in Background.

Using PowerPoint compatibility features

If you create your presentations in PowerPoint 2007 and send your presentations to users of older versions of PowerPoint, they might complain because they can't view all the latest features, like the new effects and styles, charts, tables, and SmartArt diagrams.

You can't downgrade the capabilities of your PowerPoint version, but you can decide to save your presentations to an older file format by default by following these steps:

1. **Choose Office⇨PowerPoint Options to bring up the PowerPoint Options dialog box.**

2. **Click the Save tab (shown previously in Figure 2-4).**

3. **In the Save Presentations section, select PowerPoint Presentation 97–2003 from the Save Files in This Format drop-down list.**

4. **Click OK to accept.**

Now, when you save a presentation, the PowerPoint Compatibility Checker shows you a list of compatibility issues, as shown in Figure 2-6. You can then choose how to address these issues as required on a presentation-to-presentation basis.

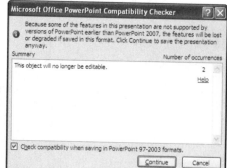

Figure 2-6:
The
Compatibil-
ity Checker.

You can switch these options back to the defaults when required if you're sure that recipients you share your presentations with are using the current version of PowerPoint.

Microsoft provides an update for older versions of PowerPoint that allows users to view all the new PowerPoint 2007 effects. In addition, this update also allows users to open the new PPTX file format using older versions of PowerPoint.

These updates will also be available for Mac users of PowerPoint so that they can exchange files with Windows PowerPoint users.

For more about PowerPoint's file formats, see the "Embracing PowerPoint File Formats" section, later in this chapter.

Showing all windows in the taskbar

What do you do if PowerPoint does some strange stuff? For instance,

- ✔ You have several presentations open in PowerPoint, and after you close the last open presentation, you find that PowerPoint still doesn't close itself.

- ✔ You want to drag a slide or an item on a slide from one presentation to the other, but where did that other presentation go?

Well, the culprit for both these behaviors is a small, unsuspecting option that you need to turn on:

1. **Choose Office➪PowerPoint Options to bring up the PowerPoint Options dialog box.**

2. **Click the Advanced tab (refer to Figure 2-5).**

3. **In the Display section, select the Show All Windows in the Taskbar check box.**

4. **Click OK to get back to PowerPoint.**

Each open presentation is now shown in the Windows taskbar, and when you close the last presentation by clicking the small X in the upper-right corner of PowerPoint, PowerPoint itself closes, too.

Enabling live previews

All the galleries on PowerPoint's Ribbon tabs can provide live previews on the slide when you hover the cursor over the preview thumbnails within the galleries. The previews show you what the option will do if you select it. However, those live previews may be turned off on some systems because all that previewing consumes more system resources than what some older computers might possess.

If you want to enable live previews (and I strongly suggest you do so), just follow these steps. If you want to go back to a life without live previews, just disable them in the same way!

1. **Choose Office➪PowerPoint Options to bring up the PowerPoint Options dialog box.**

   By default, the PowerPoint Options dialog box opens with the Popular tab active, as shown in Figure 2-7.

2. **Select the Enable Live Preview option.**

3. **Click OK to apply this option and get back to PowerPoint.**

Now when you hover your cursor over a thumbnail preview in a gallery (such as the Themes gallery on the Design tab), you see a live preview of the change on the active slide.

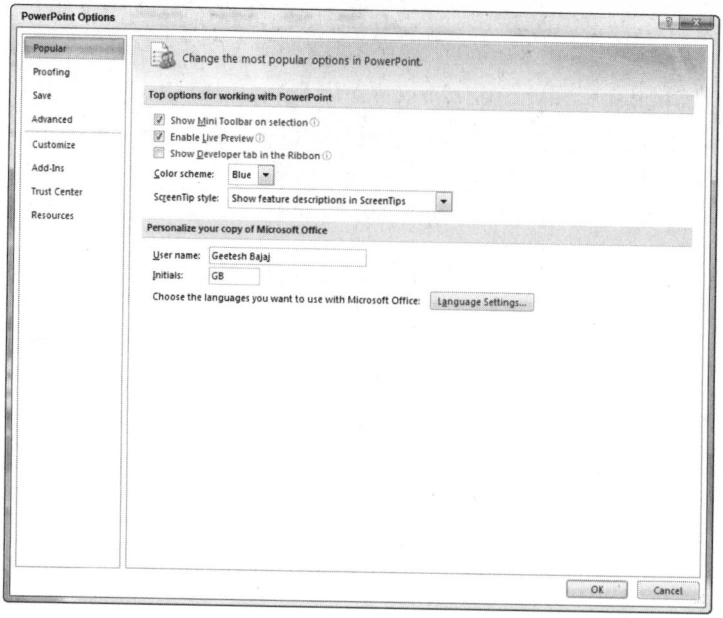

Figure 2-7:
Enable live
previews
from Power
Point's
galleries.

Adjusting automatic layouts

Does your font size keep shrinking as you type text into a placeholder? Worse, does the space between lines of text keep dwindling? This occurs when PowerPoint's AutoFit options are activated — although the results aren't half as bad as what used to happen in earlier versions of PowerPoint where the line spacing between the text would shrink so much that it cut off the top and bottom of some letters!

To change how this works, follow these steps:

1. **Choose Office⇨PowerPoint Options, click the Proofing tab, and then click the AutoCorrect Options button.**

   The AutoCorrect dialog box appears.

2. **Click the AutoFormat As You Type tab (see Figure 2-8).**

3. **Remove (or place) check marks next to the boxes for these options:**

   • AutoFit Title Text to Placeholder

   • AutoFit Body Text to Placeholder

4. **Click OK to accept.**

Figure 2-8:
Do you need
automatic
layouts?

More gotchas

Here are a couple more housekeeping tips and productivity ideas:

- ✔ **Embedding fonts:** Remember, not all font types can be embedded. To find out more about font embedding issues, turn to Chapter 8.

- ✔ **Enable error info:** If you use PowerPoint add-ins to extend your PowerPoint capabilities, you might want to turn on the display of add-in errors. By default, this is turned off, and you will have no clue about why a particular add-in did nothing!

  To see those error messages, choose Office➪PowerPoint Options. Then click the Advanced tab and scroll down to the General options. Now, select the Show Add-In User Interface Errors check box.

Keeping PowerPoint Updated

If you want to do yourself a favor today, download the latest Service Pack for your version of PowerPoint (and Microsoft Office). But what is a Service Pack? And where do you download it?

Service Packs

Most releases of popular applications are followed by releases of Service Packs that address some bugs and add some new features. These Service Packs need to be downloaded from the Microsoft site, or in some cases, they can also be ordered on a CD, which is especially useful if you don't have a broadband Internet connection.

But wait! You might have some Service Packs already applied. To find out what's already applied, choose Office⇨PowerPoint Options. Then click the Resources tab and click the About button. This brings up a dialog box similar to what you see in Figure 2-9.

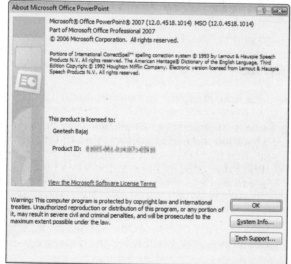

Figure 2-9:
Do you have
Service
Packs
installed?

The first line of this dialog box identifies the PowerPoint version and the Service Pack number applied. (At the time of printing, PowerPoint 2007 was so new that no Service Packs were yet available.) To acquire new Service Packs, you need to visit Microsoft's OfficeUpdate site.

OfficeUpdate

Updating your Service Pack at the OfficeUpdate site is really quite easy, although it does require a connection to the Internet:

1. **Choose Office⇨PowerPoint Options.**

2. **Click the Resources tab and then click the Check for Updates button.**

   This opens the OfficeUpdate site within your default Web browser. Not surprisingly, this update service works best if you're using Microsoft Internet Explorer as your browser.

Keep your original CD (or other installation medium) within reach just in case the Service Pack installation asks for it — you don't want to abandon the installation of the Service Pack midway just because the installation medium isn't handy!

Assembling Everything in One Folder

Working with PowerPoint is one of the few instances when you want to put all your eggs in one basket. Saving all of a presentation's elements in one folder is so important for overcoming link problems that I risk sounding like a parrot by repeating this tip often throughout this book.

You should save all of a presentation's assets in one folder because you don't want PowerPoint to have to remember any paths. PowerPoint isn't too good at remembering the location of linked files. Heaven forbid that you ever have to copy your presentation to a laptop just before an important presentation only to have PowerPoint throw up a message that it can't find your linked file! So just put everything in one folder before you link or insert those files from within PowerPoint. Then, when the presentation needs to move, copy that whole folder.

So how do you assemble everything in one folder? Here's how:

1. **Create a new folder and name it after your project.**

2. **Create your basic, bare-bones presentation (probably a one-slide presentation or just an outline) and save it within this folder.**

3. **Copy all the elements that you want to link to this presentation into this folder:**

   • Sounds and videos

   • All the other documents you want to hyperlink from within the presentation, such as other PowerPoint presentations, Word and PDF documents, and Excel spreadsheets

4. **Work on your presentation again and start inserting or linking the documents, sounds, videos, and other files.**

5. **If you need to copy your presentation to another computer, just copy the entire folder.**

Making a habit of creating a new folder for every new presentation ensures an almost uninterrupted workflow in which you can concentrate on the creative part of the presentation without having to worry about linking problems later.

Embracing PowerPoint File Formats

The file format most commonly associated with PowerPoint 2007 is .pptx, but PowerPoint creates and uses a number of file formats to provide a plethora of presentation possibilities:

PowerPoint's file types:

✔ .pptx: This is the default PowerPoint presentation file type in PowerPoint 2007. Unless you tampered with any associations in Windows, double-clicking a .pptx file opens it in PowerPoint. Of course, that's assuming you have PowerPoint installed on your system!

✔ .ppsx: This is the PowerPoint show format. Again, unless you tampered with any file associations, double-clicking a .ppsx file results in the presentation playing.

The only difference between .pptx and .ppsx files is one letter. Yes, it is only the *t* and *s* that make them different file types. Even if you rename those extensions from one to the other a thousand times, you'll still see the same slides! Now that you know this, I wish you happy renaming.

By default, double-clicking a .pptx file opens it in PowerPoint, ready for editing. On the other hand, double-clicking a .ppsx file opens it in Show mode — without the PowerPoint interface.

Other PowerPoint file formats:

✔ .potx: A .potx file is a PowerPoint template that contains information about the Slide Masters and the various theme presets like Theme Colors and Theme Fonts. It might or might not include preset animation and transition choices.

Double-clicking a .potx file results in PowerPoint creating a new, unsaved presentation based on that template.

Check out Chapter 3 for the lowdown on Theme Colors, and see Chapter 4 for a quick lesson in masters, templates, and themes.

✔ .thmx: These are Office Theme files that let you apply the same font, color, and effects themes in Word, Excel, and PowerPoint.

✔ `.pptm`, `.potm`, and `.ppsm`: .These file types are essentially the same as a `.pptx`, `.potx`, and `.ppsx` files, respectively. The only difference is that these file types contain at least one macro. These three file types are normally called *macro-enabled files*.

✔ `.ppam`: This lesser-known file type is used mainly to store advanced macro and programming routines. `.ppam` files are usually PowerPoint add-ins that add new features to PowerPoint.

✔ PowerPoint HTML Output: PowerPoint creates a fairly nice HTML output that looks more or less like the original presentation.

Recognizing All the Pieces and Parts of PowerPoint

The following list orients you to all the terms that you'll hear in the rest of this book:

✔ **Presentations:** A presentation is what PowerPoint creates, much in the same way that Word creates documents and Excel creates spreadsheets. Every presentation comprises one or more *slides*.

✔ **Slides:** The individual screens in a presentation — almost like pages in a book.

✔ **Placeholders:** Special container frames you insert information into. You type text in a text placeholder and insert a picture (image) into a picture placeholder. Title placeholders contain slide titles.

In addition to text placeholders, you can add almost any number of text boxes to a slide. These text boxes function just like regular text placeholders apart from one important difference: The text contained in text boxes is never a part of the presentation's *outline*.

✔ **Layouts (also called slide layouts):** Special preset arrangements of placeholders contained on individual slides. For example, one arrangement might contain a single title placeholder and a single chart placeholder. Or you might have an arrangement with title and text placeholders — or even an arrangement with no placeholders at all.

✔ **Outlines:** The text part of the presentation that's contained within the title and text placeholders. Any other text in the presentation is not part of the outline. Thus if your slide has a title and a text placeholder, all the text within those placeholders is part of the outline for the slide.

- ✔ **Shapes:** Shapes include patterns like rectangles, circles, lines, and more exotic representations. They are like cookie cutters that you can insert on a slide with one click — their power lies in their simplicity. They are the building blocks of PowerPoint.

- ✔ **Charts:** Charts are graphics that are driven by data and statistics.

- ✔ **Diagrams:** Diagrams, known as *SmartArt* in this version of PowerPoint, are logical drawings that show relationships.

- ✔ **Theme Colors:** Theme Colors are preset color combination values that influence the color of all PowerPoint elements, such as the background, charts, text, diagrams, shadows, and hyperlinks.

  Each presentation can contain multiple Theme Colors, and you can change the Theme Colors to create a new look for your presentation.

- ✔ **Slide Master:** When you create a preset slide type and select a slide background, you'll want to save it within the Slide Master. Slide Masters can also influence other elements in a presentation, such as text formatting.

- ✔ **Handout Master and Notes Master:** PowerPoint has two more master types that influence handouts and notes. Not surprisingly, those masters are called Handout Master and Notes Master.

- ✔ **Templates:** You can save a combination of Theme Colors and masters as a template that you can implement across any number of presentations.

- ✔ **Themes:** PowerPoint 2007 adds more options in the form of Theme Fonts and Theme Effects. This is a very powerful feature that can help you create consistency of look across presentations and other Office documents. Themes created in PowerPoint 2007 also work in Word and Excel versions of Office 2007.

Chapter 3

Color Is Life

. . . .

. . . .

Audiences develop lasting opinions the moment you project the first slide in your presentation. Many times, that's before you say the first word. Color can win over the audience's opinion or lose it in that first moment.

Color is powerful stuff: Ignore it at your own peril. But don't worry. This chapter shows you how to pick the right color palette for your presentation.

Color theory is art and science working together. Don't run away — I have no ambitions to convert you into a color theorist. I won't even suggest that you buy another book on color theory; you probably don't have that sort of time. Instead, I provide you with a set of no-brainer guidelines on using color effectively in your presentations. Don't be skeptical about all these wonderful color things — let your inspiration soar and touch the rainbow. (I know that was pretty sappy. You can stop rolling your eyes now.)

Why Color Is So Important

The French painter Yves Klein said, "Color is sensibility turned into matter, matter in its primordial state."

Nothing could be truer in the world of PowerPoint. When I'm asked to name just one thing that can make a limp, uninspiring presentation look dazzling and cutting edge, I answer *color*.

Color and contrast affect the readability of your slides

In PowerPoint-land, color expresses its omnipresence through combinations and contrasts between these two key elements:

- The slide background
- The foreground elements (everything else in PowerPoint, such as text, diagrams, charts, and shapes)

Contrast is king. The first basic color rule in PowerPoint is to make sure that your background and foreground colors are as different as night and day. The reason is basic: The more contrast you have between the background and foreground, the easier it is to read any text in the foreground. The examples in Figure 3-1 show how contrast makes text more legible.

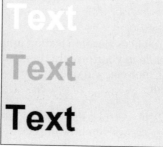

Figure 3-1:
Color can
help
improve
contrast and
readability.

For the best contrast and readability, use

- Light text over a dark background
- Dark text over a light background

For clarity of text, avoid

- Similar text and background colors
- Light text on a light background
- Dark text on a dark background

Color Plate 3-1 (see the color pages in this book) shows you how text and background colors work so much better with contrast.

Even if your actual presentation is shown in full color, checking the contrast in grayscale can be helpful. Often, color prevents you from accurately judging contrast.

If colors have good contrast in grayscale, they work well together in color.

Use these steps to control PowerPoint's grayscale:

1. **Start the grayscale preview by clicking the View tab of the Ribbon and then clicking the Grayscale option.**

   This activates the Grayscale tab of the Ribbon. (See Figure 3-2.)

   The Grayscale tab provides several types of Grayscale previews — such as light and inverse grayscales, black, white, and so on — but for most purposes, the Automatic option works great.

2. **To get back to the normal color view, click the Back to Color View button on the Grayscale tab of the Ribbon.**

Changing the view settings in the Grayscale tab of the Ribbon, as shown in Figure 3-2, doesn't change any of your color slides — it affects only the grayscale view.

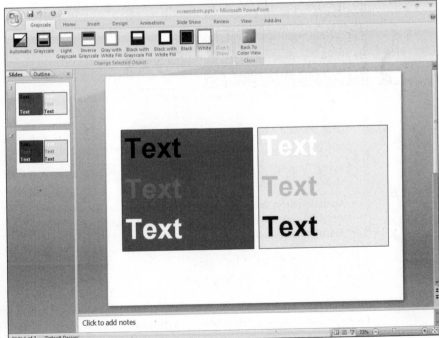

Figure 3-2:
The Grayscale view magnifies contrast.

Color influences mood

Colors are associated with moods. Although the rules are often broken, you should still know the essential psychology of color to make the best color choices for your presentations.

Any color family can be used successfully in presentations, but some colors are more appropriate than others for certain subjects or audiences.

Safe choices

It's hard to go wrong when you use these colors in your presentations:

- **Blue** signifies *endurance, capability, depth,* and *vastness.*

  The color of tranquil skies and water is reassuring. You can also use blue-green shades like turquoise or teal.

- **Green** denotes *trust.* It's a great choice for presentations to new audiences. Use it for banking, industry, and government sectors.

  Avoid fluorescent greens. Opt for paler tints and shades of the color.

- **White** denotes *peace* and *blank space.*

  White works well for such purposes as research, nonprofit organizations, education, venture capital, funding, and IPOs.

- **Black** signifies *sophistication.*

  Black works very well in visually rich presentations for fields such as fashion, art, jewelry, space research, and many sciences.

- **Violet and purple** denote *luxury* and *opulence* and provide a *spiritual fervor.*

  Shades of violet and purple are good choices for presentations intended for travel, interior design, self-improvement, and alternative medicine.

- **Gray** denotes *balance* and *stability.* Gray works well with visuals of differing styles.

  Gray is the color to deliver bad news because it is among the most neutral colors. However, this doesn't mean that you can't use gray in happier situations!

Risky choices

These colors can work in your presentation if you take necessary precautions:

✔ **Red** is suitable for internal presentations that *call for action.*

In its pure saturation, red is a screaming color totally unsuited for presentation backgrounds. If you want to use red in your backgrounds, tone down the red by mixing in black (to create a shade) or white (to create a tint). Red can be made to work as a background by using a predominantly red texture, as you can see in a sample within Color Plate 3-4.

✔ **Orange** denotes *authority* and *influence.* It's a nice choice to neutralize a disadvantage.

Use a pale shade of orange and combine it with dark blue text because both white and black text might not work with a pale orange background.

✔ **Brown** is associated with *growth* and *lifestyle.*

Again, opt for paler shades of brown. Also, experiment with brown-beige textures.

✔ **Yellow** indicates *youth, warmth,* and *optimism.* Use it for education, royalty, travel, and design.

Be wary of using the more saturated values of yellow. If a particular yellow value is too bright, stay away from it.

✔ **Pink** is a controversial color often associated with the feminine look.

Pink in various shades and tints is used for spheres such as haute couture, decorative arts, and even finance. You can also use shades between pink, violet, and brown that provide an interesting look.

Choosing the Background Color

Please don't tell me that you plan to use a chocolate-to-magenta gradient as the background for your next presentation. A bad background color choice can ruin a presentation more than anything else. Fortunately, changing the background color is one of the most effective makeovers possible.

Many times, you won't even have to bother about the background because it might be contained as part of the *template* or *theme* on which you base your PowerPoint presentation. This book teaches you about themes and templates as well, and the good design principles you discover in this chapter can help you create and use suitable background choices.

To find out more about templates and themes, head to Chapter 4.

Replicate nature

Why are blue and green the most common background colors in PowerPoint presentations? You find blue in the skies and the seas; green pervades forests and meadows. It's almost as if nature starts with a blue or green canvas and then paints everything over these colors. No wonder we humans subconsciously re-create the same effect on our PowerPoint slides!

Imitate nature if you can. That's the second color rule in PowerPoint-land.

Tints, shades, and textures

You might be unable to replicate nature if your company colors are deep orange and dark purple. Okay, you probably know of some exotic tropical bird that has just these colors, but then you don't have the advantage of sunlight making those colors look magical on a PowerPoint slide! On your slides, you might also have strict instructions to not change any colors. Luckily, you can cope with that situation in a lot of ways.

I give you the basics on tints, shades, and textures in the following subsections. For more details about tints, shades, textures, and color terminology, check out this book's companion Web site at www.cuttingedgeppt.com/colortheory.

Tints and Shades

PowerPoint lets you choose from millions of colors. Any given color has hundreds of variations. In color theory, these variations in color are known as

- ✓ **Tint:** You create a tint by mixing white with the color (*lightening* it).

  All pastel colors are tints.

- ✓ **Shade:** You create a shade by mixing black with the color (*darkening* it).

- ✓ **Pure:** You get a pure color with the original color values; pure colors are the basis for creating tints and shades by mixing with white and black, respectively. Pure colors are also called *saturated* colors.

Using either tints or shades makes the background color less saturated and ensures that either white or black text is easily readable over the background. Color Plate 3-2 shows you some pure colors with their tints and shades. Using tints and shades is a good way to increase contrast, as you can see in Color Plate 3-3. Don't be afraid to use pure colors, however.

Favorite background colors

An online survey on my Web site asked visitors to vote for their favorite presentation background colors. The results make very interesting reading:

✔ If *blue* is your favorite background, you aren't alone. Nearly 42 percent of the respondents polled provided the same answer.

✔ *Green* fared well with 16 percent of the votes.

✔ *Black, white, violet,* and *purple* polled between 7 and 9 percent each.

✔ *Red, brown, yellow,* and *orange* were the least favored colors.

PowerPoint 2007 uses tints and shades extensively. Each time you select a color in PowerPoint, you can now choose a tint or shade of the same color.

Textures

If you need to use a bright, saturated color like red or yellow as a background, use a *texture* as the background. Textures let you play with a wide gamut of values and saturations while leaving the color hue unchanged.

Color Plate 3-4 shows you some sample textures. You'll see that these textures fill the entire image area, yet they don't look as overwhelming as a pure, solid color because they show different values and saturations of the same color.

Unless you want to create a rainbow or kaleidoscope on your PowerPoint slide background, stay away from multicolored textures! Of course, you might love overpowering or psychedelic effects, or you might be creating a presentation that is intended to create headaches and squinted eyes for the audience — in that case, feel free to go nuts with the colors!

You can find textured backgrounds the use difficult colors like red and yellow in the Chapter Files folder on the *Cutting Edge PowerPoint 2007 For Dummies* CD.

Picking Out Theme Colors

Every PowerPoint slide element (such as background, text, chart, shapes, and lines) is associated with a *default* color. These default colors are stored in palettes within PowerPoint called *Theme Colors.*

Theme Colors are part of a larger feature called Office Document Themes — also known as Office Themes or just Themes. However, Microsoft made the Theme Colors feature fairly independent so that you can use it even if you don't know the whole skinny about Themes, which, incidentally, is covered in Chapter 4.

You can quickly make over a presentation by changing its Theme Colors. To see how Theme Colors can change the look of a presentation, check out Color Plates 3-5 and 3-6 in the color insert in the middle of this book.

The source presentation for Color Plates 3-5 and 3-6 is included in the Chapter Files folder on the *Cutting Edge PowerPoint 2007 For Dummies* CD — it's called `themecolors.pptx`.

Theme Color sets

PowerPoint 2007 contains several sets of Theme Colors.

Follow these steps to access the Theme Color sets available in PowerPoint:

1. **Make sure you have a presentation open.**

2. **On the Design tab of the Ribbon, click the Colors button in the Themes group to see a drop-down gallery of Theme Color sets available, as shown on the left in Figure 3-3.**

   If you worked with Color Schemes in older PowerPoint versions, you know that they're included within the presentation or template itself. So what happens if you open an older PowerPoint presentation and you want to use your Color Schemes? Microsoft retains those Color Schemes within the presentation, and they show up as part of the Theme Color gallery, as you can see on the right side of Figure 3-3.

3. **Hover the cursor over each Theme Color set to see how it affects the active slide.**

The color swatches

Although the Theme Color gallery that I explain in the preceding section shows only 8 swatches per Theme Color set, the actual sets contain 12 color swatches each. Some colors aren't shown in the gallery. These colors can be seen by following these steps:

1. **In the Design tab of the Ribbon, click the Colors button in the Themes group to view the Theme Colors gallery (refer to Figure 3-3).**

2. **Click the Create New Theme Colors option to summon a dialog box of the same name.**

   This dialog box shows you all 12 color swatches, along with info on what these swatches represent, as shown later in this chapter in Figure 3-5.

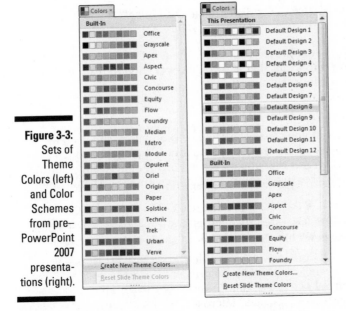

Figure 3-3: Sets of Theme Colors (left) and Color Schemes from pre–PowerPoint 2007 presentations (right).

On Color Plate 3-9, I show you the relationship between the Theme Colors in the Color gallery and the Create New Theme Colors dialog box.

These Theme Colors are so well chosen that they work all the time, and they're also based on sound color principles — this means that they look good, too. In the following sections, I explain all 12 swatches contained in a Theme Color set that are used for particular slide elements.

Background and text (swatches 1 to 4)

PowerPoint now provides two colors each for backgrounds and text in a Theme Color set — that's a total of four colors.

All put together, you have two light colors and two dark colors. When you use any of the dark variants for a background, PowerPoint automatically uses the light variant for the text on the slide to maintain contrast. Similarly, when you use a light variant for the background, PowerPoint uses the darker color for the text elements on the slide. Most of the time, the first two colors are black and white, and these colors don't make it to the Theme Colors gallery. The other light and dark colors, however, do make it to the gallery and are the first two color swatches that you see there. You can see this in Color Plate 3-9.

The two darker colors are always visible over the two lighter colors or vice versa. You know how important that is if you've ever tried to read medium grey text over a charcoal background!

Accent colors (swatches 5 to 10)

The other six colors that you see in the Theme Color gallery are used as accent colors. These six colors are used as the first six fill colors for any charts or SmartArt diagrams that you create in PowerPoint. Again, refer to Color Plate 3-9 to view how these colors are set up within the Theme Colors feature.

If your chart or diagram uses more than six series or elements, PowerPoint automatically creates new colors using tints and shades of the six accent colors.

Hyperlink (swatch 11)

This is the color used for hyperlinked text.

Followed hyperlink (swatch 12)

This color is used for a followed (visited) hyperlinked text.

Applying Theme Colors

Every presentation and slide already has Theme Colors applied. You can open a presentation and change the Theme Colors for a whole presentation or for specific slides. Later in this chapter, I show you how to create and customize Theme Color sets.

Follow these steps to assign Theme Colors in PowerPoint 2007:

1. **On the Design tab of the Ribbon, click the Colors button.**

   This activates the Theme Color gallery (refer to Figure 3-3).

2. **Hover the cursor over the Theme Color sets to see a live preview of the change on the active slide.**

   If you want to see a more dramatic change, make sure your active slide contains a chart or SmartArt graphic.

3. **Click any of the Theme Color sets in the gallery to change the Theme Color for all the slides in the presentation.**

   If you inadvertently clicked a Theme Color set that you don't want to use, press Ctrl+Z to undo the change.

You can experiment with applying different Theme Color sets on the `themecolorschange.pptx` presentation in the Chapter Files folder on the *Cutting Edge PowerPoint 2007 For Dummies* CD.

If you want to select a Theme Color set for specific slides in a presentation, follow these steps:

1. **On the View tab of the Ribbon, click the Slide Sorter button.**

   This shows you all your slides in Slide Sorter view.

2. **Select the individual slides you want to change.**

   - To select *consecutive* slides, select the first slide and then Shift+click the *last* slide in the sequence.

   - To select slides *out of sequence,* select the first slide and then Ctrl+click *individual* slides.

You can also select slides by using the same techniques in the Slides pane within Normal view — this is especially handy if you don't have too many slides to select.

3. **On the Design tab of the Ribbon, access the Theme Colors gallery by clicking the Colors button. When your cursor is over the Theme Color set that you want to use for the selected slides, right-click and then choose the Apply to Selected Slides option, as shown in Figure 3-4.**

If you click over a Theme Color set that you don't want to use, press Ctrl+Z to undo the change.

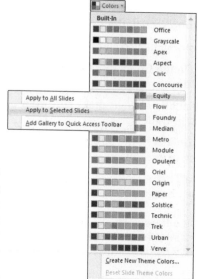

Figure 3-4:
Applying
Theme
Colors to
selected
slides.

Creating Theme Color sets

Seeing a slide metamorphose from one family of colors to another might look like magic. You can be a part of this magic by creating your own Theme Color set.

To create a Theme Color set, follow these steps:

1. **Click the Colors button on the Design tab of the Ribbon.**

   This activates the Theme Color gallery (refer to Figure 3-3).

2. **Choose the Create New Theme Colors option at the bottom of this gallery to summon the Create New Theme Colors dialog box, shown in Figure 3-5.**

RGB and the colors of light

When most people think of mixing colors, they probably recall mixing paint in art class. Mixing yellow and red paint, for example, creates orange.

Guess what — if you tell your computer or resident geek that red and yellow make orange, you'll be zapped through the keyboard! That's because computers mix the colors of light to create new colors. All colors in your computer come from the three primary colors of light: red, green, and blue.

I'm sure you've guessed that *RGB* stands for red, green, and blue. RGB is a *color model* that computers understand. Each color has a numeric value that ranges from 0 to 255.

- ✔ When all three RGB values are 0, you get *black*.
- ✔ When all three RGB values are 255, you get *white*.

You can use different combinations of any three numbers between 0 and 255 to create about 16 million colors. These are some common color values:

- ✔ **Blue:** R:0; G:0; B:255
- ✔ **Green:** R:0; G:255; B:0
- ✔ **Red:** R:255; G:0; B:0
- ✔ **Yellow:** R:255; G:255; B:0
- ✔ **Orange:** R:255; G:153; B:0

Color Plate 3-7 (see the color insert pages in the middle of the book) is an RGB Color Reference chart.

3. **Click any of the 12 swatches to open a color chooser, as shown on the right in Figure 3-5.**

4. **Select a color from the color chooser as follows:**

    - *The Theme Colors area* lets you choose from 12 existing theme colors and an additional 60 tints and shades of these 12 colors.

    - *The Standard Colors area* lets you choose from some popular colors.

    - *The Recent Colors area* shows any recent colors you have used. If you haven't used any colors recently, this area won't be visible.

5. **(Optional) To create a custom color, click More Colors on the color chooser and then choose additional colors.**

    The Windows Colors dialog box, with its two tabs, appears.

    - The Standard tab lets you choose from a hive of 127 colors. In addition, you can choose from black, white, and 15 shades of gray. Take a peek at how the Standard tab looks on the left side of Figure 3-6.

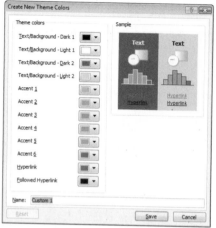 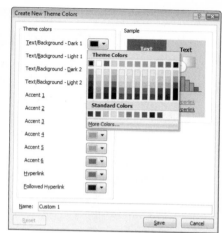

Figure 3-5:
The Create
New Theme
Colors
dialog box
(left) and
the color
chooser
(right).

- If you prefer more control over your colors, you'll love the Custom tab. This lets you mix your own colors or enter specific color values using the RGB and HSL color models. You can see how the Custom tab looks on the right side of Figure 3-6.

  The sidebars, "RGB and the colors of light" and "HSL and the human eye color system," explain more about RGB and HSL.

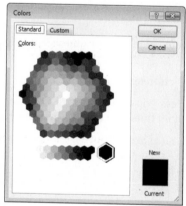 

Figure 3-6:
The
Standard
tab in the
color
chooser
(left) and the
Custom tab
(right).

6. **After you have chosen colors for all 12 swatches, you can save the group of them as your own Theme Color set by typing a name in the Name text box and clicking the Save button.**

   If you don't type in a name, PowerPoint automatically names the set Custom 1, Custom 2, and so on.

HSL and the human eye color system

The HSL color system stands for *hue, saturation,* and *luminosity.*

✔ **Hue is the *pure color* value.**

This value can be any numeric value between 0 and 255. Changing this value moves the hue in the color spectrum.

✔ **Saturation is the *strength* of the color.**

If a color is too *bright,* just reduce the saturation value.

✔ **Luminosity (or Luminance) denotes light or dark values.**

Colors can be mixed with white to make tints or mixed with black to create shades.

HSL works like the human eye, so most designers and purists prefer using it to RGB.

The accompanying figure shows the Custom tab of the Color Chooser with the HSL color model selected. It's easy to manipulate the HSL model:

✔ Changing the Hue value moves the crosshair in the color spectrum horizontally.

✔ Changing the Saturation value moves the crosshair in the color spectrum vertically.

✔ Changing the Luminosity value moves the arrow in the Luminosity bar vertically.

Color Plate 3-8, in this book's color insert, is an HSL Color Reference chart.

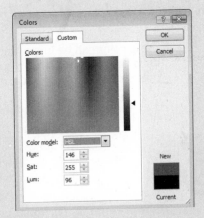

Choosing Colors

Creating your own Theme Color sets is easy — but then it's almost as easy to create Theme Colors without visual meaning. That's why Microsoft has provided so many built-in Theme Color sets — and I don't say that to discourage you from creating your own Theme Colors! These ideas for choosing colors will help you all the time:

✔ **Build on an existing Theme Color set:** Most of PowerPoint's built-in Theme Colors were created from sound color principles. If you find a Theme Color set that suits your presentation and identity, just go ahead and use it. Even if you need to create a new set, it's a good idea to use the existing schemes as a foundation to build upon.

To do that, make sure that the Theme Color set that you want to alter is applied to all slides in your open presentation. Then, on the Design tab of the Ribbon, click the Colors button to open the Theme Colors gallery. Choose the Create New Theme Colors option so that PowerPoint lets you create a new set by altering the theme's existing colors.

✔ **Extend your identity:** Your company might already have visual style guidelines that are used for stationery, on Web sites, and in advertisements — build a Theme Color set around that identity.

Color Design Guidelines

Using color can be fun — and most of the time, experimenting with combinations, layouts, and ideas is a good plan. However, combine those ideas with these guidelines, and you can't go wrong:

✔ **The background should stay in the background.** Don't use any color in the background that's too bright, fluorescent, or garish. The background color shouldn't distract the viewer from the foreground text and objects.

If neither white nor black text shows well over the background color, you've made a poor background choice.

✔ **Use the same Theme Colors for an entire presentation (or a set of presentations).** Your company might require that all presentations use a single set of Theme Colors to maintain consistency.

✔ **Limit your color palette.** Use a single hue and vary the saturation and luminance.

✔ **Experiment with the single grayscale set of Theme Colors available in PowerPoint.** This provides more control if you need to print to a black-and-white presentation.

✔ **Use the HSL (instead of RGB) model to mix your colors.** This lets you observe and understand color theory more closely.

✔ **Be wary of using red and green next to each other.** Many people are red-green colorblind, so these two colors look alike to them.

Chapter 4

Masters and Layouts, Templates and Themes

In This Chapter

▶ Applying consistency with masters and templates

▶ Understanding the types of masters

▶ Creating and applying masters

▶ Starting with templates

▶ Doing more with templates

*I*f you evolve a presentation through edits, you might end up with something that has as much consistency as unbaked lasagna. In a presentation, this lack of consistency shows up in many ways:

✔ Differing font sizes and styles

✔ Diverse layouts

✔ Charts and graphs in noncomplementing colors

✔ Dissimilar backgrounds across successive slides

Such inconsistency on your slides will make your audience unhappy. And you won't be able to blame it on the lunch! Correcting each individual slide for inconsistency problems can be laborious and time-consuming, especially if you need to do it for many slides or for multiple presentations. If you want to change things very often, your woes are multiplied. Does this sound familiar?

Thankfully, PowerPoint 2007 makes it more difficult to create inconsistent slides because it practically holds your hand by providing coordinated *styles* and *themes*. Even prior to releasing PowerPoint 2007, Microsoft has provided a simpler solution to these problems in the form of *masters* and *templates*. If you change a master, all slides based on that master change instantly!

Masters, Templates, and Themes

Masters and templates act like frameworks that let you create presentations that are consistent in look and layout. In addition, *themes* which are new for this version of PowerPoint are like templates on steroids.

✔ **Masters are contained within the presentation.**

You can think of masters as design boilerplates that influence slides. Even if you aren't aware of it, PowerPoint uses a master for every new slide.

✔ **Templates are essentially a collection of masters that might or might not contain any slides. Typically, they are saved as separate files.**

You can identify PowerPoint templates by their `.potx` file extension, which is different from PowerPoint's regular `.pptx` file extension.

When you apply a template to a presentation, it's stored within that presentation as a distinct set of masters. The presentation no longer relies on the original template file. Later in this chapter, you find out how to create and apply templates.

Mastering Masters

To really benefit from using masters, you must start with a presentation from scratch and then fine-tune the masters before creating or inserting new slides.

Color Plate 4-1 (see the color insert pages in this book) shows a basic presentation — it contains almost no formatting other than titles and bulleted lists that use the Arial typeface for text elements.

Now look at Color Plate 4-2. This is the same presentation shown in Color Plate 4-1. The only difference is that some self-congratulating PowerPoint guru probably followed these steps to end up with this inconsistent deck of slides:

✔ Formatted each slide background individually using all the background fill types that PowerPoint provides.

✔ Used a different font type for each text placeholder.

✔ Changed the alignment and placement of all slide elements so that all slides looked different from each other.

If you don't want to end up with such an inconsistent pack of slides, your best bet is to peek at the masters within PowerPoint. That's something I show you later in this chapter.

Now that you have seen the colossal misadventure that is caused without exploring masters, head to the color insert section in this book and check out Color Plate 4-3. This is again the same presentation, as shown in the earlier two color plates. Only this time, the presentation creator used the masters feature in PowerPoint to give it a consistent, professional appearance.

Types of masters

PowerPoint can create and store three types of masters:

- ✔ Slide Master
- ✔ Handout Master
- ✔ Notes Master

If you're wondering about what happened to the Title Master, that's now just another *layout* within the Slide Master.

Slide Master

The Slide Master influences the layouts of all slides in a presentation. Any customization in the Slide Master shows up on all slides of your presentation, although you can override this on individual slides. (I show you how later in the chapter.)

Follow these steps to edit or create a Slide Master:

1. **Choose Office⇨New to bring up the New Presentation dialog box that you see in Figure 4-1.**

2. **Click the Blank Presentation button to create a blank, new presentation, and then click the Create button.**

   This step gets you back to PowerPoint. You see a single slide presentation that's blank except for two placeholders for the title and subtitle.

3. **Click the View tab of the Ribbon, and then click the Slide Master button.**

   The Slide Master view opens, as shown in Figure 4-2.

   PowerPoint automatically places a default master in the left pane showing a larger thumbnail with several, indented, smaller thumbnails below it (see Figure 4-2). The smaller thumbnails represent the individual preset layouts that are inserted as the default subset of each Master. Remember — these masters and the individual layouts can be edited. In fact, you can even create your own layouts within the masters. I cover layouts in more detail later in this chapter.

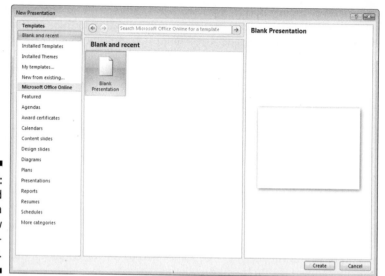

Figure 4-1:
Get started
with a
blank, new
presenta-
tion.

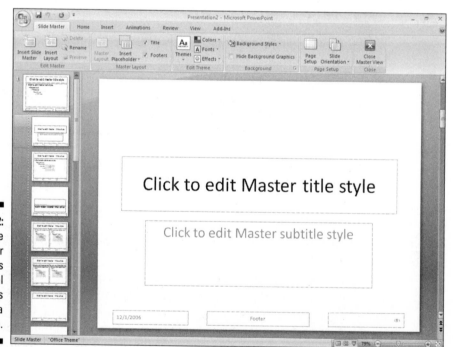

Figure 4-2:
The Slide
Master
shows
several
layouts
and a
blank slide.

The main design thumbnail on the left pane is larger than the other slide layouts — any changes applied while you have this master thumbnail selected get applied to all the layouts that are placed beneath it, unless you go and add individual edits to one of the layouts. When you make an individual edit to one of the layouts, the link between the Master and the layout for that element is broken. So, for example, if you change the background image for one of the slide layouts, changing the background image on the Master will have no impact on that particular layout. On the other hand, if you change the text formatting in the Master, that slide layout will still reflect the change because only the link for the background image change was broken — everything else is still related. You'll understand this concept better when you play with the possibilities.

4. **Click the top thumbnail to select it and then add a background to the Master.**

   Format the slide background of the master, and change the slide look. To quickly do that, right-click the master thumbnail, and choose the Format Background option to summon a dialog box of the same name.

   The options in this dialog box are explained later in this chapter. Look at the section "Background effects," to find ways to add some pizzazz to your presentation.

5. **Format the text on the master.**

   Select the text in any of the placeholders within the master, and alter the size or formatting of the font.

   This can be easily done by right-clicking the selected text, and making changes in the Mini Toolbar that pops up, or by using the font formatting options on the Home tab of the Ribbon.

   You might want to make some text bold or italic — whatever you want to do, this is your chance to make PowerPoint realize that you're the boss. If you want to change the font altogether, it would be best to make changes to the *Theme Fonts,* which I cover later in this chapter.

   Although you can change the font color here, it's best if you leave them to their default color values and change those defaults by altering the Theme Colors, as explained in the previous chapter. Chapter 7 offers more information on dressing up all the text.

6. **Add more elements like a picture or a text box — anything inserted in the Slide Master shows up on all slides based on the particular Slide Master.**

   You can find all the insert options on the Insert tab of the Ribbon.

7. **Get back to Normal view by clicking the View tab of the Ribbon and then clicking Normal.**

Alternatively, just click the Close Master View button on the Slide Master tab of the Ribbon.

8. Save your presentation.

You can have more than one Slide Master, as discussed later in this chapter in the "Multiple masters" section.

Handout Master

The Handout Master decides the look of presentation handouts that you print and distribute. Chapter 14 covers handouts.

Follow these steps to edit the Handout Master:

1. **To go to the Handout Master view, click the View tab on the Ribbon and then click the Handout Master button.**

2. **Edit and customize the Handout Master.**

   Within the Handout edit area, you find four editable regions (on the four corners of the page), as shown in Figure 4-3. These are the header, footer, number, and date. You can edit all four regions; because you're doing all edits on the Handout Master, you see the results in every printed handout.

3. **Edit the background as required.**

   Click the Background Styles option on the Handout Master tab of the Ribbon, and choose from any of the background options in the resultant Background Styles gallery.

4. **To view how your Handout Master looks with a given number of slide thumbnails, choose all the options available within the Slides Per Page option on the Handout Master tab of the ribbon.**

5. **Click Normal on the View tab of the Ribbon to exit the Handout Master view.**

Notes Master

The Notes Master defines the look of printed notes. Follow these steps to edit the Notes Master:

1. **Get into Notes Master view by clicking the View tab on the Ribbon and then clicking the Notes Master button.**

2. **Edit and customize your Notes Master.**

   Within the Notes edit area, you find four editable regions on the four corners of the page, as shown in Figure 4-4. These are header, footer, number, and date.

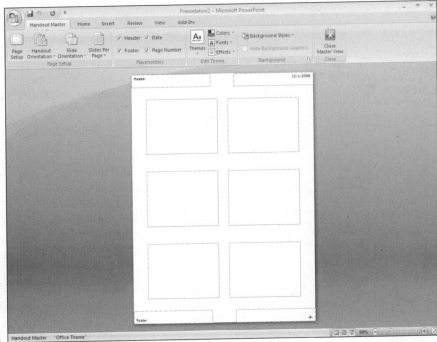

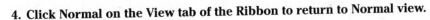

Figure 4-3:
Editing the
Handout
Master.

3. **Indulge yourself and edit as required.**

   You can also select the text in the Notes area below the slide and change the font as required. To do that, select the Notes area box, and change font on the Home tab of the Ribbon.

4. **Click Normal on the View tab of the Ribbon to return to Normal view.**

PowerPoint's capacity to store masters depends on the type of master:

✔ Slide Masters are stored inside both PowerPoint presentations and templates.

✔ PowerPoint 2007 can create and store multiple Slide Masters.

   You can find more about using multiple masters later in this chapter.

✔ Handout and Notes Masters are stored only inside presentations (PPTX files) — templates (POTX files) just ignore them.

   All PowerPoint presentations (PPTX files) can store only one instance each of the Handout Master and Notes Master.

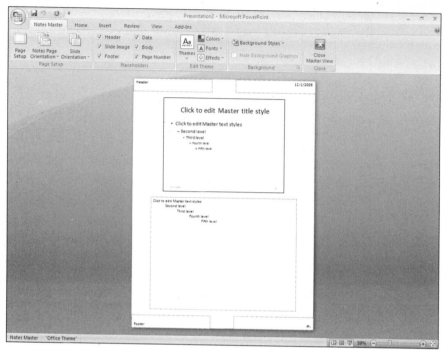

Figure 4-4:
Editing the
Notes
Master.

Arrange your slides with layouts and placeholders

Layouts are as simple as they sound — the arrangement of placeholders in a slide. You can change the layouts as often as you want.

More often than not, you'll tweak these layouts within the Slide Master view, as explained in the preceding section. Tweaking (or customizing) these layouts is a big improvement in this version of PowerPoint — also the implementation is simple and intuitive and allows you to arrange your slides the way you want them to look. If only you could rearrange the furniture in your home as easily!

I first show you how you can explore these layouts and placeholders. Then I show you how you can use these in your presentation and create your own customized layouts.

Built-in layouts

PowerPoint 2007 includes several built-in layouts — and because layouts are contained within the presentation or template, different presentations might not even have the same layouts, almost in the same way that no two rooms in your home have the same furniture layout.

To view the layouts available in any presentation, on the Home tab of the Ribbon, click the Layout button. This brings up the Layouts gallery shown in Figure 4-5.

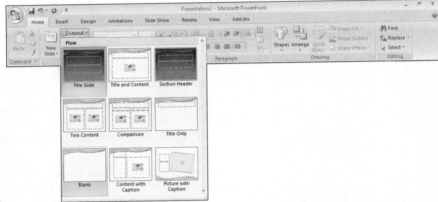

Figure 4-5:
The Layout gallery.

Later in this chapter, I'll show you how you can apply these layouts and create new ones — but before that, you can explore placeholders!

Placeholder types

Each layout is essentially a collection and arrangement of placeholders. PowerPoint provides ten placeholder types:

- ✔ **Title:** Contains the slide title.
- ✔ **Text:** Contains bulleted or non-bulleted text.
- ✔ **Picture:** Holds a graphic image, such as a photo.
- ✔ **Chart:** Contains a chart that you copied from Excel.
- ✔ **Table:** Holds a table.
- ✔ **SmartArt:** Places a SmartArt graphic.
- ✔ **Media:** Places a sound or movie file.
- ✔ **Clip Art:** Holds a clip art image.
- ✔ **Footers:** Places a date, slide number, and copyright footer.
- ✔ **Content:** Contains a content placeholder, a kind of multifaceted place-holder that contains six icons — one each for table, chart, picture, clip art, SmartArt, and video. Click the icon for the content type that you want to place.

The following section shows you how different arrangement of these place-holders can make layouts — in that respect, placeholders are almost like the building blocks of PowerPoint.

Layout styles

Each individual thumbnail in the Layout gallery (refer to Figure 4-5) represents a layout style available in the presentation. You can have tens and hundreds of layout styles, but here are the most important layout styles that are included in almost every PowerPoint presentation:

- **Title Slide:** Comprises a title and subtitle placeholder. This layout is best used for the opening slide, and occasionally for the last slide.

- **Title and Content:** Contains a title and content placeholder. This layout is what you will use most of the time.

- **Section Header:** Contains a title and subtitle placeholder, similar to the Title slide, but used as a cover slide for sections inside a presentation. This layout works best in longer presentations by creating distinct parts within the presentation.

- **Two Content:** Includes a title with two content placeholders, placed next to each other. This layout is great when you want to place two visuals — or a visual with descriptive text — next to each other.

- **Comparison:** Includes a title, two content placeholders, and two text placeholders. This layout is intended for use in situations when you need to compare two objects or concepts.

- **Title Only:** Includes a title with a large, blank expanse underneath. This is the layout style you'd use if you wanted to insert an uncommon object like a Flash movie in a slide. Chapter 13 shows you how you can insert Flash movies in PowerPoint.

- **Blank:** Contains no placeholders, not even the title (although the footer placeholders are still available). Use this layout when you need a blank canvas and you're sure that you don't even need a title for the slide. If you need a title but don't want it to be visible, use the Title Only layout and drag the title placeholder off the slide area so that it exists even if it isn't visible while the presentation is shown.

- **Content with Caption:** Contains placeholders for title, text, and content. This layout works great if you need a text area to describe the content you are going to place on a slide.

- **Picture with Caption:** Contains placeholders for title, text, and picture. This layout works best for displaying your pictures — even the title placeholder in this layout is unobtrusive so that the picture can command all the attention.

Using and changing layouts

Most of the time, you'll want to specify a layout style at the time you insert a new slide. Fortunately, the New Slide button on the Home tab of the Ribbon opens a small gallery that shows you the layout styles available — this allows you to both insert a slide and specify its layout style at one go. Figure 4-6 shows you what this gallery looks like.

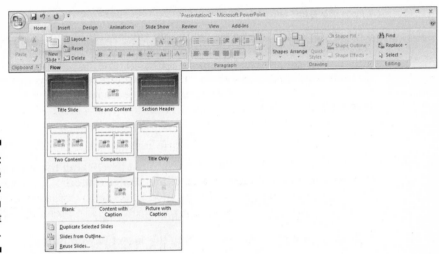

Figure 4-6:
Choose
layouts
when you
insert
a slide.

You might not be as lucky all the time, or you might end up having to improve a presentation that someone else created — and maybe the original creator used all the wrong layouts! I show you how easy it is to change the layout of an existing slide — in fact, you have at least two quick ways to do just that:

✔ Right-click the slide and choose Layout from the contextual menu to see the Layout gallery. Click the layout you want to apply to the slide.

✔ Make sure that the active slide is the one for which you want to change the layout. Then click the Home tab on the Ribbon and then click the Layout option to access the Layout gallery. Click the layout you want to apply to the slide.

Although changing slide layouts is easy, you might not want to do it all the time just because it's easy! Reasons to avoid changing the layout include

✔ The slide has too much content already, and it might be better to divide the content in two or more slides before changing layouts.

✔ You might end up applying the blank layout to a slide that contains title and text — the title and text will be still there on the slide, but the place-holders will be converted (read downgraded) to mere text boxes.

Any text within a text placeholder is part of the outline, and text that is within a text box is not a part of the outline.

✔ The arrangement and alignment of placeholders might change in the slide.

Creating new layouts

Think of the presentation as your home, the layouts as the rooms, and the placeholders as the furniture. Say you really want to buy new furniture for your home or rearrange or throw out the old furniture. PowerPoint lets you do that — and it also lets you whip up a few more rooms in your existing home and duplicate your furniture! You can even rename your customized layouts.

Follow these steps to create new layouts:

1. **Get into the Slide Master environment by clicking the View tab on the Ribbon and then clicking the Slide Master button.**

   PowerPoint is suddenly in rearrangement mode; note that the selected tab on the Ribbon is now the Slide Master tab.

2. **Insert a new layout by clicking the Insert Layout button.**

   PowerPoint places a new layout that will be highlighted in the left pane.

3. **Rename the layout by right-clicking the slide in the left pane and choosing Rename Layout, as shown in Figure 4-7.**

   This action summons the Rename Layout dialog box, as shown in Figure 4-8.

4. **Type a new name in the Layout Name text box and click the Rename button.**

Figure 4-7:
Right-click
and choose
the Rename
Layout
option.

Figure 4-8:
Type a
descriptive
name.

Rename Layout

Layout name:

My Picture Layout

Rename

Cancel

5. Remove or reposition the title.

By default, PowerPoint places a title placeholder. Remove it or reposition as required. I decided to rotate my title placeholder and placed it on the left of the slide, as you can see in Figure 4-10 (later in this chapter).

6. Add some placeholders by clicking the Insert Placeholder button and selecting a placeholder type, as shown in Figure 4-9.

I chose a Picture placeholder, and the cursor turned into a cross-hair — I then dragged and drew an area for the picture placeholder.

Add more placeholders as required. Remember to keep it as simple as possible because too many placeholders might make your finished slide look cluttered.

I just added a text placeholder and replaced the dummy text on the placeholder with my own text because I was going to use this text placeholder as a caption area for the picture. Figure 4-10 shows my finished layout.

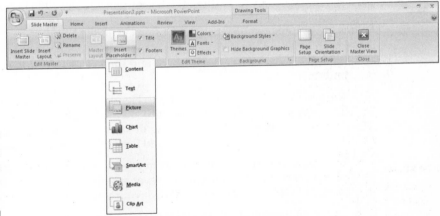

Figure 4-9:
Add some
place-
holders.

7. Get back to Normal view by clicking the Close Master View button on the Slide Master tab.

8. Save your presentation.

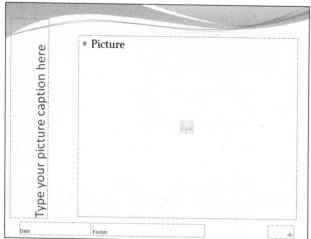

Figure 4-10:
A new
layout.

Background effects

PowerPoint allows you to use different fill effects options as slide backgrounds, such as a solid fill, a gradient fill, and a picture or texture fill.

As often as possible, change the background for the slides in the Slide Master view rather than in Normal view. PowerPoint uses the background options specified in the master (or slide layout) for all slides unless you override the background choice by formatting the background of any slide in Normal view.

Follow these steps to alter the backgrounds in Slide Master view:

1. **Click the View tab on the Ribbon, and then click the Slide Master button.**

   The Slide Master view opens (refer to Figure 4-2). In the Slides pane, click the larger slide preview if you want to alter the background for the master and all slide layouts inherited below, or select one of the smaller previews if you want to change the background for a particular slide layout.

   You might have more than one master — so if you want to change the background of another master (or even a slide layout), scroll down the pane and select the master or slide layout you want.

2. **Check the background styles by clicking the Background Styles option on the Slide Master tab.**

   You see the Background Styles gallery, as shown in Figure 4-11.

   You could just click any of the options in this gallery — when you hover your cursor over any of the thumbnails, you see a live preview of how that particular background looks on your slide.

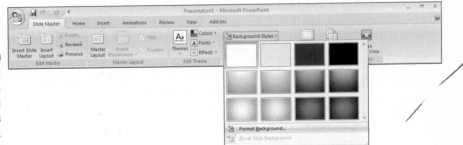

Figure 4-11:
The
Background
Styles
gallery.

3. **To customize the background, click the Format Background option at the bottom of this gallery.**

The Format Background dialog box appears, as shown in Figure 4-12.

Figure 4-12:
The Format
Background
dialog box.

The Format Background dialog box has two tabs — Fill and Picture. The Fill tab allows you to select

- Solid Fill
- Gradient Fill
- Texture or Picture Fill

4. **Select the option you want and click the Apply to All button.**

The following sections give all the details for each of the background fill types.

Solid color

A solid fill is a solid block of color for the entire background of the slide. To apply a solid-color background to a Slide Master, follow these steps:

1. **Access the Format Background dialog box as described in the preceding section, "Background effects."**

   Refer to Figure 4-12.

2. **In the Fill tab of this dialog box, select the Solid Fill option.**

3. **Click the Color button to access the color chooser, as shown in Figure 4-13.**

4. **Select one of the Theme Colors or Standard Colors or choose the More Colors option to summon the Colors dialog box, shown in Figure 4-14.**

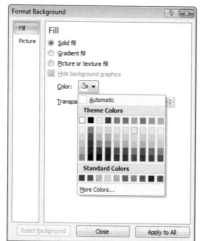

Figure 4-13:
The color chooser.

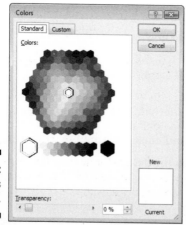

Figure 4-14:
The Colors dialog box.

5. **Select any of the colors from the color hive in the dialog box, and then click OK.**

   If you want to use a color that isn't available in the hive, click the Custom tab, which lets you choose any color from a spectrum. For the lowdown on color, see Chapter 3.

6. **Click Apply to All to apply to all Masters and layouts in the presentation.**

   The Reset Background option is only available if you select a slide layout rather than the Master, and applies the background associated with the Master to a particular slide layout.

7. **Click Close to get back to your slide with the background choice applied to the chosen Master and its layouts.**

Gradient fill

Gradient fill backgrounds are a quick way to escape the plain look of a solid color.

Using gradient fill backgrounds might improve the *performance* of your computer compared to picture backgrounds (which I explore next) because

- Gradient fills aren't as processor-intensive as textured or full-screen picture backgrounds.
- Gradient fills keep file sizes small.

Follow these steps to apply a gradient as a background:

1. **Access the Format Background dialog box as described in the earlier section, "Background effects."**

   Refer to Figure 4-12.

2. **Select the Gradient Fill option.**

   This changes the options in the dialog box, as shown in Figure 4-15.

3. **Select the options for the gradient.**

   The deceptively simple-looking dialog box hides a slew of options normally found in high-end graphic programs:

   - *Preset Colors:* This opens a fly-out gallery with several preset gradients that are part of PowerPoint's fill engine — some of these gradients use more than two colors.
   - *Type:* You can choose from Linear, Radial, Rectangular, Path, and Shade from Title options for the gradient type. The background of the slide in Figure 4-16 uses the Shade from Title option, while the rectangles within the slide show you samples of the remaining four types.

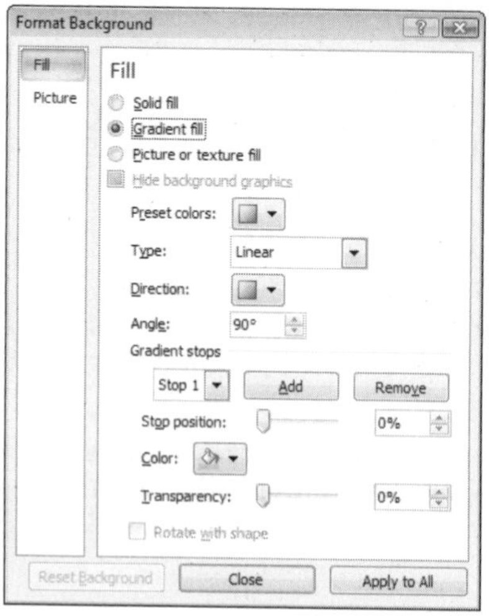

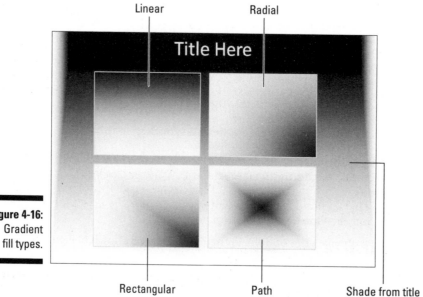

Figure 4-15:
Gradient
fill options.

Linear   Radial

Title Here

Figure 4-16:
Gradient
fill types.

Rectangular   Path   Shade from title

- *Direction and Angle:* Choose from eight gradient directions — or just type the angle of the direction you want in the Angle text box.

- *Gradient Stops:* You can choose from Stop 1 and Stop 2 or click the Add and Remove buttons to add and delete stops. *Stops* are basically a new color that forms a gradient with another color. You can also alter the start position and transparency of each stop — so you could create a gradient that ranges from pink to blue and violet — and each of the colors could have different transparencies and stop positions. Truly powerful stuff!

- *Rotate with Shape:* This option allows the gradient fills to rotate if the shapes themselves rotate. You might wonder how you can rotate a background! Rest assured, you can't do that — just ignore this option!

4. **Click Close to get back to the Slide Master view, with your changes visible on the chosen Master and its layouts. Click Apply to All to apply the changes to all Masters and layouts in the presentation.**

Gradient backgrounds have a couple of drawbacks:

✔ **Gradients are unsuitable for presentations with numerous elements.** Many slide objects work better with a solid-color background rather than a gradient that uses two (or more) colors.

✔ **Gradients don't display similarly across different systems.** Some machines might display banding. *Banding* is the visibility of distinct lines of colors being mixed between the two gradient colors — this normally happens when you're running your computer in 8-bit color (that's 256-color mode). Almost all computers shipped in the last five years can display millions of colors.

Picture or texture fill

Picture backgrounds are the most attractive and versatile of all backgrounds, whereas textured backgrounds use seamless tiles to repeat a pattern all over the slide background. The same picture can be used as a picture fill or texture fill for the slide background.

Follow these steps to apply a picture or texture fill:

1. **Access the Format Background dialog box as described in the earlier section, "Background effects."**

   Refer to Figure 4-12.

2. **Select the Picture or Texture Fill option.**

   This changes the options in the dialog box, as shown in Figure 4-17.

Figure 4-17:
Picture
or Texture
fill options.

3. Choose the options for the texture:

- *Texture:* Click the Texture option to see a fly-out gallery of PowerPoint's built in textures. Click any of them to apply it as a background.

- *Insert from File:* Allows you to browse and select any picture in your system as a background.

- *Insert from Clipboard:* Uses a picture copied to the Clipboard as the background.

- *Insert from Clip Art:* This opens the Select Picture dialog box that you can see in Figure 4-18. Essentially, this is almost the same as the Clip Art task pane. You can find out more about the Clip Art task pane in Chapter 9.

- *Tile Picture as Texture:* This option, when selected, tiles a selected picture almost like a texture. Unlike PowerPoint's built-in textures, these textures might not be seamless.

   The accompanying CD contains hundreds of seamless textures ready for you to use as fills in your presentations.

- *Tiling Options:* Allows you to choose offset and scale coordinates. You can also opt to align as required and to mirror the picture or texture, which can provide interesting pattern-like results and works very well if you use a small picture that ends up looking like a repeating pattern.

- *Transparency:* Allows you to set the transparency of the picture or texture.

Figure 4-18:
The Select
Picture
dialog box.

- *Rotate with Shape:* This option is more relevant for shapes in PowerPoint that use the same background fill options (and dialog box). It allows the gradient fills to rotate if the shape themselves rotate.

4. **Click Close to apply the changes to the chosen Master and its layouts. Click Apply to All to apply the changes to all Masters and layouts in the presentation.**

Changes in this version of PowerPoint are applied in real time, so clicking the Close button in the Format Background dialog box just removes the dialog box. In fact, you can also use other options in PowerPoint, and keep the Format Background dialog box open, a real possibility if you have more screen estate, such as a dual monitor setup. Otherwise, the dialog box can be a screen real estate pig — just click Close to send it away!

Avoid picture backgrounds if your presentation consists of a lot of elements, unless the picture you're using is very *neutral, faded,* or *blurred.*

Usually, you have to tweak picture backgrounds in an *image editor* — a separate application that allows you to edit and create images. The most well-known image editor is Adobe Photoshop, but plenty of free and low-priced alternatives also exist. You can find many options listed on this book's companion site at

`www.cuttingedgeppt.com/imageeditors`

Within your image editor, experiment with adjustments in brightness, contrast, and saturation to attain an image that can be an acceptable background. You might also want to use the image editor to resize the background.

Size dimensions for an ideal presentation picture background are 1,024 x 768 pixels or 800 x 600 pixels. These size dimensions are for normal 4:3 monitors and projectors — wide-screen displays require different dimensions.

While designing your backgrounds, try creating variations for your slide and title slides and a coordinated print-suitable background that includes large areas of white.

On the CD accompanying this book, you can find over a hundred ready-to-use presentation backgrounds.

Multiple masters

PowerPoint supports using more than one Slide Master within a single presentation. Follow these steps to add more Slide Masters in PowerPoint:

1. **Click the View tab on the Ribbon and then click the Slide Master button.**

   The Slide Master view opens (refer to Figure 4-2).

2. **Click the Insert Slide Master button to add a new Slide Master.**

3. **Format as required using the options explained in the "Slide Master" section, earlier in this chapter.**

4. **Right-click the Master thumbnail in the Slides pane, and choose Preserve Master if that option is not already selected.**

   This option ensures that your Masters are not deleted even if none of the slides in the presentation actually uses them.

5. **When you are done, click the Close Master View button.**

You can add, delete, and edit slide layouts to this new Slide Master.

Applying masters

The following subsections provide the steps to apply masters to individual and specific slides in PowerPoint.

Complete presentation

Follow these steps to change the master for all slides in a presentation:

1. **Access the Themes gallery by clicking the Design tab on the Ribbon and then clicking the down-pointing arrow beside the Themes gallery, as shown in Figure 4-19.**

   In the top area of the gallery are several master previews in the This Presentation area.

   If you can't see more than one master preview in the **This Presentation** area, your presentation doesn't have multiple masters. Refer to the "Multiple masters" section, earlier in this chapter, to create more masters.

2. **Click the appropriate master preview to apply the master to all slides in the presentation.**

   If you inadvertently click a preview icon that you don't like, press Ctrl+Z to undo the change.

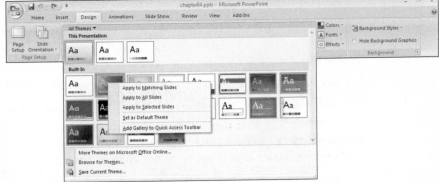

Figure 4-19:
The Theme gallery.

Specific slides

If you want to apply a master to specific slides in a presentation, follow these steps:

1. **Click the View tab on the Ribbon and then click the Slide Sorter button to access Slide Sorter view.**

2. **Choose the individual slides that you want to change:**

   - To select slides in a sequence, select the first slide and then Shift+click the last slide in the sequence.

   - To select slides out of sequence, select the first slide and then Ctrl+click individual slides.

3. **Access the Themes gallery by clicking the Design tab on the Ribbon and then clicking the downward-pointing arrow in the bottom-right of the Themes gallery (refer to Figure 4-19).**

   In the top area of the task pane are several master previews in the This Presentation area.

   If you can't see more than one master preview in the This Presentation area, your presentation doesn't have multiple masters. Refer to the "Multiple masters" section, earlier in this chapter, to create more masters.

4. **Right-click any of the master previews in the gallery and choose the Apply to Selected Slides option to change the master for selected slides.**

   You also have the Apply to Matching Slides option (refer to Figure 4-19) that changes the master for all slides based on the same slide master. Again, this option might not be available if you don't have multiple masters in the open presentation.

If you inadvertently click a preview icon you don't like, press Ctrl+Z to undo the change.

Masters: Design guidelines

Masters ensure that your presentations remain consistent in design, layout, and form. These guidelines can help you attain that goal:

- ✔ **Overriding masters:** For a certain slide, you might want to override the master with your own settings. While in Normal view, you can use the options in the Background Styles gallery on the Design tab to change the background of the active slide. This change at the slide level overrides the master settings — any changes you make to the master aren't reflected on that slide, text box, or placeholder thereafter.

- ✔ **Company logos in masters:** You can place a company logo within a slide master if the logo is available in a picture format that PowerPoint can import. (See Chapter 9 to find out all about pulling pictures into your presentations.)

- ✔ **Footers in masters:** Editing footers in masters allows you to add the time, date, author name, and/or slide number to all slides that are based on that particular master.

- ✔ **Renaming masters:** Within the Slide Master view, you can right-click a master thumbnail within the left pane and choose Rename from the contextual menu to provide meaningful names to all your masters.

Transforming Masters into Templates or Themes

You've created masters, and all your placeholders are positioned and format-ted exactly as you want them. The colors work great, and you love the back-ground choices you made. Now you want a few (or a few thousand) PowerPoint users to maintain the same look and identity in their presentations.

This is simple enough: Just evolve your master to become a template or theme. Every master's lifelong dream is to someday become a template or theme!

Differentiating between templates and themes

So what's the difference between templates and themes? Let me tell you first what Microsoft calls them: Templates are PowerPoint Templates, and themes are Office Themes. That in itself makes the distinction complete — whereas templates are limited to being used within PowerPoint itself, themes are design looks that work in other Microsoft Office applications such as Word and Excel.

Apart from that difference, the way templates and themes work in PowerPoint isn't too different. In fact, many times the terms are used interchangeably.

Housekeeping

Before you save to a template or theme, you should do some housekeeping so that your template or theme is well organized and not as bloated as a hip-popotamus. Clean up your template or theme by following these steps:

1. **Include the Properties information for the template by choosing Office⇨Prepare⇨Properties.**

   The Properties pane appears.

2. **Click the Document Properties text link on the top of the pane and then click Advanced Properties from the menu that appears.**

   This brings up the Properties dialog box shown in Figure 4-20.

3. **Click the Summary tab in the Properties dialog box and describe your template or theme.**

   The Summary tab provides a slew of text boxes to describe everything you want to about your template or theme. You don't have to fill in every text box, but be sure to enter a name for the template in the Title text box and to include your name in the Author text box.

Figure 4-20:
The Properties dialog box.

4. **Delete all slides in the presentation.**

   Even if you delete the slides, the masters don't get deleted. This works as long as you preserved the masters, as explained in the "Multiple Masters" section earlier in this chapter.

   Removing all slides makes the final output more compact.

   Don't save the presentation yet — the following steps show you how you can save the presentation as a template or theme.

Saving as a template or theme

To save a template or theme, follow these steps:

1. **Choose Office⇨Save As.**

   This opens the Save As dialog box.

2. In the Save as Type drop-down list, select either PowerPoint Template (*.potx) or Office Theme (*.thmx), as shown in Figure 4-21.

By default, PowerPoint automatically saves templates and themes in a specially designated folder, although you can opt to save to any other folder instead.

3. Click the Save button.

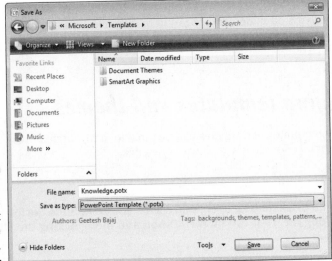

Figure 4-21:
Save as
PowerPoint
Template
or Theme.

Microsoft has created a distinction between masters, templates, and themes in the file format within which they're saved:

- ✔ **Regular PowerPoint presentations are usually named with the `.pptx` or `.ppsx` extensions.** Such presentations can include masters.
- ✔ **Templates are saved with the `.potx` extension.**
- ✔ **Themes are saved with the `.thmx` extension.**

Customizing templates and themes

PowerPoint ships with many ready-made templates (and themes) that you can customize as required to create new variations. Such customization is a good idea because most existing PowerPoint templates can look canned because everyone else is using them — you've probably seen all PowerPoint templates at one meeting or another by now!

Beyond Microsoft's own offerings, hundreds of other vendors create templates — a simple online search provides several links to both free and commercial sites. You can find many such resources at this book's companion site:

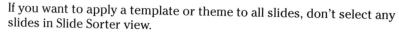
www.cuttingedgeppt.com/templates

This book's accompanying CD contains over 100 free PowerPoint templates that you can use.

You can opt for ultimate customization by commissioning your own PowerPoint template or theme — many professional template designers can do this for you.

Applying templates and themes

Applying templates and themes can be fun. I love to watch a presentation metamorphose into a new look with one click.

The steps to apply a template or theme are easy:

1. **With a presentation open, make sure you're in Slide Sorter view by clicking the View tab on the Ribbon and then clicking the Slide Sorter button.**

2. **If you want to apply a template to selected slides, select them individually in Slide Sorter view.**

    Use the Ctrl or Shift key to select more than one slide.

    If you want to apply a template or theme to all slides, don't select any slides in Slide Sorter view.

3. **Access the Themes gallery by clicking the Design tab and then clicking the down-pointing arrow in the bottom of the Themes gallery.**

    This reveals a drop-down gallery (refer to Figure 4-19). In the top area of the gallery are several thumbnails under the headings Customs and Built-In.

4. **Live preview the templates and themes by hovering the cursor over a thumbnail.**

5. **Click the thumbnail that you want to apply as a template or theme.**

    You aren't limited to using the templates or themes that show up in the Themes gallery. If you want to apply another template or theme from your hard drive, just click the Browse for Themes link below the thumbnail previews and choose any PowerPoint Template (.potx) or Office Theme (.thmx) on your computer.

You aren't limited to using templates and themes, either. You can browse to any PowerPoint presentation (.pptx) file on your computer and apply that as a template to a presentation!

If you inadvertently click a preview icon that you don't like, press Ctrl+Z to undo the change.

Creating templates from existing presentations

If you like the look of an existing presentation, you can save it as a template. Yes, PowerPoint allows you to choose any .pptx file on your computer and convert it to a template.

It's easy to create a template from an existing presentation — you might first want to create a backup copy of the presentation involved:

1. **Delete all slides within the active presentation.**

2. **Insert two blank slides by pressing Ctrl+M twice and accepting the defaults.**

   PowerPoint automatically inserts one slide each, based on these layouts:

   - Title Slide

   - Title and Content

   Leave these slides unaltered.

3. **Save as a PowerPoint template (.potx) file:**

   a. Choose Office⇨Save As.

   b. Select PowerPoint Template (*.potx) from the Save as Type drop-down list (refer to Figure 4-21).

   c. Click the Save button.

Using blank or default templates

When you start PowerPoint, you can create a blank presentation.

Such blank presentations are based on PowerPoint's default blank template that has just one Slide Master and uses Calibri as the default font.

The best part of this blank presentation ability is that you can use any template to create your blank presentation. Imagine how much time you could save if PowerPoint would default to your own custom template that you use all the time.

Assuming you've formatted your default presentation exactly as you want, follow these steps to create your default template:

1. **Choose Office⇨Save As.**

2. **Select PowerPoint Template (*.potx) as the file type.**

    PowerPoint saves the template in the default Templates folder.

    Don't change the location!

3. **Name your template.**

    Name your template **Blank.potx**.

4. **Click the Save button.**

Sometimes you might apply a custom template to a presentation but then want to go back to a plain template presentation — something that contains black text on a white background. To do this, create a boilerplate blank template (under a different name than the default template) and apply it to the active presentation.

If you want to use any of PowerPoint's built-in Themes as a default template, just right-click the Theme thumbnail within the Theme gallery, and choose the Set as Default Theme option. The Theme gallery can be found on the Design tab of the Ribbon.

Part II
Achieving Visual Appeal

The 5th Wave   By Rich Tennant

"Look-what if we just increase the size of the charts?"

In this part . . .

This part is all about the visual element in PowerPoint. From the basic building blocks of PowerPoint to the text content, and from pictures to diagrams, this part covers all the stuff that you see on a typical PowerPoint slide.

Chapter 5

Shape Magic

· ·

In This Chapter

▶ Creating supernatural shapes

▶ Making your shapes behave

▶ Copying formatting with the Format Painter

▶ Creating connections in your presentation

▶ Exploring more ways to use shapes

· ·

*P*resentation graphics can emphasize your essential message and keep your audience's attention. But great presentation graphics often take time that you can better spend on other tasks in your business (especially if you aren't already an expert designer — or maybe you just need more time to study astronomy).

PowerPoint shapes can give your presentations the pop you need with just a few simple steps. This chapter shows how you can quickly create and customize presentation graphics with shapes.

And if you're a seasoned PowerPoint user who's wondering what happened to PowerPoint's AutoShapes, rest assured that they're still there — now they're called shapes!

Shapes use PowerPoint's basic fill, effect, line, color, and font tools. If a tool in this chapter is unfamiliar, it's covered elsewhere in this book. Colors, for example, are covered in Chapter 3; fonts and text are in Chapter 8; and fills, lines, and effects are detailed in Chapter 6.

Why Shapes?

Shapes are preset, intelligent patterns like circles, arrows, stars, and callouts — even lines that you can use to draw almost anything inside PowerPoint. Think of them as cookie cutters!

Figure 5-1 shows some of these shapes. Combine these to create amazing visual content so fast that your colleagues will be left blinking and dazzled.

With shapes, you can

- ✔ Draw circles, rectangles, arcs, hexagons, cubes, and many other polygons (both 2-D and 3-D).
- ✔ Place a thought bubble beside a picture of Aunt Eliza and make her think (for a change).
- ✔ Combine several shapes to create diagrams, flowcharts, and timelines.
- ✔ Draw an exotic thunderbolt shape fit for Harry Potter's forehead.
- ✔ Draw stars with more points than you can count.

If you want to create better presentations, you'll love shapes.

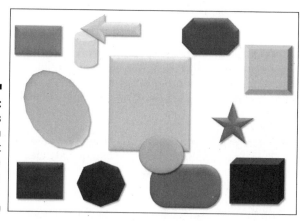

Figure 5-1:
Shapes might seem trivial, but they're the tops in PowerPoint.

You can create professional-looking drawings on your slides even if you've led an uneventful, boring, or sinister life that required no artistic expression. If you've led a moral and eventful life full of artistic vision, you'll still love shapes because Microsoft tested this technology with all sorts of guinea pigs (er, users).

Although shapes are versatile, you can't get too far in your presentations by using them as they are. After all, how much impact can a set of green cookie-cutter patterns on a white background make? Not to worry — in Chapter 6, you find out how to combine shapes with exotic fills, lines, and effects. In fact, you discover the easiest route to create cutting-edge PowerPoint presentations that scream *wow!*

Types of shapes

You access each type of shape from the Shapes gallery, as shown in Figure 5-2.

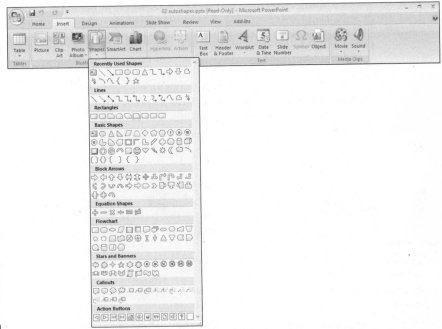

Figure 5-2:
The Shapes gallery.

PowerPoint offers nine types of shapes:

- **Lines:** Lines (with or without arrows), curves, freeform paths, and scribbles. (Chapter 6 shows you more about drawing lines and paths.)

  In addition, lines also work as connectors — these connect individual shapes with straight and curved branches. You can have arrowheads on either, none, or both ends of the connectors.

- **Rectangles:** PowerPoint provides several types of rectangles other than the ubiquitous squares and rectangles — these include rounded and snipped corner rectangles.

- **Basic Shapes:** Create circles, cubes, hearts, and many not-so-basic shapes.

- **Block Arrows:** An assortment of arrow styles will make sure that you move in the right direction and sequence.

- **Equation Shapes:** A new category of shapes in PowerPoint 2007 that comprises common mathematical equation symbols.

- **Flowchart:** Create a number of standard flowchart shapes, such as *process, decision,* and *data.*

- **Stars and Banners:** Draw stars, explosions, scrolls, and banners.

- **Callouts:** Insert comic book–style speech bubbles, as well as line callouts.

- **Action Buttons:** Add push-style buttons that allow you to add navigation between slides. See Chapter 13 for more information on navigation.

On top of all these shape types in the Shapes gallery, you find a selection in the Recently Used Shapes area. Most of the shapes you've used recently are also visible in their normal locations in the Shapes gallery.

Drawing shapes

Shapes can be found in the Shapes gallery on the Home and Insert tabs of the Ribbon. Click the down-pointing arrow within this gallery to see the Shapes gallery in all its splendor, as visible earlier in Figure 5-2.

You can draw a shape in two ways:

- Choose any shape in the Shapes gallery and click the desired location on the slide to place a default-sized shape.

- Choose any shape in the Shapes gallery and then drag and draw on the slide to place a shape of the size and proportion you require.

PowerPoint automatically applies a default fill and line to the shape. Yes, you can change those defaults. (See the sidebar in Chapter 6.)

After you've created a shape, you can change its orientation and position — and even its visibility! That's all covered later in this chapter.

Text within shapes

To add text to a shape, draw a shape and start typing immediately thereafter. Anything you type shows up within the shape.

You can't use this technique to add text to shape types such as lines and Action Buttons. If you try, PowerPoint pops up the Action Settings dialog box before you can type a word!

To type or edit text within an existing shape, follow these steps:

1. **Click the shape to select it.**

2. **Right-click the shape and choose Edit Text.**

3. **Start typing your text to input new text (and delete the existing text, if any). If you want to edit the existing text, click anywhere within the text and edit as usual.**

In many ways, shapes function in the same way as regular text placeholders. That isn't surprising; any new text box you create on a slide is actually just a rectangle shape with special characteristics.

"Sticky" shape tools

Sometimes, you want to pull your hair out because PowerPoint insists on making you work more. This is particularly true if you want to draw 100 stars on your slide. (Now why do you want to do that?) PowerPoint insists that you reselect the star shape after drawing each star. (Is that because PowerPoint doesn't want you to daydream?) That means you're clicking within the Shapes gallery 100 times! Maybe it's just easier to imagine a sky without stars?

Or maybe you should tame PowerPoint and get your work done fast — I show you how to do just that.

PowerPoint changes the shape crosshair cursor to the default arrow cursor soon after you draw a single shape. If you want to draw 100 stars, don't go back to the Basic Shapes section in the Shapes gallery 100 times. Do this instead:

1. **In the Shapes gallery, choose the category you need (such as Stars & Banners).**

2. **Choose the exact shape you need.**

3. **Right-click the Shape icon and choose the Lock Drawing Mode option (see Figure 5-3) so that the icon remains "sticky."**

   Now you won't have to go to the Shapes gallery again!

4. **Draw your 100 or so shapes.**

5. **Click the star icon once again (or any other icon) or just press Esc to get your hands off this sticky mess.**

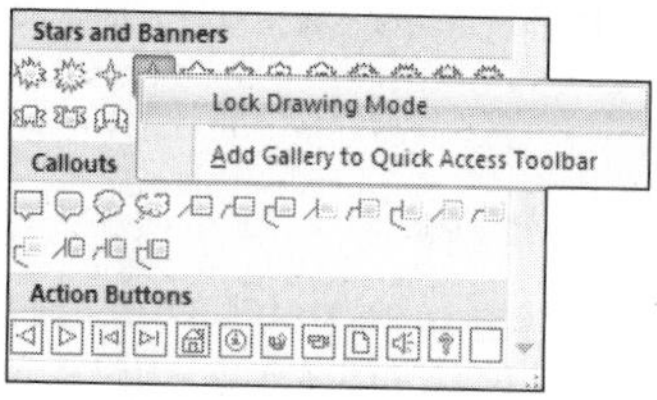

Figure 5-3:
Make your
chosen
shape
sticky.

Supernatural shape abilities

Shapes in PowerPoint have special attributes and supernatural powers. Some of them are such show-offs that they even sport yellow diamonds when selected. And some even sport more than one of those diamonds!

You can't steal those diamonds, but you can certainly put them to good use. For example:

✔ Dragging the diamond above a rounded rectangle shape from left to right (or top to bottom) increases the "rounded" value of the rectangle, as shown in Figure 5-4.

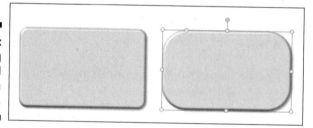

Figure 5-4:
Increasing
the rounded
value of a
rectangle.

✔ Dragging the diamond up or to the right on a parallelogram, octagon, hexagon, or trapezoid alters the shape further. If you drag it to the maximum extent, you end up with almost a diamond shape. On the other hand, dragging to the left (or bottom) gives you almost a rectangle — look at Figure 5-5.

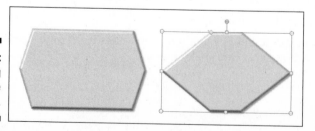

Figure 5-5:
Adjusting
a shape
is easy.

✔ Dragging the diamond down or to the right on a cube, bevel, or can (otherwise known as a cylinder) alters the three-dimensional angle of the shape. Drag to the left (or top) to make the shape more two-dimensional, as illustrated in Figure 5-6.

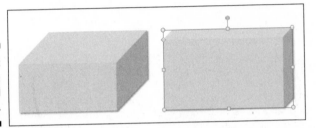

Figure 5-6:
Controlling
the third
dimension.

✔ You can adjust the size of the various parts of an arrow by dragging its yellow diamond, as shown in Figure 5-7. Most arrows have two diamonds — one each to alter the arrowhead and the line.

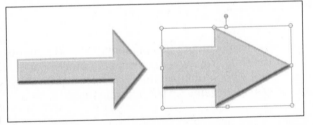

Figure 5-7:
Make your
arrows
behave.

✔ All stars have diamonds — pull them toward the center to create a star with a smaller center. Drag outward to create larger centers. In fact, if you drag the 32-point star's diamond outward, you end up with an oval — almost. Figure 5-8 shows you more.

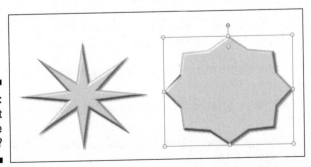

Figure 5-8:
Stars that
behave like
ovals?

✔ With callouts, pulling the diamond around the shape moves the tail of the callout. If you can't see the diamond, look at the bottom end of the tail! (See Figure 5-9.)

Figure 5-9:
See who's
talking with
those
callouts.

Experiment with any shape you use in a presentation and pull those diamonds all over the slide. You never know what unique shapes those diamonds can cause! And if you don't like the changes, you can always undo your last few changes by pressing Ctrl+Z multiple times.

Changing shapes

Sometimes you end up using the wrong shape — or maybe somebody else used the wrong shape and sent the presentation to you. By the time you realize the mistake, you've already added a fill and applied some animation and don't want to delete and start all over again.

Follow these steps to change the shape itself without altering the fill, effects, or animation associated with the shape:

1. **Double-click the shape to access the Drawing Tools Format tab of the Ribbon.**

2. **Click the Edit Shape icon to see the contextual menu shown in Figure 5-10.**

3. **Choose the Change Shape option to access a variation of the Shapes gallery (see Figure 5-10).**

4. **Click the shape you want to change to.**

Figure 5-10:
Change
your
shapes, and
no one will
be wiser!

Keeping Your Shapes (And Everything Else in PowerPoint) Tidy

If you leave your things all over the place and then forget where you put them, you already know the virtues of keeping everything tidy. Things aren't too different in PowerPoint-land, other than the fact that you won't be able to find that elusive shape in front of an audience while you're presenting! And your shapes will be scattered all over the slide because they were never aligned to each other!

To avoid such disasters, read and implement each trick I explain in this section!

Although I discuss the resize, rotate, flip, nudge, move, align, and distribute options using shapes, bear in mind that most other slide elements, including photos, charts, and even videos, can be manipulated in the same way.

Double-click any shape to summon the Drawing Tools Format tab of the Ribbon. At the far right of this tab is a Size group, and clicking the dialog box launcher here opens the venerable Size and Position dialog box with three tabs (see Figure 5-11).

On the Size tab, you find options to resize and rotate shapes. Use this dialog box if you need to enter exact coordinates or resize percentages. If you don't need to be so exact, you can use faster and easier ways of keeping your shapes in order. For now, click Close to get rid of this dialog box.

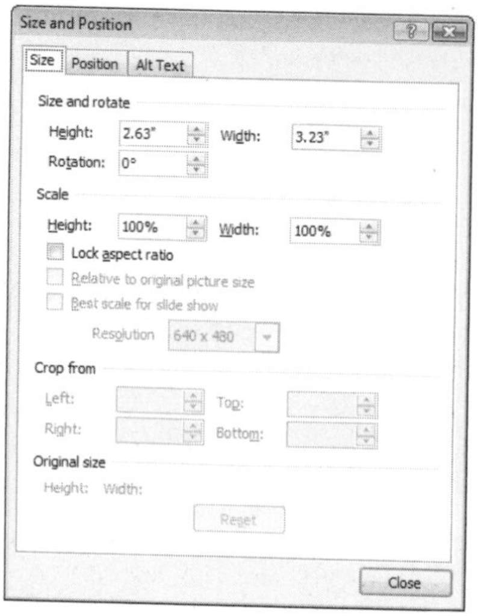

Figure 5-11:
The Size
and Position
dialog box.

PowerPoint uses three types of organizing processes to keep shapes in line:

- Selection
- Orientation
- Positioning

In the following sections, I explain the individual tasks that are part of these processes.

Selection

Before you change the orientation or reposition anything on a PowerPoint slide, you must select it. It's easy to select a single object, such as a shape, unless it's placed behind several other objects.

Or maybe you need to select multiple objects. Whatever you need to do, I now explain how you can make the selection process quicker and easier — and more intuitive.

Selecting one shape

This is what you'll do most of the time:

- Click a shape to select it.
- If you want to select a shape that's behind some shapes and not easily selected, press the Tab key to rotate between all shapes and other objects on the slide until the shape you want is selected.

✔ Take advantage of PowerPoint's new Selection and Visibility task pane. See the "Using the Selection and Visibility task pane" section, later in this chapter.

Selecting multiple shapes

To select more than one object, use any of these options:

✔ Click a shape to select it and then Ctrl+click another shape to select it. You can also use Shift+click to do the same thing, but your cursor won't show the "plus" graphic!

✔ Draw a marquee with your cursor over some shapes to select them all — this works best when only the shapes you want are placed next to each other.

✔ Select all the shapes and other objects on a slide by pressing Ctrl+A. Then Ctrl+click every shape or other object that you don't want to be part of the selection to deselect them. You end up with all the shapes you want selected.

✔ Use PowerPoint's new Selection and Visibility task pane that I explain next.

Using the Selection and Visibility task pane

The Selection and Visibility task pane is new for this version of PowerPoint, and it replaces the Select Multiple Objects tool in earlier PowerPoint versions.

Follow these steps to access this task pane:

1. **Double-click any shape to access the Drawing Tools Format tab of the Ribbon.**

2. **In the Arrange group, click the Selection Pane option to bring up this task pane, as shown in Figure 5-12.**

   You can also get to this option from anywhere the Arrange option shows up, such as on the Home tab of the Ribbon.

3. **Use the Selection and Visibility task pane as described in the bulleted list following these steps.**

4. **When you're done with working in this pane, click the same option again to hide it, or click the X in the upper-right corner of the pane.**

The task pane lists every single object on the active slide, including shapes, text boxes and placeholders, WordArt, and even sounds and movies. If any particular object on the slide doesn't show up on the task pane, that object is either part of the Slide Master or is the background of the slide. (To find out more about masters, take a look at Chapter 4.)

Figure 5-12:
Select and
hide your
shapes!

Follow these guidelines to use the Selection and Visibility task pane:

- ✔ Click a shape in the task pane to select it on the slide.
- ✔ Ctrl+click to select more shapes in the pane (and on the slide).
- ✔ You can also combine selecting shapes on the pane and on the slide at the same time. Again, you can use Ctrl+clicking to work more efficiently.
- ✔ Right-click a selection of shapes on the slide (not on the pane) to access a contextual menu that allows you to group shapes. I cover grouping in more detail later in this chapter in the "Group, ungroup, and regroup" section.
- ✔ Click a shape twice (not in quick succession so that it isn't a double-click) in the pane and type a new name if you want to add more descriptive names to your shapes — for example, Blue Square might sound better than Rectangle16!
- ✔ Reorder any selected object in the pane by clicking the up and down arrow buttons at the bottom of the pane.
- ✔ Click the eye icon next to a shape's listing on the task pane to make it invisible. Click again to toggle the visibility.

Can't see the eye icons in the Selection and Visibility task pane? Drag the edge of your task pane to make way for the eye!

✔ Click the Show All and Hide All buttons at the bottom of the pane to show or hide all objects on a slide — be careful with this one!

Orientation

When selected, most shapes have several handles, as shown in Figure 5-13:

✔ Four blue handles on the corners

✔ Four more blue handles on the sides

✔ A green rotation handle can be found over the top-middle handle

✔ A yellow diamond handle that I explain earlier in this chapter in the "Supernatural shape abilities" section

All these handles help you change the orientation of your shapes, as I show you next.

Figure 5-13: Resize and rotate handles keep your shapes on a leash.

Resize

It's easy to make shapes teeny-tiny or humongous. You can resize the shape by dragging one of the eight blue handles. For more control when you resize, here are your options:

✔ **To resize while maintaining the shape's proportions,** hold the Shift key while you drag one of the four corner handles.

✔ **To resize from the center of the shape,** hold the Ctrl key while you drag one of the four corner handles.

✔ **To resize from the center and still maintain proportions,** hold both the Shift and Ctrl keys while you drag one of the four corner handles.

✔ **To resize only one side,** drag the corresponding side handle.

✔ **To resize opposite sides,** hold the Ctrl key while you drag a side handle.

Rotate

To rotate shapes, select a shape and do the following:

✔ Drag the green rotation handle to the right or left to rotate around the center of the shape.

✔ Hold the Shift key and drag the rotation handle to rotate in 15-degree increments.

✔ If you want to rotate in 90-degree increments, double-click the shape to access the Drawing Tools Format tab of the Ribbon. Click the Rotate button within the Arrange group to access the Rotate gallery, and then choose either Rotate Right 90° or Rotate Left 90°.

Within the Rotate gallery, you can also choose the More Rotation Options to access the Size and Position dialog box. You can enter a new value here or type a zero rotation value to restore the original placement.

Flip

Start flipping your shapes like pancakes:

✔ **Select any of the side handles of a selected shape and drag toward the other end of the shape.** Don't stop — keep dragging beyond the shape on the other side to flip an object. Although this is quick and easy, I prefer the next option because it more precisely maintains the shape's size and proportion.

✔ **Double-click the shape to access the Drawing Tools Format tab of the Ribbon.** Then click the Rotate button within the Arrange group to access the Rotate gallery, and then choose either Flip Vertical or Flip Horizontal.

Positioning

The position of a shape (or any object) on a slide in relation to itself and other objects can be manipulated by using the options discussed in the following subsections.

Group, ungroup, and regroup

You can perform many PowerPoint tasks easier and faster with grouped objects. Perhaps you want to animate a group of shapes all at once, or you want to move every shape an inch to the left. PowerPoint provides functional grouping and ungrouping abilities:

✔ **Grouping** in PowerPoint places more than one object in a collection so that you can change the characteristics of objects contained within the group at one go. It's also easier to manage four or five groups rather than 200 objects on a slide!

✔ **Ungrouping** in PowerPoint breaks a grouped collection back into individual objects.

✔ **Regrouping** in PowerPoint remembers which objects comprised an ungrouped group so that you can regroup them all again without having to select all the individual shapes (or other objects).

Follow these steps to group your shapes (or anything else):

1. **Select all the shapes you want to group by using one of these methods:**

   • Select one shape and then hold down the Shift or Ctrl key while you select other shapes.

   • Drag a marquee around the shapes you want to be grouped.

   • Use PowerPoint's new Selection and Visibility task pane (which I explain earlier in this chapter).

2. **Group the shapes by right-clicking the selection, and then choosing Group⇨Group from the contextual menu. You can also group by pressing Ctrl+G.**

   Now you can change the position, color, size, and various other attributes of all the grouped items simultaneously.

Follow these steps to ungroup your grouped shapes:

1. **Select the grouped shapes you want to ungroup.**

2. **Right-click and choose Group⇨Ungroup from the contextual menu, or press Ctrl+Shift+G on your keyboard.**

Follow these steps to regroup previously grouped (and then ungrouped) shapes:

1. **Select any one of the previously grouped shapes.**

2. **Right-click and choose Group⇨Regroup from the contextual menu.**

Nudge or move

PowerPoint provides more than one way to nudge or move your shapes:

- ✔ Select a shape and press the arrow keys on the keyboard to nudge the shape.

- ✔ To nudge in even smaller increments, hold down the Ctrl key while you press the arrow keys.

- ✔ To move the shape anywhere around the slide, just select and drag it anywhere on or off the slide.

- ✔ To move in a straight line, hold the Shift key and then select the shape and drag it horizontally or vertically.

- ✔ To move it to an exact coordinate position on the slide, double-click the shape to access the Drawing Tools Format tab of the Ribbon. Click the dialog box launcher in the Size group to bring up the Size and Position dialog box (refer to Figure 5-11). On the Position tab (see Figure 5-14), enter the exact horizontal and vertical coordinates.

Figure 5-14:
Position
your
shapes.

Align

Say that you have three shapes on a slide. Select all three shapes (by clicking the first one and then Shift+clicking the other two) and click any of the top six align options in the Align gallery. You can find the Align gallery by clicking the Align option in the Arrange button on the Home tab of the Ribbon. You can also find the Align gallery on the Drawing Tools Format tab of the Ribbon (see Figure 5-15). This Ribbon tab appears whenever you have a shape (or shapes) selected on the slide.

Figure 5-15:
The Align
gallery.

The Align gallery provides the following options:

- **Align Left:** Aligns the left edge of all the shapes. The leftmost shape determines the left anchor. See the second column of shapes in Figure 5-16.

- **Align Center:** Aligns all shapes vertically along their centers. The anchor is determined by the median center of all the shapes. See the first column of shapes in Figure 5-16.

- **Align Right:** Aligns the right sides all the shapes. The rightmost shape determines the right anchor. See the third column of shapes in Figure 5-16.

- **Align Top:** Aligns the tops of all shapes. The topmost shape determines the top anchor.

- **Align Middle:** Aligns all shapes horizontally along their midlines. The anchor is determined by the median center of all the shapes.

- **Align Bottom:** Aligns the bottoms of all the shapes. The bottommost shape determines the bottom anchor.

If the alignment doesn't work as expected, you might have the Align to Slide option selected in the Align gallery — change that to the Align Selected Objects option.

Center a shape (or shapes)

Follow these steps to center a shape on a PowerPoint slide:

1. **Select the shape.**

2. **Make sure that the Align to Slide option is selected in the Align gallery.**

3. **Click the Align Center and the Align Middle options one after the other.**

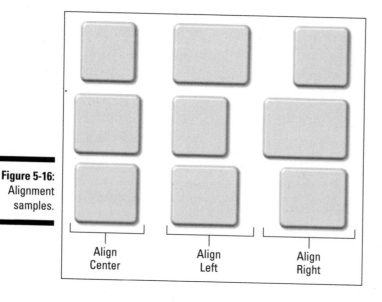

Figure 5-16:
Alignment
samples.

Follow these steps if you need to center several shapes on a PowerPoint slide without altering their distances from each other:

1. **Select all the shapes.**

2. **Group the shapes.**

   To do this step, right-click the selected shapes and choose Group⊅Group from the contextual menu.

3. **Make sure that the Align to Slide option is selected in the Align gallery.**

4. **Click the Align Center and the Align Middle buttons one after the other.**

5. **Ungroup the selected shapes (if required) by right-clicking them and choosing Group⊅Ungroup from the contextual menu.**

Distribute

Distributing shapes is a great way to make sure that they're perfectly lined up. For example, if you want a row of 12 evenly spaced stars, you use the Distribute command. Figure 5-17 illustrates how distributed shapes look.

To distribute shapes horizontally:

1. **Place all the shapes beside each other.**

2. **Select the shapes and choose Distribute Horizontally from the same Align gallery (refer to Figure 5-15).**

To distribute shapes vertically:

1. **Place all the shapes one below the other.**

2. **Select the shapes and choose Distribute Vertically from the Align gallery (refer to Figure 5-15).**

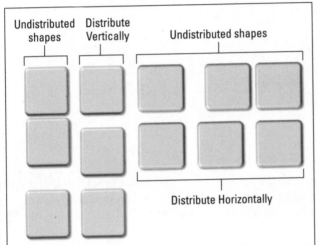

Undistributed shapes   Distribute Vertically   Undistributed shapes

Distribute Horizontally

Figure 5-17:
Distribute
samples.

Order

Ordering brings your shapes behind or above each other. You can choose an ordering option in the Arrange group on the Home tab of the Ribbon. Alternatively (and more easily), you can right-click a shape to access the contextual menu, as shown in Figure 5-18.

Select any shape and choose any of the four ordering options.

- **Bring to Front⇨Bring to Front:** Moves the selected object in front of *all* objects on the slide.

- **Bring to Front⇨Bring Forward:** Moves the selected object *up* one layer.

- **Send to Back⇨Send to Back:** Moves the selected object behind *all* objects on the slide.

- **Send to Back⇨Send Backward:** Moves the selected object *down* one layer.

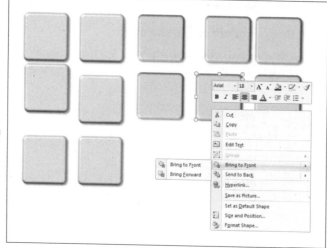

Figure 5-18:
Reorder
your shapes
(and
anything
else).

You can also use the up and down arrows in the Selection and Visibility task pane to reorder objects on a slide, as I explain in more detail earlier in this chapter in the "Using the Selecting and Visibility task pane" section.

The Format Painter

Imagine that you just formatted a shape with the fill and line you want, and the text inside the shape is formatted using a particular font style and color. Now you need to apply the same formatting to 25 more shapes within the presentation. What do you do?

You could manually format each shape the same way and have no time for lunch — and even then, you're human and could miss some details! Or you could use the Format Painter and also have time for dessert and coffee at lunch — and imagine your supernatural capabilities!

Follow these steps to use the Format Painter:

1. **Select the shape whose attributes you want to copy.**

2. **Copy the attributes by selecting the Format Painter:**

    • If you want to apply the attributes to one shape, click the Format Painter icon on the Home tab of the Ribbon — look for this icon in the Clipboard group. This button looks like a paintbrush loaded with paint.

    • If you want to apply the attributes to several shapes, double-click the Format Painter icon so that it remains selected (or *sticky*).

3. **Click the shape(s) where you want the attributes copied.**

4. **If you double-clicked the Format Painter to make it sticky, get rid of the stickiness by**

   - Clicking the Format Painter button again.

   - Pressing the Esc key.

Here are some guidelines for using the Format Painter:

   ✔ **You can use the Format Painter to copy attributes to other shapes on the same slide, the same presentation, or across other presentations.**

   ✔ **The Format Painter works beyond shapes.** You can use the Format Painter to copy characteristics of placeholders, tables, and charts.

Smart Connectors

Connectors are shapes found in the Lines category within the Shapes gallery. They're a special line type, but they look just like conventional lines — the only difference is in how you create them, as I show you later in this section.

And even though connectors are part of the Lines category in the Shapes gallery, many PowerPoint users simply aren't aware of connectors and how they differ from conventional lines. It isn't unusual for users to place lines between two shapes to show a relationship — but a connector would have been a better choice!

Lines and connectors might look the same in some instances, especially if all you need is to draw something linking two shapes. In reality, there are subtle differences between them:

   ✔ If you place a line so it's attached to a shape but later move the shape, the line will never move.

   ✔ If you attach a connector to a shape and later move the shape, the connector moves with the shape. No wonder they're called connectors!

Using connectors and basic shapes, you can create any type of relationship chart inside PowerPoint. Figure 5-19 shows you an unconventional diagram that was created using just rectangles and connectors.

Although connectors are just another shape type, they have no fill attributes. However, all line formatting options, including line thickness, dash styles, and arrowheads, are available. For more on line formatting options, turn to Chapter 6.

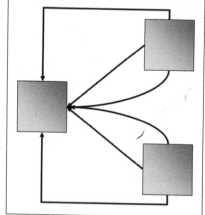

Figure 5-19:
Connector
samples.

Types of connectors

PowerPoint provides three types of connectors, and each of these connectors has three variants, as shown in Table 5-1.

Table 5-1	Connector Types and Variants		
Connector Type	*No Arrows*	*Arrows on One End*	*Arrows on Both Ends*
Straight			
Elbow			
Curved			

Drawing connectors

Draw the connectors only after your shapes are in place. If you draw them earlier, your connector will end up being a mere line!

To draw a connector between shapes, follow these steps:

1. **Click the Insert tab on the Ribbon and select a connector type from the Shapes gallery.**

   Look in the Lines section of the gallery — you can use any of the first nine variants as a connector.

   The cursor turns into a crosshair, and the instant you move your cursor near a shape, you find several red, square handles highlighted on the shape, as shown in Figure 5-20.

2. **Click one of the handles to determine the start point of the connector.**

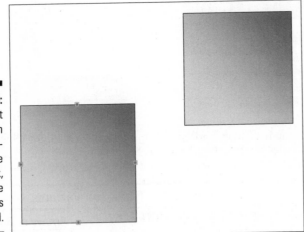

Figure 5-20:
You can't tell it from this black-and-white book, but those handles are red.

3. **Move the cursor toward the shape you want to connect.**

   The red squares are highlighted on that shape.

4. **Click any of the red handles to set the connector's closing point.**

Changing the connector type

To change the connector type, right-click the connector, choose the Connector Type option in the contextual menu, and then click the new connector type from the fly-out menu, as shown in Figure 5-21.

Using the yellow diamonds

Curved and elbow connectors, when selected, sport yellow diamonds that allow you to change the elbow location in elbow connectors and the curvature in curve connectors. Straight connectors need no manipulation — so those poor things have no diamonds.

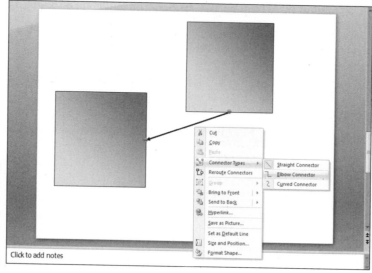

Figure 5-21:
Change
your
connector
types.

After manipulating the curve and elbow connectors, you might want to change their shapes so that they connect the shapes using the shortest route possible. Just right-click the connector and choose Reroute Connectors from the contextual menu to achieve that cause.

Adding, changing, or reversing arrowheads

Unless you created a connector that already had arrowheads on one or both ends, you might want to add them later — or even remove the arrowheads from an existing connector. You might also want to reverse the arrowheads in a connector.

Follow these steps to add, change, or reverse arrowheads:

1. **Select the connector that you want to edit, right-click, and choose Format⇨Shape.**

   This summons the Format Shape dialog box. On the Line Style tab, the bottom half of the dialog box is concerned exclusively with arrowheads.

2. **You can set the begin and end styles for the arrowheads and also make the arrowheads smaller or larger in the drop-down lists for these options.**

3. **When you're done, click Close.**

Moving connectors and attached shapes

Follow these guidelines when you need to move shapes and their attached connectors:

✔ When you move a shape with an attached connector, the connector moves with the shape and automatically becomes longer or shorter to accommodate the distance between shapes.

✔ Connector ends attached to a shape have a red circle handle. Unattached connector ends have a light blue circle handle.

✔ To remove a connector, first select the connector and then drag one of the ends away so it is unconnected. Or you can just drag it to another shape, and connect to that.

Expanding your chart horizons

You can combine shapes and connectors to create any sort of chart in PowerPoint. For most data-based charts, you can use PowerPoint's own charts. However, for other types of charts, the shape-and-connector approach works very well.

Some examples of this approach include

✔ Relationship charts

✔ Mind maps

✔ Flowcharts

✔ Callouts

✔ Concept charts

Connectors: Design guidelines

Follow these guidelines to create better connectors:

✔ **Experiment with connector formatting options — especially line thickness and color.** Dark-color connectors work well over light background colors, and vice versa.

✔ **Use a consistent line color and thickness for the shapes and connectors on the same slide to maintain a unified design look.**

✔ **Animate connectors in sequence with the shapes to create a sequential build.**

More Shape Ideas

Almost everything on a PowerPoint slide has something to do with shapes — working with all these shapes can help you discover usability tricks and great ideas. Even then, some ideas are better than others. Here are some of my favorite shape ideas.

Transparent fills

All fill styles can be made transparent to varying degrees. To change the transparency value, follow these steps:

1. **Right-click the shape, and choose the Format Shape option in the contextual menu to open the Format Shape dialog box.**

2. **On the Fill tab, select the Solid Fill option, and then drag the Transparency slider to show any value between 0 and 100 (see Figure 5-22).**

Figure 5-22:
Creating shape ghosts with the Transparency slider.

You can find many more fill tricks in Chapter 6.

A tale of tables

PowerPoint's native tables can't be animated in sequence; that is, one row or column at a time. You can animate a table, however, if you first convert the table to shapes. Follow these steps to convert a table into shapes:

1. **Draw your table and select it or choose an existing table.**

2. **Save the table as a picture by right-clicking it and choosing Save As Picture.**

3. **In the resultant Save as Picture dialog box, make sure that you choose Enhanced Windows Metafile (*.EMF) in the Save as Type drop-down list. Save it to a location on your computer.**

4. **On the same slide, or preferably on another slide, insert the picture by clicking the Insert tab on the Ribbon and then clicking the Picture button.**

5. **In the Insert Picture dialog box, select the EMF picture file you saved in Step 3, and then click the Insert button.**

6. **Ungroup the picture by right-clicking it and choosing Group⇨Ungroup from the contextual menu.**

   PowerPoint warns you that you're about to discombobulate a picture, but that's one warning you can ignore because you're just working with a copy of the original table.

7. **If your table isn't yet ungrouped to individual shapes, choose Group⇨Ungroup once again.**

   You're now free to animate the individual cells of the table as you see fit.

You might want to group some of the cells into rows and columns that you can animate more easily.

Quick drawings

You can combine shapes to create quick drawings even if you need to use them outside of PowerPoint. For example, you can combine

- ✔ Five or six ovals to create a flower
- ✔ Several hexagons to create a honeycomb pattern
- ✔ Two or more donuts to create a target or dartboard

Other quick drawings you can create with shapes include clocks, road maps, and geometric abstracts. This can be a very helpful and quick alternative to conventional clip art.

Callouts

Callouts are a category of shapes that allows you to create comic book–style text and thought balloons. Combine them with drawings or photos of human or animal characters to create something that's different, yet universally appealing. Figure 5-23 shows you how this coin-tossing man is coping with three callouts!

Figure 5-23:
Call out for callouts.

To use a callout, follow these steps:

1. **Draw or insert the character associated with the callout.**

2. **In the Shapes gallery on the Insert tab (or the Home tab) of the Ribbon, select any of the shapes within the Callouts category.**

3. **Click anywhere on the slide.**

4. **Type text inside the callout shape and format the font as required.**

5. Resize the callout to fit the entire text content.

6. Drag the diamond handle of the callout toward the character associated with the callout.

Export your shapes

You might end up creating something that needs to be used outside of PowerPoint. Follow these steps to export shapes to a graphic file format:

1. **Select all the shapes, right-click carefully so that you don't deselect a shape, and then choose Group⇨Group from the contextual menu.**

   Alternatively, you can select all the shapes, and then choose Arrange⇨Group on the Home tab of the Ribbon.

2. **Right-click the grouped graphic and choose Save Picture As.**

3. **In the Save As dialog box, choose the graphic format you need from the Save as Type drop-down list.**

4 **Type a name for your graphic in the File Name text box and then click Save.**

Not all graphic file formats that you can save as are created equal. While PNG and TIF will retain transparency areas, JPG and BMP won't. And if you want to export to a vector file format, choose EMF rather than WMF to get a cleaner output. Chapter 9 discusses what a vector file format is.

Designers often need to move their compositions to high-end drawing and page-layout applications. To export your graphic to an industry-standard format, such as EPS, you need to have Adobe Acrobat (the full version, not just the Reader) and Adobe Illustrator installed on your system.

Follow these steps to export a drawing from PowerPoint as an EPS file:

1. **Select all the shapes, right-click carefully so that you don't deselect a shape, and then choose Group⇨Group from the contextual menu.**

2. **Print the slide(s) containing the shapes to a PDF document by using the Acrobat printer driver. You can also print to PDF using any other PDF compatible driver.**

   Make sure that each slide that contains your composition is saved as a separate PDF document. All versions of Adobe Illustrator can't import multipage PDFs.

3. **Open the single-page PDF inside Adobe Illustrator and edit as needed; then save the drawing as an EPS graphic.**

   EPS graphics can be used in page-layout programs like Adobe InDesign and Quark XPress.

Beyond shapes

If you love the shape concept, you might want to explore Microsoft Visio and SmartDraw. Both applications use the shape metaphor to create diagrams. Both Visio and SmartDraw work very well with PowerPoint.

Chapter 6

Working with Fills, Lines, and Effects

. . . .

. . . .

*I*f shapes are the building blocks that you place on your slides in PowerPoint, the finishes are entirely created using PowerPoint's revamped graphic technology — the new fills, lines, and effects can leave you and your audiences mesmerized!

All these effects can be applied to slide objects in two ways:

> ✔ **By using the galleries to preview the effect on the selected object(s):** The options in the galleries are all based on the theme options, such as colors, effects, fonts, and so on, and so they work well with themes — which is great if you don't have much artistic inclination.

> ✔ **By using the advanced options by bringing up the Format Shape dialog box:** This allows you to refuse PowerPoint's helping hand and use your own brush on your own canvas.

And frankly, you don't have to use just one approach all the time — feel free to try them both as I show you in this chapter!

PowerPoint's ability to present richly colored and textured elements is based on the OfficeArt fill, line, and effects technology. OfficeArt is a shared graphic component used across the programs in the Microsoft Office suite.

Apart from shapes, PowerPoint's fills, lines, and effects work the same way across other slide objects, such as WordArt, backgrounds, and charts.

Working with PowerPoint's Fills

PowerPoint provides four types of fills:

- ✔ Solid colors
- ✔ Pictures
- ✔ Gradients
- ✔ Textures

Color Plate 6-1 (see the color pages in this book) shows how versatile the fills can be.

By default, any shape you draw has a solid fill. You can change the fill either through the options on the Drawing Tools Format tab of the Ribbon or through the Format Shape dialog box.

I suggest you use the Drawing Tools Format tab of the Ribbon because

- ✔ It's quicker, and the numerous options are specifically designed to work well within the gamut of each theme.
- ✔ Hovering over the fills, lines, and effects options on the Drawing Tools Format tab of the Ribbon shows you a live preview on the selected shape.

Default fills and Theme Colors

Whenever you create a new shape, PowerPoint uses a default fill color. This color is determined by the first accent color specified in PowerPoint's *Theme Colors* option for the active open presentation. Theme Colors are covered in Chapter 3 — however, you can follow the rest of this chapter even without reading that section now.

The advantage or disadvantage (whichever way you look at it) of using a default color from a Theme Colors is that when you apply another set of Theme Colors, all your fill colors change, too. If you don't want your fill colors to change, don't use a color from the Theme Colors swatches in the Shape Fill gallery.

Changing default fills and lines

You can override Theme Colors and change the default fill, line, and effect for shapes in any presentation as follows:

1. Draw any shape or select an existing shape.

2. Format the fills, lines, and effects as required.

3. Right-click the shape to summon the contextual menu.

4. Select the Set as Default Shape option.

The Shape Styles gallery

Later in this chapter, I show you how you can individually alter the fills, lines, and effects for any selected shape (or shapes). Although it's a great idea to find out how to format these characteristics individually, PowerPoint allows you to format all of them at one go using the *trés* cool Shape Styles gallery. To see this awesome gallery, check out Color Plate 6-4 in the color insert of this book.

Follow these steps to apply any of these ready-made effects to a selected shape (or shapes):

1. **With your shape selected, click the Drawing Tools Format tab on the Ribbon.**

2. **Click the down-pointing arrow in the Shape Styles group to access this gallery.**

   This same gallery is also available in the Home tab of the Ribbon — only there, it's called the Quick Styles gallery.

3. **Click the style that you want to apply.**

These styles are theme-specific, so if you change the theme of the presentation, you'll end up changing to new shape styles as well!

Now that I have introduced you to the Shape Styles gallery, read on to find out more about the fills, lines, and effects you can apply to shapes.

The Shape Fill gallery

To access the Shape Fill gallery:

1. **Double-click any shape to bring up the Drawing Tools Format tab of the Ribbon.**

2. **Click the down-pointing arrow next to the Shape Fill icon to open the Shape Fill gallery, as shown in Figure 6-1.**

Figure 6-1:
The Shape Fill gallery.

Solid colors

You use the Shape Fill gallery (see Figure 6-1), to fill a shape with a solid color. You can choose from:

- ✔ Ten Theme Colors swatches
- ✔ Ten Standard Colors swatches
- ✔ Up to ten swatches in the Recent Colors area
- ✔ An absolute color value by clicking the More Fill Colors option

  Clicking the More Fill Colors option opens the standard Windows Colors dialog box, where you can choose or mix any RGB color — which means you have almost 16 million color choices.

  The PowerPoint color chooser has two tabs, Standard and Custom (refer to Chapter 3 to see both of these tabs).

  - The **Standard tab** offers 127 colors, black, white, and 14 shades of gray. You can also change the transparency value of the color so that whatever is behind your shape shows through.

  - On the **Custom tab,** you can click a color from a spectrum and then adjust the color's luminosity with the slider on the right. You can also enter specific HSL or RGB values to create a specific fill color. (For the skinny on RGB and HSL, refer to the relevant sidebars in Chapter 3. And check out the Color Plates for Chapter 3, as well.)

Gradient fills

To change or apply a gradient fill, select the shape, open the Shape Fill gallery, and choose the Gradient option to see the Gradient gallery shown in Figure 6-2. As you hover the cursor over any of the samples in the Gradient gallery, you see a live preview of the fill in the selected shape.

If the shape gets hidden by the Gradient gallery, you can move the shape to a more suitable location on the slide. When you're done applying the gradient fill, move the shape back to its original location.

To view more gradient fill options, click the More Gradients option in the Gradient gallery to summon the Format Shape dialog box. On the Fill tab of this dialog box, click the Gradient Fill option to find many more options. The section about gradient fills in Chapter 4 fully covers these options.

Creating gradients can take a lot of time. The CD attached to this book contains over 1,000 gradient swatches for you to copy and use. All gradient swatches are contained in a PowerPoint presentation. Follow these steps to use these swatches:

1. **Copy any swatch you like and paste it in your active presentation.**

2. **With the copied swatch selected, click once on the Format Painter icon on the Home tab of the Ribbon.**

   The Format Painter icon looks like a little paintbrush.

3. **Click a shape to apply that gradient to the shape.**

4. **Delete the copied swatch.**

Follow these guidelines for gradient fills:

- ✓ **Experiment with gradients between hues of the same color.** I often use a medium-to-dark blue gradient as a fill, which works great if I need to place some white text inside the shape.

  Make sure that any gradient fill you use works well with either black or white text.

- ✓ **If you don't need to place any text in the shape, you can use gradients composed of light and dark colors.**

- ✓ **If you need to focus attention on a single shape on a slide that contains many elements, use a gradient fill with a contrasting color.** For example, on a slide filled with blue gradient elements, I'd use a red-to-black gradient to focus on a single shape.

- ✓ **Experiment with using white as one of the gradient colors.** This works especially well if you're creating a presentation with a white background.

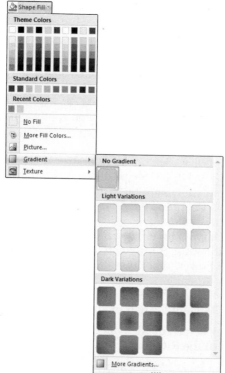

Figure 6-2:
The
Gradient
gallery
shows
several
gradient
types.

Picture or texture fills

Before you use a picture or texture to fill a shape, you need to know how pictures and textures differ from each other:

- **Textures:** In PowerPoint parlance, *textures* tile across and down to form a fill. It goes without saying that such textures need to be *seamless.* PowerPoint includes several built-in textures, and you can also use any *picture* as a texture.

  Seamless textures wrap all over the slide to create an uninterrupted pattern when tiled. If your texture (or picture) isn't seamless, you can see the edges of the textures as they tile against each other.

- **Pictures:** Pictures make great fills — you can obtain pictures from digital cameras, scans, online photo galleries, or CD-ROM clip art collections. Many pictures are included within Clip Organizer, a media cataloging program that's part of Microsoft Office.

Here's how you change or apply a picture or texture fill:

1. **Select the shape.**

2. **Click the Drawing Tools Format tab on the Ribbon, and from the Shape Fill gallery, choose the Texture option to view the Texture gallery shown in Figure 6-3.**

3. **Choose either of these options:**

   - Select any texture in the Texture gallery to apply a seamless texture to the shape.

   - Choose the More Textures option to summon the Format Shape dialog box. On the Fill tab, click the Picture or Texture Fill option. You'll find several options for picture and texture fills here.

   Head to Chapter 4 for a more complete coverage of these options in the section about picture or texture fills.

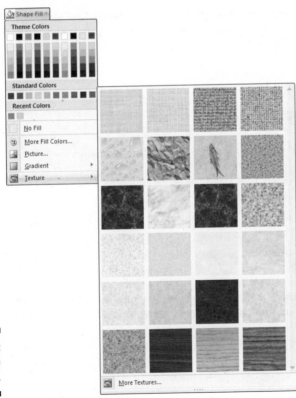

Figure 6-3:
The Texture gallery.

The CD that accompanies this book contains hundreds of seamless textures ready for you to use as fills in your presentations. The CD with this book also contains several royalty-free pictures for you to use. You can access the pictures from the CD, or you can copy all the picture folders to your hard drive and access them from there.

Because textures are small files that tile seamlessly across a shape, using textures doesn't balloon your PowerPoint file size.

Follow these guidelines for texture fills:

✔ **Don't use textures as fills for shapes that also contain text.**

✔ **If you want to design your own seamless textures,** use an application like Corel Painter that has specific features suitable for their creation.

✔ **You can find tons of seamless textures available on the Internet.** Check out www.ppted.com/001100/back for a collection of over 800 seamless textures.

✔ **Create design elements with small, texture-filled shapes.** Often, you can enliven a drab presentation by inserting such shapes in the corners or sides of the slide area. You can also use seamless textures as fills for charts.

PowerPoint's Lines

The lines in PowerPoint work in several different ways:

✔ As normal lines that have two ends, such as straight lines, curves, scribbles, and so on.

✔ As closed lines that form outlines of shapes such as rectangles, circles, and so on.

✔ As edges (borders) of other PowerPoint objects, such as pictures and movies.

PowerPoint provides an amazing diversity of options for creating and editing all these types of lines. Some simple, straight lines are shown in Figure 6-4.

PowerPoint uses the terms *line* and *outline* interchangeably.

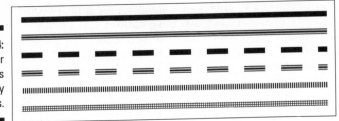

Figure 6-4:
Options for
line types
are nearly
limitless.

The Shape Outline gallery

Almost all the formatting you do for lines in PowerPoint will be through the Shape Outline gallery. You can access the Shape Outline gallery in any of the following ways:

✔ Select a line or any shape that includes an outline. Click the Drawing Tools Format tab of the Ribbon, and then click the Shape Outline option.

✔ Double-click a line or a shape that includes an outline to activate the Drawing Tools Format tab of the Ribbon. Then click the Shape Outline option.

✔ If you need to apply an outline to a picture, double-click the picture to activate the Picture Tools Format tab of the Ribbon, and then click the Picture Border option.

Any of these actions opens the Shape Outline gallery, shown in Figure 6-5.

Depending on whether you selected a line, a closed shape, or a picture, the Shape Outline gallery might have some options missing or grayed out. For example, the Arrow option is available only for lines that don't comprise any closed shape like a circle or square.

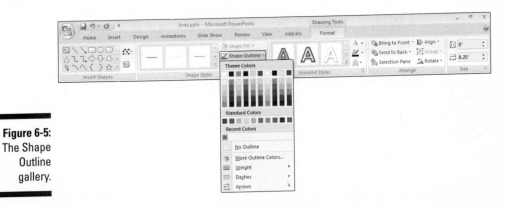

Figure 6-5:
The Shape
Outline
gallery.

Within the Shape Outline gallery, you can find four principal options:

- Color
- Weight
- Dashes
- Arrow

Each of these options is discussed in more detail in the following sections. Remember, you will have to access the Shape Outline gallery to work with these options.

Line color

You can choose from several line color options in the Shape Outline gallery (refer to Figure 6-5), including

- Ten Theme Colors swatches
- Ten Standard Colors swatches
- Up to ten color swatches in the Recent Colors area
- No outline at all using the No Outline option
- An absolute color value by clicking the More Outline Colors option

  Clicking the More Outline Colors option opens the standard Windows Color dialog box, where you can choose or mix any RGB color — which means you have almost 16 million color choices.

  The PowerPoint color chooser has two tabs, Standard and Custom (refer Chapter 3).

Line weight

By changing the weight of a line, you can alter the thickness attribute of a line all the way from a miniscule, almost-invisible hairline to a chunky, thick border-style that almost overpowers everything else on the same slide.

To alter a line weight, click the Weight option in the Shape Outline gallery to open the Line Weight gallery, as shown in Figure 6-6. The Line Weight gallery provides different line styles — each has a different thickness (weight) value. Select any of these preset weights, or click the More Lines option to summon the familiar Format Shape (also the Format Picture or Format Chart Area) dialog box that allows you choose a line weight, as well as more compound type lines such as double-ruled lines. These options are explained in the "More line formatting" section, later in this chapter.

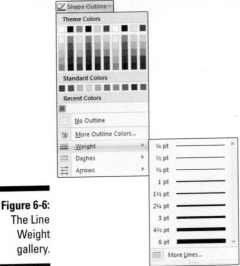

Figure 6-6:
The Line
Weight
gallery.

Line dashes

A dashed line can sometimes work better than a conventional line in design terms, especially when you're using plenty of lines in a slide. Here are some scenarios:

- ✔ Use conventional lines as callouts and relationship indicators — and use dashed lines for proposed indicators.

- ✔ Use dashed lines as a border line when you want something more understated.

- ✔ You might be printing to black and white and need different line types — combing dashed lines with conventional lines provides more choices.

- ✔ Select a different dash pattern to create even more variations in the lines.

Follow these steps to alter a line dash style:

1. **Open the Shape Outline gallery and choose the Dashes option to access the Dashes gallery, as shown in Figure 6-7.**

2. **Choose from any of the different dash styles or choose the More Lines option to access the Format Shape dialog box.**

   The line options in this dialog box are explained in the "More line formatting" section, later in this chapter.

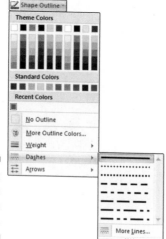

Figure 6-7:
The Line
Dashes
gallery.

Line arrows

A line with an arrowhead on one or both ends can be a useful design indicator, and such lines can add value to a layout in a PowerPoint slide:

- ✔ Lines with arrowheads on one end can portray a sense of direction or sequence.

- ✔ Lines with arrowheads on both ends can portray a sense of continuity and relation.

Not all lines in PowerPoint can have arrowheads — only open lines such as straight lines, curves, scribbles, and so on, can have them.

Follow these steps to equip your lines with arrowheads:

1. **Open the Shape Outline gallery and choose the Arrows option to access the Arrows gallery, as shown in Figure 6-8.**

2. **Choose from any of the preset arrow styles for lines or choose the More Arrows option to bring up the Format Shape dialog box with more line options.**

   These are discussed in the next section.

More line formatting

Like almost every other gallery in PowerPoint, the Shape Outline gallery provides the nicest and the safest choices so that your lines look good in most scenarios. It's almost as safe as walking atop a bridge over a huge expanse of water.

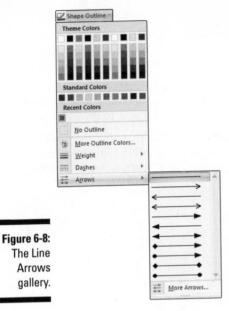

Figure 6-8:
The Line
Arrows
gallery.

But what if you don't want to play it safe? What if you're more interested in experiencing the exhilaration of bungee jumping from that bridge? In that case, you want to explore the other line options in the Format Shape dialog box — and frankly, even if you aren't interested in bungee jumping, you should still explore the other line options that I explain!

Follow these steps to access the Format Shape dialog box:

1. Select the line (or an object with a line) you want to format.

2. Right-click and choose the Format Shape option.

The Format Shape dialog box appears.

3. Select the Line Style tab of this dialog box, as shown in Figure 6-9.

This is the same dialog box that you access when you click the More Lines or More Arrows options in the Weight, Dashes, and Arrows galleries in the Shape Outline gallery, as I explain earlier in this chapter.

The Format Shape dialog box provides the following options — and almost everywhere, you can see a live preview of the change made to the selected line:

- **Width:** Enter a new thickness or use the more and less arrow buttons to increase or decrease the width.

- **Compound Type:** Select from a simple line or different variations of double-ruled and triple-ruled lines.

- **Dash Type:** Select a dash type.

- **Cap Type:** Select a square, round, or flat line end type — for dashed lines, this affects all the dashes. This option works only with open shapes because closed shapes have no ends, and thus require no caps (edges).

- **Join Type:** Select round, bevel, or miter — this affects the joins, edges, or points of a shape, such as the corner of a rectangle. In shapes such as straight lines and circles, this option won't appear to do anything.

- **Arrow settings:** Click the four buttons within this area to access drop-down lists. Select an arrowhead for each end of the line from the Begin Type and End Type lists; select the size of the arrowhead(s) in the Begin Size and End Size lists.

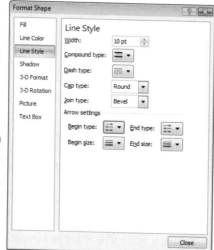

Figure 6-9:
The Line
Style tab of
the Format
Shape
dialog box.

Follow these guidelines for formatting lines:

- Just because PowerPoint includes a line by default on every shape you draw is no reason to live with it. Face it — sometimes lines just get in the way. If that's the case with some of your presentation visuals, set the line attribute in the Shape Outline gallery to No Outline.

- Taking this further, you can achieve a great effect by adding a shadow to a shape that has no line. The "Shadow" section, later in this chapter, shows you how to apply a shadow to a shape.

- Sometimes, you can achieve a nice effect by using the same color for both line and fill. You might want to darken the line color just a little bit.

- Explore gradient lines. They make great frames for images — you can discover them in the next section. If you're wondering about what happened to patterned lines, that's covered next!

PowerPoint 2007 no longer allows you to create patterned lines, but if you have a presentation from an older version of PowerPoint that contains shapes or other slide objects with patterned lines, this version lets you retain those lines. You can still edit the width and other parameters of those lines without doing anything to the pattern in PowerPoint 2007 — the only thing you can't do is change the pattern or add a new patterned line!

If you want to get your hands on a presentation that has patterned lines, check out the CD with this book.

Gradient lines

A *gradient line* is a line with a gradient applied to it. Every element in PowerPoint has a fill and line attribute — gradient lines are just another line attribute, and yes, they're new for this version of PowerPoint.

Figure 6-10 shows some samples of gradient lines. Color Plate 6-2 shows more gradient lines.

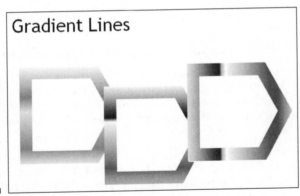

Figure 6-10: Give your lines some pizzazz by adding gradients.

Follow these steps to apply or edit a gradient line:

1. **If you haven't already done so, draw a shape on the slide.**

2. **Right-click the shape and choose Format Shape from the contextual menu.**

   This presents you with the Format Shape dialog box.

3. **Select the Line Style tab.**

4. **In the Width box, enter a nice, thick width for the line.**

   To make the gradient lines stand out, anything higher than 10 pt will work, but I chose 30 pt, as shown in Figure 6-11.

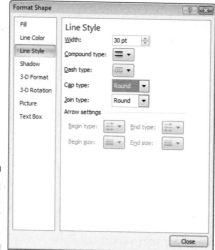

Figure 6-11:
Choose a
thicker
outline.

5. **Click Line Color tab in the Format Shapes dialog box and then select the Gradient Line option.**

   This shows you the options for gradient lines within the dialog box, as shown in Figure 6-12.

6. **Select a preset or create your own gradient pattern as follows:**

   • From the Type drop-down list, select Linear, Radial, Rectangular, or Path. As you select these or any of the other options in this dialog box, the actual shape selected on the slide shows a live preview. If you can't see the shape, drag the dialog box away to reveal the shape.

   • Change other gradient options. These options are essentially the same as for other gradients in PowerPoint. You can find a detailed explanation in the section about backgrounds in Chapter 4.

7. **Click Close.**

You can find a sample presentation containing gradient lines on the CD that's included with this book.

Follow these guidelines for gradient lines:

   ✔ Gradient lines can help color blind people differentiate between objects.

   ✔ Gradient lines look good only if you use lines with at least 10-point thickness.

   ✔ Gradient lines are ideally suited for creating quick frames for pictures inserted in PowerPoint.

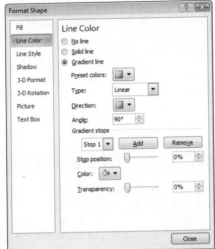

Figure 6-12:
Creating
gradient
lines.

Admiring Shape Effects

You can apply some of the most jaw-dropping effects in this version of PowerPoint to shapes on a slide. In fact, Microsoft provided a whole new attribute to shapes other than the normal fills and lines — and yes, that attribute is called *effects*.

Before you apply an effect, a shape either has an outline or not, and maybe a fill with a nice color or gradient applied to it. Effects, on the other hand, provide so many possibilities that I'm glad to show them in black and white! See Figure 6-13 to see how eight similarly shaped squares can look so different and "wow" even though this is just a grayscale image.

Figure 6-13:
Effects
make their
presence
felt.

And the same effects are absolutely eye candy in color, as you can see in Color Plate 6-3. (See the color insert pages in this book.)

So how can you apply an effect, how many types of effects does PowerPoint provide, what can you do with these effects, and how can you control them individually? If that was your question, I explain it all to you in the remaining pages of this chapter — and who'll believe that your question was just one sentence long!

Between theme effects and shape effects

PowerPoint has two effect categories: theme effects and shape effects. The effects themselves look similar, but with a subtle difference:

- **Theme effects** get applied to the entire presentation, template, or Slide Master.
- **Shape effects** get applied to selected shapes on a slide — these override the theme effects on the basis of hierarchy. Using shape effects, you can customize individual effect characteristics like reflections, bevels, and glows.

Applying an effect

You have two ways to apply an effect: to the entire presentation or to individual shapes. I show you both options.

You apply a theme effect to an entire presentation, and shape effects to individual shapes.

Apply a theme effect

Follow these steps to apply or change the theme effect of an entire presentation:

1. **Select the Design tab on the Ribbon.**

2. **In the Themes group, click the Effects button to see the Theme Effects gallery, as shown in Figure 6-14.**

3. **Hover the cursor over the thumbnails to see a preview of the changed effects on the active slide.**

4. **Click a thumbnail to apply the theme effect to the entire presentation.**

If you want to apply a different theme effect to selected slides, you will have to create a new Slide Master, and then apply a new theme to the Slide Master. Any slides based on the new Slide Master would then use the applied theme and theme effects.

Figure 6-14:
Summon
the Theme
Effects
gallery.

Apply a shape effect

Follow these steps to apply a shape effect to one or more shapes.

1. **Select one or more shapes on a slide.**

2. **The Drawing Tools Format tab appears on the Ribbon — select this tab.**

3. **Click the Shape Effects button to view its gallery, as shown in Figure 6-15.**

   You can find several subgalleries for each effect type, including a Preset gallery.

4. **Click any of the styles in the subgalleries to apply it to the shape(s).**

   Again, hovering the cursor over the thumbnails of the options shows a live preview on the slide.

All the effect types are explained in the next section.

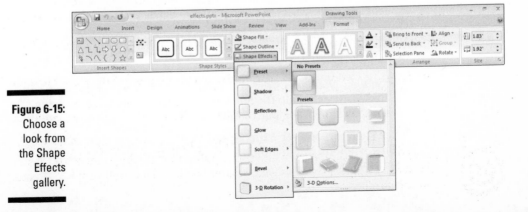

Figure 6-15:
Choose a
look from
the Shape
Effects
gallery.

Effect types

If you don't want to mess with all the effect types, you can just apply a preset effect — and because these look so cool, you might not even have to know about any individual effect types. But your state of blissful ignorance will probably last only until the day your boss asks you to change the direction of the shadow and alter the reflection! And if you are the boss and can't find any hapless employees around, read on and do it yourself. . . .

Most effect presets are a combination of effects applied to look good in most situations, and I explore the individual effect types before the presets because an understanding of individual effects can help you understand the presets better as well. Even then, if you just want to look at the presets, feel free to skip this section and head to the next section.

Now, continue on to explore the effect types.

Shadow

Like them or not, shadows seem to follow people everywhere. Follow these steps to apply a shadow effect to your selected shape or shapes:

1. **With the shape(s) selected, access the Shape Effects gallery as I explain earlier in this chapter (refer to Figure 6-15).**

2. **Click the Shadow option to view the Shadow gallery shown in Figure 6-16.**

   This gallery provides five shadow options, and at any given time, you can choose only one of these options:

   - *No Shadow* can be helpful if you want to remove the shadow from a selected shape.

   - *Outer Shadow* is almost a drop shadow that adds a slight depth to a selected shape — choose from nine styles.

   - *Inner Shadow* is more like a darkened edge for the selected object that remains within the shape area — again, choose from nine styles.

   - *Perspective* adds long shadows that can slide off outside the slide area (although there's a simple 12 o'clock variant that sits right under the shape).

   - *Shadow Options* is what you should choose if you want more control. This brings up the Shadow tab of the Format Shape dialog box, as shown in Figure 6-17.

3. **Hover your cursor over a thumbnail to see a live preview of how the shadow will look applied on the shape. Click to apply the shadow effect you want.**

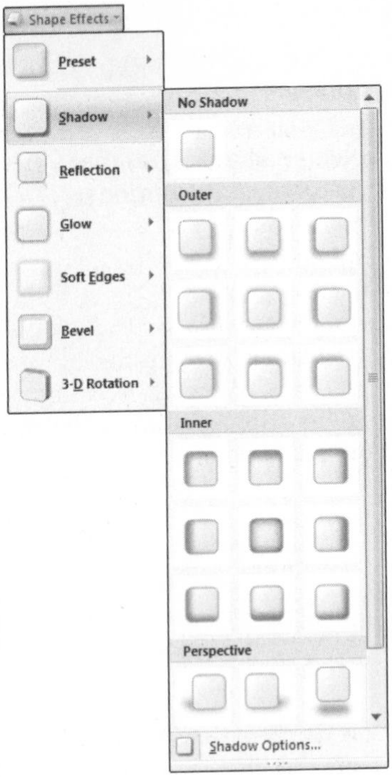

Figure 6-16:
A gallery of
Shadow
options.

If you chose the More Shadows option to gain more control over the shadow effects, read on. Here's where the shadows get more eerie! The Shadow tab of the Format Shape dialog box (see Figure 6-17) is chock-full of options that make PowerPoint almost as powerful as an illustration program — at least as far as shadows are concerned.

The following list describes what these options do — be aware though that these options format the *shadows*, not the shapes themselves:

- ✔ **The Presets drop-down list** brings up the same shadow gallery that you can see in Figure 6-16.

- ✔ **The Color chooser** allows you to alter the shadow color — remember though that shadows are almost always gray. A red shadow will look really strange!

- ✔ **The Transparency slider** allows you to alter the transparency of the shadow so that the shadow color mixes itself with the color of the slide background or any other object behind the shape — very realistic.

- ✔ **The Size slider** allows you increase the size of the shadow — that's not really a good idea unless you're going to use the Blur option as well.

- ✔ **The Blur slider** makes the edges of the shadow more feathered so that the shadow doesn't attract too much attention!

✔ **The Angle slider** changes the angle of the shadow in relation to the shape.

✔ **The Distance slider** alters the starting (and ending) point of the shadow in relation to the position of the shape.

Move the dialog box away from the selected shape(s) so that you can see the live preview of the shadow effect as you change the options.

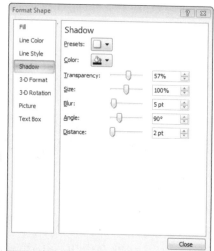

Figure 6-17:
Shadows
aren't
always
eerie.

Follow these guidelines so that your shadows always look good (and realistic):

✔ Don't apply all shadow options just because they are there — it's good to experiment, but when your shadow looks real, it's time to stop tweaking.

✔ As far as possible, use the same shadow options for all shapes (and other objects) on a slide because all the objects are essentially receiving light (and thus shadows) from the same light sources. To do that, first select the shapes and then change the shadow settings.

Of course, if your light source is right on the slide, such as a sun in the middle of the solar system, you want to use different shadow settings for all the planets (shapes on your slide) based on where and how far they're located from the sun.

✔ To make a tapered, perspective shadow, use a higher value for the transparency, blur, angle, and distance. And then use a medium value for the size.

✔ Avoid using anything other than black or gray for shadows — if you need to use another color, keep the transparency value high on the transparency slider.

✔ Shadows can make text stand out and make the text appear to be on another layer above the slide background.

✔ Shadowed tables and diagrams (especially detailed ones) just don't work because too many shape elements are trying to stand out! If you really need shadows with them, try to use a very subtle shadow.

Reflections

Reflections are indeed so much like shadows that the first thing I'm going to tell you is to not use shadows and reflections at the same time (although PowerPoint does allow you to use both if you want to).

Unlike with shadows, PowerPoint won't even let you change your reflection color. The only way that you can change the reflection color is by changing the fill color of the shape.

Although shadows can fall anywhere, reflections are visible only on reflective surfaces such as water and glass in the real world — and your slide in the world of PowerPoint!

Here's how you can apply a reflection to a selected shape or shapes:

1. **With the shape(s) selected, access the Shape Effects gallery as I explain earlier in this chapter (refer to Figure 6-15).**

2. **Click the Reflection option to view the Reflection gallery, as shown in Figure 6-18.**

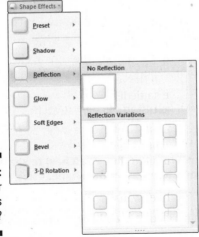

Figure 6-18: Are your shapes reflected?

This gallery provides two reflection options, but at any given time, you can choose only one of these options:

- *No Reflection* can be helpful if you want to remove the reflection of a selected shape.

- *Reflection Variations* lets you choose from nine reflection styles.

3. **Hover your cursor over the styles to see a live preview of how the reflection will look applied on the shape. Then click to apply the effect you want.**

Reflections work best for shapes in slides that don't have too many objects.

Glow

Cosmetic companies tell you that their products can bring a glow to your face that will make it look years younger. PowerPoint makes no such claims — and wisely so, because the glows in PowerPoint can be any color you want.

Follow these steps to bring a glow to selected shapes:

1. **With the shape(s) selected, access the Shape Effects gallery as explained earlier in this chapter (refer to Figure 6-15).**

2. **Click the Glow option to view the Glow gallery, as shown in Figure 6-19.**

   This gallery provides three glow options. At any given time, you can choose only one of the first two options:

   - *No Glow* can be helpful if you want to remove the glow of a selected shape.

   - *Glow Variations* lets you choose from 24 glow styles. The variations in the styles are based on glow colors and thickness widths.

     If you like a style but want to choose another color, click a style and then access this same gallery to choose the More Glow Colors option that I explain next.

   - *More Glow Colors* opens a selection of color swatches. Choose any of the colors visible or click the More Colors option to choose another color.

3. **Hover your cursor over the styles (or color swatches) to see a live preview of how the glow will look applied on the shape. Click to apply the effect you want.**

Light color glows work better with dark color slide backgrounds, and vice versa.

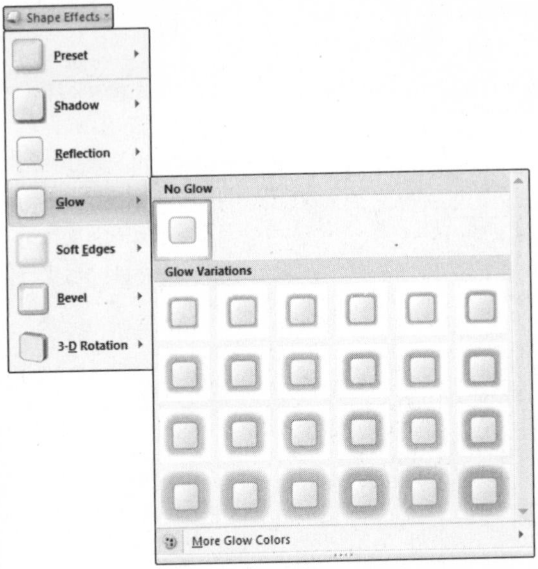

Figure 6-19:
Glowing
shapes.

Soft edges

Whereas glows add a hazed color perimeter outside the shape area, soft edges eat into the shape perimeter by making the edges of the shape feathered.

Here's how you can apply soft edges to a selected shape or shapes:

1. **With the shape(s) selected, access the Shape Effects gallery as I explain earlier in this chapter (refer to Figure 6-15).**

2. **Click the Soft Edges option to view the Soft Edges gallery shown in Figure 6-20.**

   This gallery provides several soft edge options. You can choose one of the options:

   - *No Soft Edges* can be helpful if you want to remove the soft edge effect of a selected shape.

   - *Soft Edge Variations* lets you choose from 6 styles that vary the thickness of the soft edge all the way from 1 to 50 points. However, if you apply a 50 point soft edge to a tiny shape, it won't be visible on the slide!

3. **Hover your cursor over the styles to see a live preview of how the soft edge will look applied on the shape. Click to apply the effect you want.**

In most cases, any outline attribute that's applied to a shape will no longer be visible if you apply a soft edge.

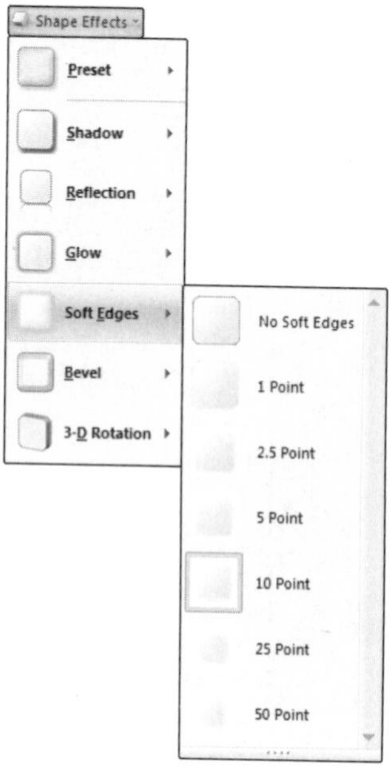

Figure 6-20:
Softer,
smoother
edges.

Bevel

At last PowerPoint has bevels, and you don't have to use Photoshop for creating simple bevel effects. In fact, PowerPoint's new bevel engine is so powerful that it looks like it's straight out of a 3-D modeling application. Fortunately, because you have so many presets, you won't need to learn any 3-D terminology unless you want to!

Follow these steps to apply a bevel to your selected shape or shapes:

1. **With the shape(s) selected, access the Shape Effects gallery as explained earlier in this chapter (refer to Figure 6-15).**

2. **Click the Bevel option to view the Bevel gallery that you can see in Figure 6-21.**

   This gallery provides three bevel options. Choose one of these options:

   - *No Bevel* can be helpful if you want to remove the bevel applied to a selected shape.

   - *Bevel* provides 12 bevel styles to choose from.

   - *3-D Options* is what you will choose if you want more control. This brings up the 3-D Format tab of the Format Shape dialog box, as shown in Figure 6-22

3. **Hover your cursor over the bevel styles to see a live preview of how the bevel will look applied on the shape. Click to apply the bevel effect you want.**

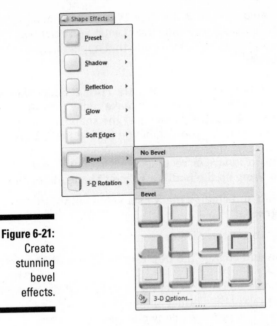

Figure 6-21:
Create
stunning
bevel
effects.

If you chose 3-D Options, the Format Shape dialog box appears with the 3-D Format tab active (see Figure 6-22). Welcome to bevel-heaven! The 3D-Format tab can keep you entertained for hours while you spend more time creating presentations in the office and earn overtime money! And because you end up creating new bevel styles all the time, no one will suspect that you had so much fun.

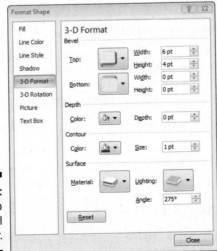

Figure 6-22:
Welcome to
my bevel
parlor.

PowerPoint considers all beveled objects as 3-D objects — even a flat square has both top and bottom attributes. On the slide itself, what you see is the top view of an object — so a square is actually a cube that appears like a square when viewed from above.

You might change 100 things in the 3-D Format tab of the Format Shape dialog box, and none of those options in the dialog box will make sense (and pre-view on the slide) because you're essentially looking at the shape from top view. Fortunately, you can overcome this problem if you follow these steps:

1. **Select a shape (preferably a square or rectangle), right-click it and choose Format Shape to bring up the familiar Format Shape dialog box.**

2. **Click the 3-D Rotation tab and change the X axis value within the Rotation area to 45 degrees.**

   Skip ahead to Figure 6-24 to see the 3-D Rotation tab.

3. **Click the 3-D Format tab and change the Depth to 30 pt or a little more.**

Now that your shape is visible as a 3-D object, let me explain what the various settings in the 3-D Format tab of the Format Shape dialog box do — remember PowerPoint shows a live preview of any changes you make:

- **Bevel:** This part of the dialog box lets you alter the bevel attributes of both the top and bottom surfaces of a selected shape.

- **Depth:** This area allows you to change the color and depth (the third dimension) of a shape.

- **Contours:** This area allows you to change the edge thickness and color.

- **Surface:** This area allows you to choose from several surface material simulations, such as matte, plastic, metal, wireframe, and so on. You can also choose from neutral, warm, cool, and special lighting styles. Below these options, you can change the angle of the lighting.

- **Reset:** This button converts a 3-D formatted shape back to a 2-D shape — such as converting a cube back to a square.

At any time, if you make a change you don't like, press Ctrl+Z to undo one step at a time — even when the dialog box is open.

3-D Rotation

This effect provides many options, but it's still probably the easiest of all effects to apply.

Follow these steps to apply a 3-D rotation to your selected shape or shapes:

1. **With the shape(s) selected, access the Shape Effects gallery as I explain earlier in this chapter (refer to Figure 6-15).**

2. **Click the 3-D Rotation tab to view the 3-D Rotation gallery shown in Figure 6-23.**

   This gallery provides five 3-D rotation options — at any given time, you can only choose one of these options:

   - *No Rotation* can be helpful if you want to remove the 3-D rotation applied to a selected shape.

   - *Parallel* rotates the selected object.

   - *Perspective* rotates the shape and alters the angle from where you view the shape so that farther edges appear smaller than nearer edges.

   - *Oblique* makes very subtle rotations so that a 2-D object merely gives an appearance of being a 3-D object.

   - *3-D Rotation Options* brings up the 3-D Rotation tab of the Format Shape dialog box, as shown in Figure 6-24.

3. **Hover your cursor over the rotation styles to see a live preview of how the rotation will look applied on the shape. Click to apply the effect you want.**

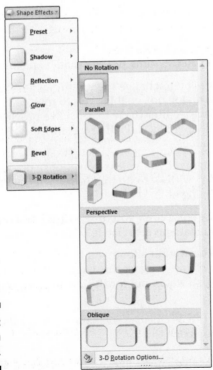

Figure 6-23:
Rotations in
3-D space.

If you chose 3-D Rotations Options, you can rotate celestial bodies and play God on your PowerPoint slide! The Format Shape dialog box appears with 3-D Rotation tab selected, as shown in Figure 6-24.

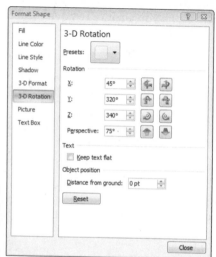

Figure 6-24:
Go ahead,
play God!

Here's an explanation for all the options:

- **Presets:** This gallery gets you the same presets that I explained in the preceding step list.

- **Rotation:** This area of the dialog box enables you to rotate the X, Y, and Z axes of object in 3-D space — alter these to see a live preview of the changes on the selected shape. You can either use the direction buttons or enter your own angle values.

  The Perspective option is grayed out unless you choose one of the Perspective presets to start with — to do that now, click the Presets gallery within the same dialog box.

- **Keep Text Flat:** This check box allows you to keep your text flat even after you rotate your shape into no semblance of its original self!

- **Distance from Ground:** This option allows you to alter the distance from the base level of the shape — again this might influence different shapes in dissimilar ways, so watch out for the live preview to ascertain what you want.

- **Reset:** This button converts a 3-D formatted shape back to a 2-D shape — such as converting a sphere back to a circle.

At any time, if you make a change you don't like, press Ctrl+Z to undo it one step at a time — even when the dialog box is open.

Chapter 7

Drawing in PowerPoint

*P*owerPoint isn't a drawing program, but it still gives you enough flexibility to let your creative juices flow. From curves and guides to shadows and 3-D effects, PowerPoint has them all!

In this chapter, I first show you how you can use rulers, guides, and grids as the building blocks of a structured presentation. I then move to PowerPoint's drawing abilities and tell you all about lines, curves, and points. Some of the stuff in this chapter builds upon techniques discussed in Chapter 6 — such as selecting stuff and applying effects. Nevertheless, you don't have to flip back the pages yet because I made sure that this chapter is self-sufficient. But in case you want to add eerie shadows that make helpless audiences squeak, go ahead and read Chapter 6!

Getting back to non-scary stuff, this chapter won't make a Walt Disney or Picasso out of you, but if you keep playing with PowerPoint's drawing tools, inspiration is never far away.

Rule Your Slides with Grids and Guides

If you want to create a structured presentation that maintains consistency of layout, look to PowerPoint's rulers, grids, and guides. With these tools, you can make PowerPoint's slide objects stay in their places all the time. For instance, you can

✔ Position text boxes and other elements identically across slides and presentations.

✔ Control ruler tabs.

✔ Manipulate the spacing between bullets and text in text placeholders and boxes.

✔ Control the snap options in PowerPoint so that slide objects snap and align to each other.

Displaying and using rulers

Rulers let you determine and measure where your objects are placed in relation to each other on one or more slides. Rulers are found to the left and above the slide area in Normal view, as shown in Figure 7-1. If your rulers aren't visible, you need to enable them.

Displaying rulers

Follow these steps to view or hide your rulers:

1. **On the View tab of the Ribbon, click the Normal button to make sure PowerPoint is in Normal view.**

2. **Also on the View tab, show or hide your rulers by selecting the Ruler check box in the Show/Hide group.**

   This option is a toggle that alternates between showing and hiding the rulers.

Do you really want the vertical ruler at all? If you want to permanently disable the vertical ruler, choose Office➪PowerPoint Options, and choose the Advanced tab. Under the Display section, deselect the Show Vertical Ruler check box.

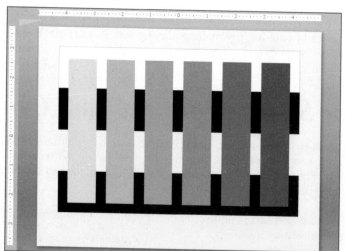

Figure 7-1:
PowerPoint
rulers.

Using rulers

Rulers can be used to

- Find and then change the position of guides.
- Tweak the indent settings in text placeholders and boxes.
- Position the spacing between the bullets and the text parts in text placeholders and boxes.

If you copy text into a PowerPoint placeholder from another application, you find that all the text formatting is goofed up. The solution is to tweak the indents and bullets by using the ruler, as I show you next.

Follow these steps to change the indents and bullet placements:

1. **Show your rulers if they aren't visible. (See the preceding section for details.)**

2. **Make sure you have a text placeholder or a text box with bulleted text on your slide.**

   Placeholders are covered in Chapter 8.

3. **Select the text you want to alter the spacing for.**

   You can select either

   - All the bulleted text (if you want to tweak the entire placeholder)
   - A single bullet or sentence

Give 'em an inch, and they'll take a kilometer

If your ruler displays inches but you want it to display centimeters — or vice versa — don't start exploring the options in PowerPoint! This setting is outside of PowerPoint. PowerPoint shows inches or centimeters based on how your operating system is set up.

To change the default units in a Windows XP system, follow these steps:

1. **Choose Start⇨Control Panel⇨Regional Settings (or Regional Options or Regional and Language options).**

2. **Click the Customize button on the Regional Options tab to open another dialog box.**

3. **In the Numbers tab of the dialog box that appears, change the Measurement System to U.S. or Metric depending upon whether you want inches or centimeters.**

If you're using Windows Vista, the steps are similar:

1. **Choose Start⇨Control Panel⇨Regional and Language Options.**

2. **Click the Customize This Format button.**

3. **In the Numbers tab of the dialog box that appears, change the Measurement System to U.S. or Metric depending upon whether you want inches or centimeters.**

4. Use the two sliders (carets) on the top ruler to adjust spacing between the text and the bullets.

Figure 7-2 shows you the sliders that you need to pull. When you pull (or drag) any of those sliders, the selected text dynamically rearranges itself to the new spacing.

- The *left slider* controls the distance between the placeholder margin and the bullet.

- The *right slider* controls the distance between the bullet and the text.

You can drag the bottommost piece of the right slider to move the two carets together.

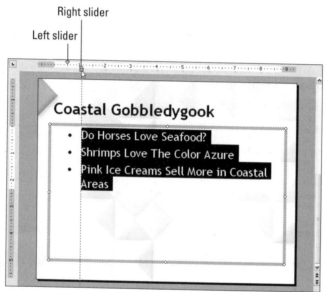

Figure 7-2:
Tweaking
indents in
the ruler.

Getting friendly with grids and guides

Think of grids and guides as a framework that lets you

✔ Align, anchor, and snap your slide objects in place.

✔ Apply the same changes to similar elements on all slides in a presentation.

The tool you should use depends on how important object placement is to you and which version of PowerPoint you're using:

✔ **Grid:** If you're happy with the default snap framework that PowerPoint provides, use a *grid.*

The grid isn't as useful as guides.

✔ **Guide:** If you want to control the placement of slide objects to the most minute level, use a *guide.*

You can use both grids and guides to get the best of both worlds.

Grids

Consider the *grid* in PowerPoint as a series of imaginary horizontal and vertical lines equally spaced over the entire slide area.

The grid can help you place slide elements in the same position on all your slides. The grid isn't as helpful as the guides because you really can't alter the placement of gridlines on the fly.

You have two quick ways to view and hide the grid:

✔ On the View tab of the Ribbon, select or deselect the Grid option.

✔ Toggle the visibility of the grid by pressing Shift+F9.

Both of these ways allow you to hide or unhide the grid — but they don't let you change any of the grid settings.

Follow these steps to change the grid settings and to view the grid on-screen:

1. **Click the Home tab of the Ribbon.**

2. **Click the Arrange button and then choose Align to view the Align gallery shown in Figure 7-3.**

3. **Choose the Grid Settings option to summon the Grid and Guides dialog box shown in Figure 7-4.**

4. **Change the snap options by selecting (or deselecting) the Snap Objects to Grid check box, as shown in Figure 7-4.**

   When the Snap Objects to Grid check box is selected, the grid becomes like a magnet that attracts slide objects to *evenly spaced points* on the slide. If you move your objects on the slide, you'll find them attaching a wee bit off from where you stopped moving them. That's the Snap Objects to Grid feature at work.

5. **Change the grid settings.**

   You can either

   • Change the default grid spacing by selecting from several preset choices in the Spacing drop-down list.

   • View the grid on the slide by selecting the Display Grid On Screen check box (see Figure 7-4).

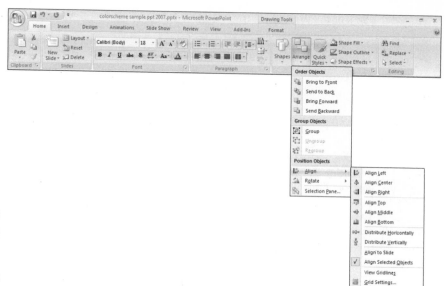

Figure 7-3:
The Align
gallery.

Figure 7-4:
The Grid
and Guides
dialog box.

Even if the grid is hidden, the Snap Objects to Grid option might be active.

Guides

Guides do so much more than grids, but you can consider them as grids that can be moved, added, or deleted.

You can have as many as eight horizontal and eight vertical guides in a presentation. By default, PowerPoint defaults to one horizontal and one vertical guide that intersect at the center of the slide, but you can add more manually, as I show you later in this chapter.

To make sure that the guides are visible, follow these steps:

1. **On the Home tab of the Ribbon, click the Arrange button and then choose Align to view the Align gallery (refer to Figure 7-3).**

2. **Click the Grid Settings option to summon the Grid and Guides dialog box (refer to Figure 7-4).**

3. **Select the Display Drawing Guides on Screen check box (refer to Figure 7-4).**

To quickly toggle the visibility of your guides, press Alt+F9.

If you need to use the same guides in all your presentations, make them visible in the Slide Master and save the presentation as a template. The guides show up in all presentations that you create using the template or theme. You can find out more about masters, templates, and themes in Chapter 4.

Creating new guides

Follow these steps to create new guides:

1. **Make sure that the guides are visible on the slide.**

2. **Place the cursor over a visible guide, press Ctrl, and drag in the direction required.**

    As you drag the new guide, you see the coordinates of the guide, which tell you how much you've dragged it away, as you can see in Figure 7-5. You can also view the coordinates within the ruler.

    If the rulers aren't visible, select the Ruler check box on the View tab of the Ribbon.

Figure 7-5:
When you
drag, you
can see the
coordinates.

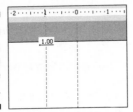

PowerPoint doesn't have a Snap to Guide option that you can turn on and off. If you set your guides to be visible, they snap all objects that venture close enough!

Moving and removing guides

To remove a guide, just select it and drag it off the slide. To move a guide, just drag it to wherever you want. Guides can't be locked into place.

Sometimes you might select a slide element rather than a guide and drag it off by mistake, especially if the slide is crowded. In that case, press Ctrl+Z to undo the original move and then pull the guide from outside the slide area.

Drawing Castles and Skyscrapers

Here are the facts about drawing in PowerPoint:

- ✔ PowerPoint doesn't have the amazing power of dedicated drawing programs, such as Adobe Illustrator and CorelDRAW.
- ✔ If you need a quick doodle or a simple drawing within your presentation, PowerPoint is best.

If you don't know how to use advanced drawing programs, don't enroll for professional training now. PowerPoint's drawing tools might be all you need.

PowerPoint can help you draw castles in the clouds. However, castles are passé — so, in the following sections, you create skyscrapers in the skies.

Adding the Shape gallery to the QAT

Getting to one of the Ribbon tabs to select all the line tools isn't very intuitive, so I like to have the entire Shapes gallery on my Quick Access toolbar.

The Quick Access toolbar (QAT) is the small toolbar that houses the Save, Undo, and Redo icons by default. However, you can add more icons to it for your convenience.

Follow these steps to place the Shapes gallery on the QAT:

1. **On the Insert tab of the Ribbon, right-click a shape within the Shapes gallery.**

2. **Choose the Add Gallery to Quick Access Toolbar option (see Figure 7-6).**

You have 12 options available for creating lines, which you can see in the Shapes gallery. Only four of these work really well for drawing lines. The other line options are for connectors that I cover in more detail in Chapter 6. These line types are shown in Figure 7-7.

The line types I cover in this chapter are

- ✔ Line (for straight, simple lines)
- ✔ Curve (for curved lines)
- ✔ Freeform (for drawing lines freehand)
- ✔ Scribble (for lines with corkscrews or random paths)

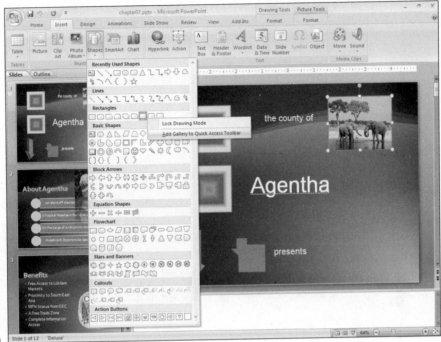

Figure 7-6:
Add the
Shapes
gallery to
the QAT.

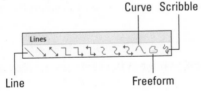

Figure 7-7:
The Line
types.

Drawing points and lines

Most dedicated drawing programs don't give you 4 (or 12) types of line tools. PowerPoint does just that so that you'll know exactly the type of line you'll end up with.

Points

In their simplest form, all lines connect two points. Before you get acquainted with lines, you must know more about points:

✔ A point is a *node* on any of the line types. Sometimes, these points are also called *vertexes*.

Every line type has a starting point and a closing point.

✔ For some lines that end up as closed shapes, the starting point is the same as the closing point. Of course, many more points exist in between.

✔ There can be several other points in between the starting point and the ending point, especially for lines that are rounded or curved — or for the places where the lines get cornered.

These in-between points can be either

- *Smooth points* (smooth curves)
- *Corner points* (sharp angles)

Drawing a line using any of the line tools is as simple as

1. Clicking the icon of the line type you want within the Lines group of the Shapes gallery.

2. Using a combination of clicking and dragging to create the points that are connected by lines.

In the following sections, I assume that you will go to the Shapes gallery and click the icon of the line type you want to draw.

Line

Follow these steps to draw a line in PowerPoint:

1. **Select the Line tool and click where you want to create the starting point of the line.**

   Don't release the mouse button.

2. **Drag the cursor to wherever you want to create the closing point of the line.**

3. **Release the mouse button.**

Lines with arrows and double arrows

Lines can automatically end with arrows:

✔ An **arrow line** has an arrowhead on one end.

✔ A **double arrow line** has arrowheads on both ends.

You draw the arrow and double arrow lines just like any other line — all you need to do is choose the single arrow or double arrow in the Lines area in the Shapes gallery.

The line, arrow, and double arrow options are all interchangeable. Just select any of these drawn lines on a slide and right-click. Then select the Format Shape option to bring up a dialog box of the same name. On the Line Style tab of this dialog box, you can find options to change the arrow styles.

Curve

Follow these steps to create a simple shape with the Curve tool:

1. **Select the Curve tool in the Lines group of the Shapes gallery.**

2. **Click anywhere on the slide to create a starting point.**

3. **Move the cursor down and to the right of the first point in a 45-degree angle and click again, as shown in the leftmost image in Figure 7-8.**

Figure 7-8:
Get them
curved in
PowerPoint.

4. **Move leftward in a straight line and click again, as shown in the middle of Figure 7-8.**

5. **Click over the first point to close the shape.**

If you don't want to close the shape, just double-click wherever you want to place the closing point of the curve.

As you just discovered, you're drawing with curved points rather than the corner points created by the Freeform Lines option. However, you can create a shape that contains both curved and corner points by using the Curve tool — just Ctrl+click to create a corner point rather than a curve point.

Freeform Line

Despite its name, the Freeform Line tool can create both freeform lines and straight lines. Its best capability might be creating a sequence of straight lines that form a shape or drawing.

Follow these steps to create freeform lines with the Freeform Line tool:

1. **Select the Freeform Line tool in the Lines group of the Shapes gallery.**

2. **Click on the slide where you want to create the starting point.**

   Don't release the mouse button yet.

3. **Drag and draw the same way you would with a pencil on paper.**

4. **End your freeform line with these options:**

   - To *stop* drawing, just double-click or press Esc.

   - To *close* the shape, click the starting point once.

Follow these steps to create straight lines (and skyscrapers) with the Freeform Line tool:

1. **Select the Freeform Line tool in the Lines group of the Shapes gallery.**

2. **Click anywhere on the slide to mark the starting point of your drawing.**

3. **Click anywhere on the slide to create another point.**

   PowerPoint draws a straight line connecting both the points.

4. **Keep adding points with connecting lines to create your own shape.**

   To do that, keep clicking to create new points and lines in between the points. Think of this as working in the same way as those connect-the-dots drawing books!

5. **When your drawing is done, click the first node (the starting point) to close the shape.**

   If you don't want a closed shape, just double-click the last node.

Figure 7-9 shows how I created a landscape of skyscrapers by using this technique.

All shapes can be formatted with PowerPoint's fills, lines, and effects. Chapter 6 has more information on PowerPoint's fills, lines, and effects.

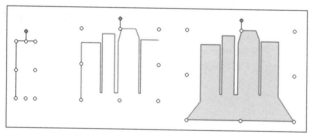

Figure 7-9:
Skyscrapers
with the
Freeform
Line tool.

Scribble Line

The Scribble Line option works the same way as the Freeform Line option but with one difference: You don't need to double-click to stop drawing — just stop dragging the cursor and the drawing ends at that position — just like a pencil! This does mean that you won't get the straight edges that can get with the Freeform line option.

Editing points

After you draw your own lines, curves, and closed shapes in PowerPoint, you might want to edit them because

- ✔ A curve needs to be more pronounced.
- ✔ A point on a smooth curve has to be converted to a corner point.
- ✔ A closed path needs to be broken up so that it becomes an open path.

Whatever your requirement might be, you'll love the Edit Points option in PowerPoint because it's so easy to use and intuitive. Not only does this allow you to alter the points on the lines, curves, and shapes that you draw, it also allows you to do the same edits on the shapes that you draw on a slide from the Shapes gallery.

However, you need to first convert those shapes to freeform shapes, and here's what you need to do:

1. **Select the shape, and click the Drawing Tools Format tab of the Ribbon.**

2. **Click the Edit Points button to open a small menu, as shown in Figure 7-10, and then choose the Convert to Freeform option.**

   Now the shape can be altered using the points on the shape. The selected shape now shows the points, as shown in Figure 7-11. Right-click one of the points to see a contextual menu (again see Figure 7-11).

Figure 7-10:
Convert shapes created from the Shape gallery to freeform, editable shapes.

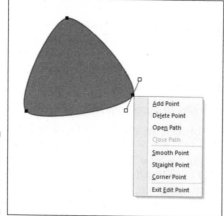

Figure 7-11:
Make and
break
points.

Here is an explanation of the options available:

- *Add Point:* Adds a new point where you right-clicked — this works best if you right-click at a spot in the line or curve where there was no existing point.

- *Delete Point:* Removes the point where you right-clicked to access this contextual menu.

- *Open Path:* Creates two points from the selected point — thereafter you can drag away those two points away from each other to make an open path from a closed path.

- *Close Path:* Closes a path by connecting to other side of the open path. In effect the closing points of both sides of an open path get connected.

- *Smooth Point:* Converts the selected point to a smooth point. Smooth points can then be smoother further by pulling the *handles* of the point. I explain handles later in this section.

- *Straight Point:* Removes the smoothen characteristic from a selected point.

- *Corner Point:* Converts a selected point to a corner point — think of this as a corner of a square or triangle to get the idea.

- *Exit Edit Points:* Gets you back to the normal editing mode in PowerPoint.

If you're happy with the changes in your shape effected with choosing any of the options explained in the preceding bullets, then that's all you need to do. Alternatively, you might want to play with the handles on each of the points when you select it.

Draw better with tablets

However good you might be at controlling the mouse, it's not as intuitive as drawing with a pen or pencil on paper. To draw more accurately and artistically, consider using a *drawing tablet* or a *Tablet PC platform* rather than a conventional mouse.

A drawing tablet lets you use a special pen on a magnetic tablet surface. Drawing tablets are often used as mouse replacements (or even coexist with mice) for desktop computers. Wacom creates the best drawing tablets — in fact, Wacom's

technology is part of the Microsoft Tablet PC platform. You can find more information at

`www.cuttingedgeppt.com/wacom`

A Tablet PC is a notebook computer that allows the screen to work as the tablet. This means you draw on the screen itself using a special pen — this is the closest simulation to paper and pen in the computer world. Microsoft creates a Tablet PC version of Windows that creates a seamless tablet interface. Find out more at

`www.cuttingedgeppt.com/tabletpc`

A *handle* is two more points attached to a point when you select the point, as shown in Figure 7-12. Dragging these handles in any direction can provide great results, so have fun experimenting with them.

When you start editing the points on lines, curves, and shapes, make a backup copy of them just in case you get overenthusiastic with the edits and then find yourself needing to get back your original stuff!

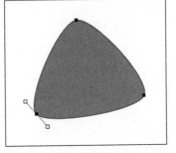

Figure 7-12:
Handles can really change the shape!

Selecting All the Teeny-Weeny Stuff

This problem happens so often! You draw a hundred shapes on your PowerPoint slide, make them all sing and dance — and then fumble when you want to do something as simple as selecting a shape. Fortunately, this section has all the help you need.

These selection techniques are almost always taken for granted:

✔ **To select an individual object, just click it.**

✔ **To deselect all objects on a slide, just click anywhere outside the slide area where no object is placed.**

✔ **To select multiple objects that aren't next to each other, Shift+click each consecutive object.**

✔ **To select multiple objects next to each other, follow these steps:**

    a. Make sure nothing is selected.

    b. Drag a marquee around the objects.

    To drag a marquee, click one corner of the area and drag diagonally (an angle of around 45 degrees) until all your objects are selected. You can even start dragging from outside the slide area.

✔ **To highlight each individual object on the slide, keep pressing the Tab key until your object is selected.**

The Tab key files through the slide objects.

Also explore the Selection and Visibility task pane, which I explain in more detail in Chapter 5.

Chapter 8

Dressing Up the Text Stuff

● ●

● ●

*I*f content is king, nothing relates to content like text in a presentation. This chapter is all about the text part of PowerPoint. I explain what all the text terms like *placeholder, text box,* and *outline* really mean — and how you can use them best. I also show you how you can create presentations from content already available as a Microsoft Word document.

You discover more about all those text niceties such as line spacing, margins, and case, and you get your bulleted and numbered lists polished. And then there are fonts. You find out how to use them as symbols and how you can make them look beautiful with WordArt.

Using Text in PowerPoint

A presentation bereft of text is like a body without a soul. Yes, you can have photo album presentations without text, but even those greatly benefit from text captions. If this prompts you to fill all your slides with 400 words of text in 10-point Arial, you need to realize that too much of anything (including text) isn't a good thing. These presentation guidelines for text usage can help:

   ✔ **Prepare your text before you begin creating a presentation.** This chapter shows you how to create a presentation from a Word document.

   ✔ **Every presentation needs a storyboard — use storyboarding principles.** This subject is beyond the scope of this book, so I've put up a link to helpful content on the companion Web site:

www.cuttingedgeppt.com/story

The *Cutting Edge PowerPoint 2007 For Dummies* CD includes a single-page storyboarding template. Print copies of the template and use it to evolve your storyboard.

- ✔ **Don't use text that's too small on a PowerPoint slide — for most fonts, less than 24 points is too small.** You can use smaller text for things you really don't want the audience to read, such as copyright notices or silly captions!

- ✔ **Don't use more than four bullet points on a slide.** If your bulleted items are *short,* five bullets might be okay on a slide.

If you have longer lists, either

  - *Combine* bulleted items.

  - *Divide* the content over two or more slides.

- ✔ **Consider not using bullets at all!** Although most presenters swear by slides filled with bulleted items, not using bullets might give you more flexibility in designing and delivering your presentation.

- ✔ **Limit text to the title.** You can also create slides where the only text content is the slide title. However, as with anything else be sure that this is suitable for the audience and the presentation — every situation is different!

All Those Text Terms

This section shows all the text nomenclature that PowerPoint uses. After you and PowerPoint start using the same language, you'll be on the same wavelength!

Placeholders and text boxes

All text placeholders are text boxes, but not all text boxes are placeholders:

- ✔ **Any container of text is called a *text box.***

- ✔ **PowerPoint includes several slide layouts.** Most of these layouts include text boxes. Because these text boxes are part of a slide layout, they're known as *placeholders.*

To view the layouts, click the Home tab on the Ribbon and then click the Layout option. This brings up the Layout gallery with thumbnail representations of all slide layouts available in the active PowerPoint presentation.

✔ **Other text boxes that you insert within a slide aren't placeholders;** they're mere text boxes.

To insert a text box in a slide, click the Insert tab on the Ribbon, and then click the Text Box button. Your cursor transforms into an insertion point. You can either

- Place the cursor anywhere on the slide to create a text box that resizes to fit any text you type.
- Drag and draw with the cursor on the slide to set the size and location of the text box.

✔ **All text boxes and placeholders are part of the shapes family.** You can use all the formatting options associated with shapes (such as shape styles, fills, lines, and effects) to spiff up your text boxes.

Chapter 5 includes more information about how you can format your shapes — and also how you can manipulate them for size, position, and orientation.

Outlines

The outline of a presentation is merely the text content of all the title and text placeholders that you see on your slides. This includes all slide titles, bulleted text, or anything that you type into the title and text placeholders. All this becomes part of the presentation's outline.

Any text outside the placeholders doesn't become a part of the outline. Include as much text content in the outline (and placeholders) as you can because most third-party tools for PowerPoint use only the text contained within the outline and ignore everything else! Even if you want to send your text to Microsoft Word, it will ignore everything outside the outlines.

To view (and edit) your presentation's outline, follow these steps:

✔ Click the Outline tab in the left pane of the PowerPoint window.

✔ If you want a better view of the outline, drag the vertical line between the slide and outline panes to resize it as required.

Putting Microsoft Word to Good Use

Creating and editing an outline in Word is easier than in PowerPoint. You can create a new PowerPoint presentation in an instant from a properly formatted Word outline. Only two conditions need to be met:

✔ **Both Word and PowerPoint must be installed on the same machine.**

Word and PowerPoint collaborate best when they have the same version number — so if you're using PowerPoint 2007, it'll work best with Word 2007.

✔ **Your Word outline needs to be formatted using Heading styles.** These styles correspond directly to PowerPoint's Title and Bullets attributes.

For the following brief tutorial, you need a Word document with some text in it. You can use the sample document called `small.doc` on the *Cutting Edge PowerPoint 2007 For Dummies* CD.

Follow these steps to create a Word document that successfully translates to a PowerPoint presentation:

1. **Remove all the gobbledygook.**

   PowerPoint often requires much less text than a Word document:

   • Remove repetitive text.

   • Prune your sentences.

   • Break long sentences into smaller sentences.

   Repeat this process any number of times to end up with a slick and effective outline.

2. **Include a return (press Enter) after each title or sentence.**

   Place only one return after each sentence. More than one return makes *blank* PowerPoint slides after the conversion!

3. **Apply Word's paragraph styles.**

   Select the text you need to apply the style to and then choose a style from the Style gallery on the Home tab of the Ribbon (see Figure 8-1).

   I've included an edited Word file with the styles applied, `edited.docx`, on the *Cutting Edge PowerPoint 2007 For Dummies* CD.

   Use only the following styles; PowerPoint ignores anything else. These Word styles translate to PowerPoint equivalents:

   • Heading 1 becomes Title.

   • Heading 2 becomes Bullet Level 1.

   • Heading 3 becomes Bullet Level 2 (a subbullet).

   • Heading 4 becomes Bullet Level 3 (a sub-subbullet).

   • Heading 5 becomes Bullet Level 4.

   In the same way, you can go right up to Heading 9 in Word, but anything below Heading 5 is actually not going to make much sense!

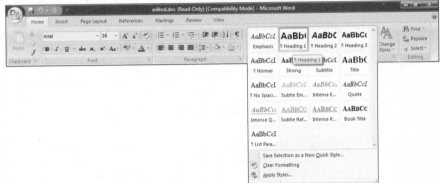

Figure 8-1:
Applying
styles in
Word.

4. **Save your outline document, preferably under a new name. Close the document and exit Word.**

5. **Launch PowerPoint, and import this outline by clicking the Home tab on the Ribbon and then clicking the arrow below the New Slide button.**

   This opens a gallery.

6. **Choose the Slides from Outline option, and in the Insert Outline dialog box that appears, select the Word document you just saved.**

   The outline translates to a presentation in PowerPoint, formatted with titles and bulleted items. Isn't this cool?

Presentations created with Word outlines are pretty basic: a default font style in black over a white background. Rarely do you want to leave your presentation in such a bare state. The easiest way to provide a sophisticated look to such a plain presentation is to apply a template or theme. Chapter 4 has more information on applying PowerPoint templates and Office themes.

You can choose from 100 PowerPoint templates on the *Cutting Edge PowerPoint 2007 For Dummies* CD!

Formatting Text Boxes

Text in a presentation might be within a placeholder, a shape, or a text box.

All text boxes (or the text that they contain) have these formatting attributes:

- ✔ Line spacing and alignment
- ✔ Case
- ✔ Margins and text wrap

✔ Character spacing

✔ Bullets and numbering

The following sections show how you can use these text attributes.

Line spacing and alignment

Line spacing denotes the spacing between sentences and paragraphs in a text box. Efficient use of line spacing is one of the most neglected options in presentations. Fortunately, it's one of the easiest things to manage in PowerPoint.

I also explore the text alignment options in this section.

Follow these steps to tweak line spacing and alignment:

1. **Select the text that you want to change.**

   You can select either

   - The entire text box (to change spacing for all the text in the box)
   - Just the text you want to format

2. **Click the Home tab on the Ribbon and then click the Line Spacing button.**

   The Line Spacing gallery appears.

3. **Choose any of the preset line spacing options or choose Line Spacing Options to summon the Paragraph dialog box shown in Figure 8-2.**

   If the dialog box covers your text box, move the dialog box to another position so that you can preview any changes you make.

Figure 8-2: Change line spacing to make text more readable.

4. **Change the following line spacing options as desired:**

- *The Alignment option* changes the alignment of the selected text — choices include left, centered, right, justified, and distributed.

    All these options are also directly available in the Home tab's Paragraph group.

- *The Indentation options* allow you to change the value of the indent before text and the hanging value. *Hanging* denotes the area between the bullet and the first text character within the bulleted list.

- *The Spacing options* change the spacing between lines of the same sentence or paragraph.

    The Before option changes the line spacing in the area above the selected text or paragraph.

    The After option changes the line spacing in the area below the selected text or paragraph.

    The Line Spacing drop-down list allows you to choose from line spacing presets such as Single, 1.5, Double, and more.

5. **Click OK to apply the changes to the selected text or paragraph.**

    If you don't like the changes, press Ctrl+Z to undo. You can then change the line spacing options again.

Reducing the line spacing value is a great idea when you need to squeeze a single, extra line on an existing text box. To do this, select Multiple in the Line Spacing drop down box, and set it to a spacing value of 0.8 or 0.85.

However, don't do this trick too often because reducing the line spacing might affect readability.

Changing case

How often have you inherited a presentation that was created by someone who seemed to love typing in ALL CAPS? If this frustrates you as much as it frustrates me, you'll love PowerPoint's Change Case option, which puts the case in your court!

Follow these steps to set your cases in order:

1. **Select the text or an entire paragraph that you want to change.**

    You can select either

    - An entire text box (to change capitalization for all text in the box)

    - Only the text you want to format

2. **Click the Home tab on the Ribbon and then click the Change Case button in the Font group.**

   The Change Case gallery appears. (See Figure 8-3.)

3. **Choose any of the five *case* (capitalization) options:**

   - *Sentence case:* Capitalizes the first letter of the first word in a sentence and uses lowercase for everything else.

   - *lowercase:* Changes the entire selection to lowercase letters.

   - *UPPERCASE:* Changes everything selected to uppercase.

     This is my worst case nightmare come true! Never use it unless you have a sound reason to do so.

   - *Capitalize Each Word:* Capitalizes the first letter of each word in a selection. In previous versions of PowerPoint, this option was called Title Case.

     Yes, it capitalizes the *by*s and the *a*s. Change them back manually to lowercase after using this option.

   - *tOGGLE cASE:* Reverses every letter's original case. For instance, PowerPoint would become pOWERpOINT.

   PowerPoint applies the changes instantly — to undo something that you don't like, press Ctrl+Z to undo the last change.

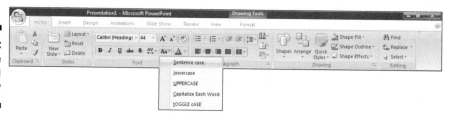

Figure 8-3:
What case
can I
provide?

Margins and text wrap

Margins are the bare areas on the perimeter of the text boxes that provide some breathing space to the text.

Text wrap is an option that enables your text to flow within the text box so that text that can't fit within the width of the box automatically flows to the next line.

If your text suffers from a lack of oxygen or if your text is so rigid that it can't flow, you just have to follow these steps and let it breathe more easily:

1. **Select the text box, right-click and choose the Format Shape option.**

2. **In the resulting dialog box, click the Text Box tab (as shown in Figure 8-4).**

3. **If you want to alter the direction in which the text is placed in a text box, change the text anchor point in this dialog box from the Vertical Alignment drop-down list.**

   A _text anchor point_ relates to the location of the text within the text box.

4. **Change the left, right, top, and bottom margin values as required for your selected text within the Internal Margin section.**

5. **If the Wrap Text in Shape option isn't selected, place a check mark next to it so that your text wraps and flows within the text box.**

6. **Click Close to get back to your slide.**

   If you don't like the changes, press Ctrl+Z immediately to undo.

Figure 8-4:
Margin
magic and
wrap wows.

The same dialog box offers more formatting options for niceties like auto-fitting text and text direction. Play with these options and review them — remember to undo the changes by pressing Ctrl+Z immediately if you don't like them.

Character spacing

PowerPoint finally has character spacing — this is a great solution when you want that extra word in the paragraph to fit within the existing four lines rather than living lonely on the fifth line.

Page layout designers call those extra words orphans and widows.

Follow these steps to adjust the character spacing of text in PowerPoint:

1. **Select the text, sentence, or an entire text box.**

2. **Click the Home tab on the Ribbon and then click the Character Spacing button.**

   This will bring up the Character Spacing gallery shown in Figure 8-5.

3. **Choose from any of the presets or click the More Spacing option to bring up the dialog box shown in Figure 8-6.**

Figure 8-5:
Choose a preset character spacing option . . .

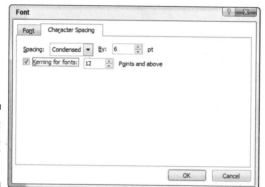

Figure 8-6:
. . . or tweak it on your own!

4. **Make your choices as explained here:**

   • From the Spacing drop-down list, select from Normal, Expanded, or Condensed. Normal is regular text spacing, Expanded is loose fitting text, and Condensed is text placed close to each other.

   • Set the By option for your Spacing attribute. If you choose Condensed and then set the By option to 6 pts, you get very tight-fitting text. If you set the By option to 25 pts, you might not even be able to read your text anymore — the characters will be almost squeezed against each other!

- Select the Kerning for Fonts check box and enter a value in the Points and Above text box. If you choose 12 points or above, only text that is above 12 points will obey any character spacing rules that you specify. (*Kerning* is the spacing of text characters based on the information contained within the font.)

5. **Click OK to accept the changes or click Cancel to exit this dialog box without any changes.**

Bullets and numbering

Do you take all those bullets and numbering for granted just because PowerPoint takes care of them seamlessly? Truly, you don't know what you're missing. Try experimenting with some of the style options to find great new ways to make your presentation look unique.

Bullets

Follow these steps to change the bullet style:

1. **Select the text to be changed.**

   You can select either

   - Bulleted items that you want to format
   - A sentence without bullets that you want to be bulleted

2. **Click Home tab on the Ribbon, and then click the arrow next to the Bullets button (located in the Paragraph group).**

3. **Choose an option from the Bullets gallery or choose the Bullets and Numbering option.**

   If you chose the Bullets and Numbering option, the Bullets and Numbering dialog box opens, as shown in Figure 8-7.

Figure 8-7:
Bullets don't have to be boring.

4. **Select your bullet character.**

   To choose a preset bullet style, just select one and click OK.

   To choose a picture bullet, follow these steps:

   a. *Click the Picture button.*

   A dialog box opens with many picture bullets.

   b. *Select a picture bullet and then click OK to apply it.*

   To use another symbol as the bullet character, follow these steps:

   a. *Click the Customize button.*

   The Symbol dialog box opens.

   b. *Use the dialog box to select any character from any installed font as the bullet.*

   Use a common font like Wingdings for your bullets. This ensures that all recipients of your presentation can view the bullets as you intended. If you use an uncommon font, recipients of the presentation who don't have the font installed on their computers might end up seeing an annoying box instead of a bullet!

5. **(Optional) If required, use the Bullets and Numbering dialog box (refer to Figure 8-7) to change the bullet color or size:**

   • The Size text box lets you increase or decrease the bullet size in proportion to your text size.

   By default, the bullet size is 100% of the text size because it makes so much design sense. Don't change it to 40% or 400% unless you have a compelling need for variation in size!

   • The Color option lets you change the bullet color from the default text color.

   If you change the color, you can change it back to the *default* by selecting the Automatic Color option. Make sure that the bullet color contrasts well with your slide background.

6. **Click OK to accept or click Cancel to exit without any changes.**

Numbering

Changing the format of numbered bullets gives you an excuse to choose from a small mob of numbering styles. Follow these steps to change the number style:

1. **Select the text you want to format as a numbered list:**

   • Numbered items that you want to format

   • Sentences that you want numbered

   • A bulleted list that you want to convert to a numbered list

2. **Click the Home tab and then click the arrow next to the Numbering button in the Paragraph group.**

3. **Choose an option from the Numbering gallery, or choose the Bullets and Numbering option.**

   If you choose the Bullets and Numbering option, the Bullets and Numbering dialog box appears (refer to Figure 8-7).

4. **Click the Numbered tab if that's not already active, as shown in Figure 8-8.**

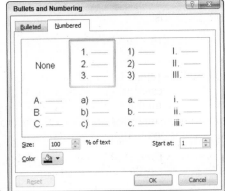

Figure 8-8:
Are your
bullets
numbered?

5. **Choose from any of the preset styles.**

6. **(Optional) You can choose a different color and size for the number, as I explain in the preceding "Bullets" section.**

7. **In the Start At text box, enter a starting number.**

   The default is to start the numbered list at 1. You can enter any number you want, however — you can start your numbered list at 6,754, so that the next number in the list is 6,755 instead of 2.

8. **Click OK to accept or click Cancel to exit without any changes.**

Playing with Fonts

Did you ever end up using a font that looks like the letters are running away! Or maybe the font you used looks just like a movie title? It might look good on a home poster, but use it in a presentation and the audience might run away. Using the right fonts for your presentation is very important.

Font types

Fonts can be classified into five types:

- ✔ **Serif** fonts are typefaces that have *serifs* (little hook edges that make them easier to read in print). Figure 8-9 shows you a few serif fonts.

  Serif fonts are used mainly by the print media for body type. Examples of such fonts include Times New Roman, Georgia, and Book Antiqua.
- ✔ **Sans serif** fonts, which are also shown in Figure 8-9, are typefaces without serifs.

  Sans serif fonts are suited for headings and electronic media (such as PowerPoint) because they're easier to read on your computer screen. In addition, they also project well. Examples of common sans serif fonts include Arial, Trebuchet MS, and Tahoma.
- ✔ **Monospace** fonts are much like typewriter imprints. In these fonts, all characters are the same width, including the spaces.

  Courier is an example of a monospace font. 
- ✔ **Script** fonts typically resemble brush scripts, calligraphy, or handwriting.

  These normally aren't suitable for PowerPoint presentations.
- ✔ **Dingbats** are character fonts that don't include the alphabet. Each keystroke produces a basic line drawing or illustration.

  A quick search of the Internet reveals thousands of free dingbat sets that you can download. In PowerPoint, dingbats are used for bullets. Examples of such fonts include Wingdings and Webdings.

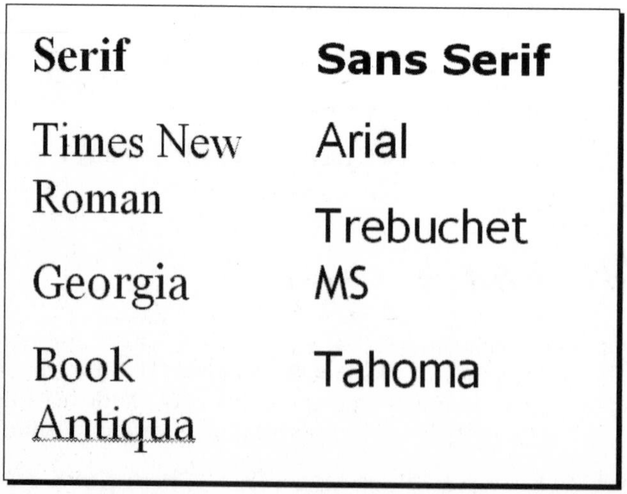

Figure 8-9: Serif and sans serif fonts.

Serif	Sans Serif
Times New Roman	Arial
Georgia	Trebuchet MS
Book Antiqua	Tahoma

Color Plate 3-1: Contrast aids readability of text over a background, whether you use lighter or darker text.

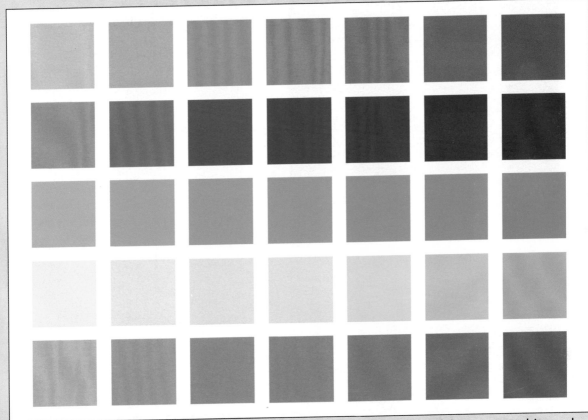

Color Plate 3-2: Pure colors are in the center column. The tints on the left have more white and the shades on the right have more black.

Color Plate 3-3: A slight change in tints and shades can significantly increase contrast and readability.

Color Plate 3-4: Textures can be magical. These textures are infinitely more interesting than plain colors.

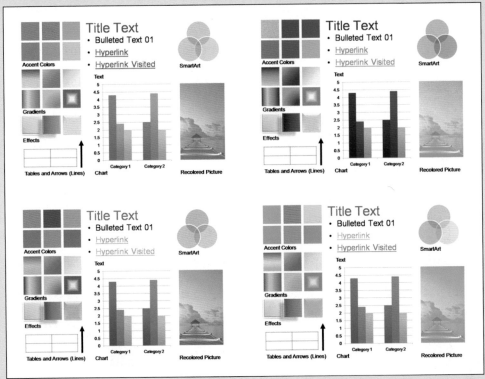

Color Plate 3-5: Change your Theme Colors, and everything changes in a blink!

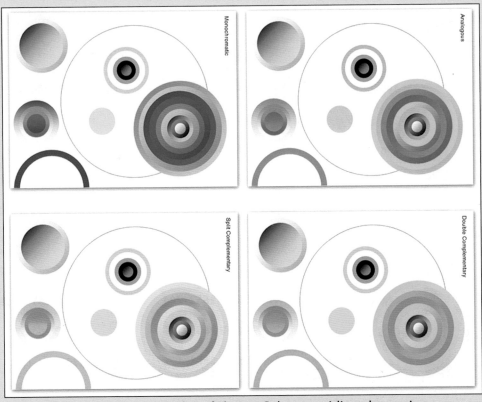

Color Plate 3-6: More examples of Theme Colors providing change in a slide design.

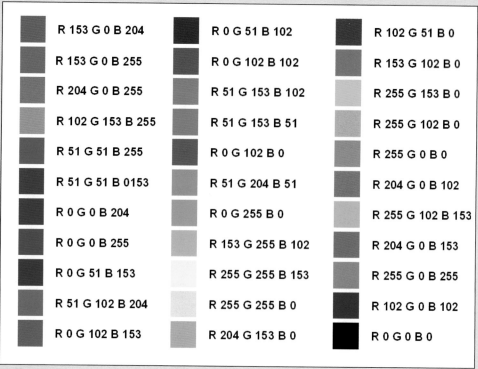

R 153 G 0 B 204	R 0 G 51 B 102	R 102 G 51 B 0
R 153 G 0 B 255	R 0 G 102 B 102	R 153 G 102 B 0
R 204 G 0 B 255	R 51 G 153 B 102	R 255 G 153 B 0
R 102 G 153 B 255	R 51 G 153 B 51	R 255 G 102 B 0
R 51 G 51 B 255	R 0 G 102 B 0	R 255 G 0 B 0
R 51 G 51 B 0153	R 51 G 204 B 51	R 204 G 0 B 102
R 0 G 0 B 204	R 0 G 255 B 0	R 255 G 102 B 153
R 0 G 0 B 255	R 153 G 255 B 102	R 204 G 0 B 153
R 0 G 51 B 153	R 255 G 255 B 153	R 255 G 0 B 255
R 51 G 102 B 204	R 255 G 255 B 0	R 102 G 0 B 102
R 0 G 102 B 153	R 204 G 153 B 0	R 0 G 0 B 0

Color Plate 3-7: RGB Color Reference Chart.

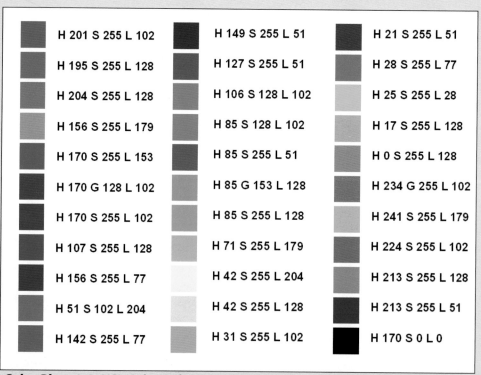

H 201 S 255 L 102	H 149 S 255 L 51	H 21 S 255 L 51
H 195 S 255 L 128	H 127 S 255 L 51	H 28 S 255 L 77
H 204 S 255 L 128	H 106 S 128 L 102	H 25 S 255 L 28
H 156 S 255 L 179	H 85 S 128 L 102	H 17 S 255 L 128
H 170 S 255 L 153	H 85 S 255 L 51	H 0 S 255 L 128
H 170 G 128 L 102	H 85 G 153 L 128	H 234 G 255 L 102
H 170 S 255 L 102	H 85 S 255 L 128	H 241 S 255 L 179
H 107 S 255 L 128	H 71 S 255 L 179	H 224 S 255 L 102
H 156 S 255 L 77	H 42 S 255 L 204	H 213 S 255 L 128
H 51 S 102 L 204	H 42 S 255 L 128	H 213 S 255 L 51
H 142 S 255 L 77	H 31 S 255 L 102	H 170 S 0 L 0

Color Plate 3-8: HSL Color Reference Chart.

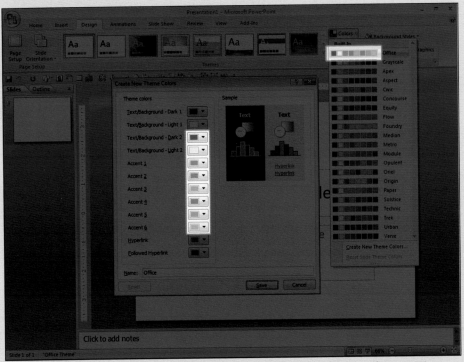

Color Plate 3-9: Only 8 of the 12 colors in a Theme Color set show up in the Theme Colors gallery.

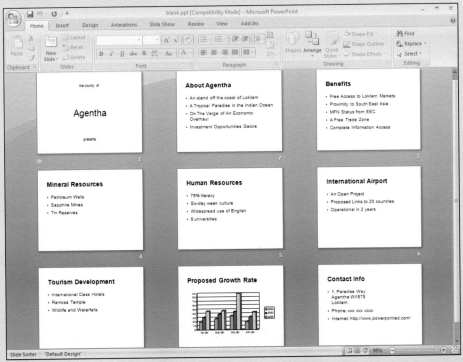

Color Plate 4-1: Before: A basic, boring presentation.

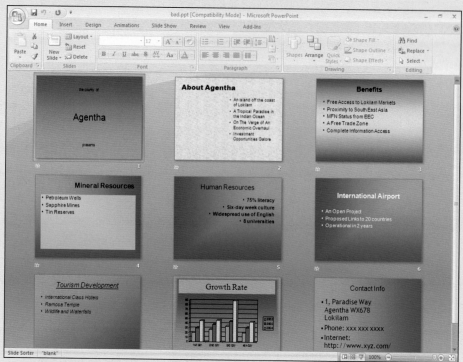

Color Plate 4-2: After: Formatting without Masters is a recipe for disaster.

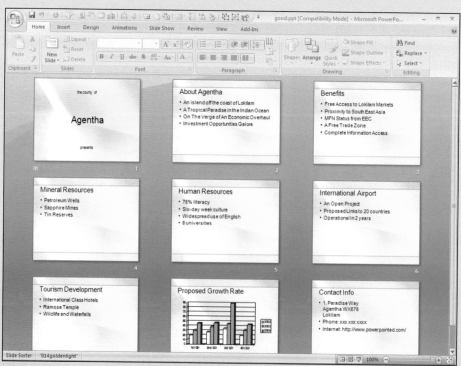

Color Plate 4-3: After: Using a template makes for a consistent, professional presentation.

Color Plate 6-1: PowerPoint's fill options control color and texture.

Gradient Lines

Color Plate 6-2: Gradient Lines make great frames and borders.

Color Plate 6-3: Just add the effect you want for your shapes!

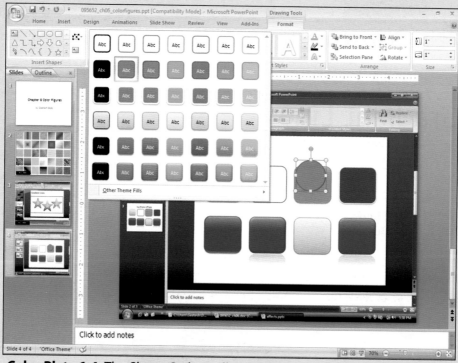

Color Plate 6-4: The Shape Styles gallery provides a bewildering array of options to embellish your shapes.

Font formats

All fonts in Windows are actually files that you can find by double-clicking the Font icon inside the Control Panel. Table 7-1 lists the common font formats for Windows PCs.

Table 7-1	Common Windows Font Formats
Format	**Windows Versions**
TrueType	Vista, XP, 2000, NT, 98, 95
Type 1 PostScript	Vista, XP, 2000, NT, 98, 95 (older versions require Adobe Type Manager)
OpenType	Vista, XP

Theme Fonts

PowerPoint 2007 includes a new Theme Fonts feature that lets you determine a default font for the titles and text boxes within any PowerPoint presentation that is based on the applied theme.

To create your own Theme Fonts set for an open presentation, follow these steps:

1. **Click the Design tab on the Ribbon and click the Fonts button to bring up the Fonts gallery, as shown in Figure 8-10.**

2. **Choose the Create New Theme Fonts option to bring up a dialog box of the same name, as shown in Figure 8-11.**

3. **Choose fonts for the heading and body from the Heading Font and Body Font drop-down lists.**

   • Heading fonts are mainly used in slide titles.

   • Body fonts are used for all other text.

4. **In the Name text box, enter a descriptive name for your theme fonts set.**

5. **Click Save to finish creating the Theme Fonts set.**

   Your Theme Fonts set is now available in the Fonts gallery — in fact, you can even apply the same Theme Fonts set to any of your presentations by clicking the relevant option in the Fonts gallery.

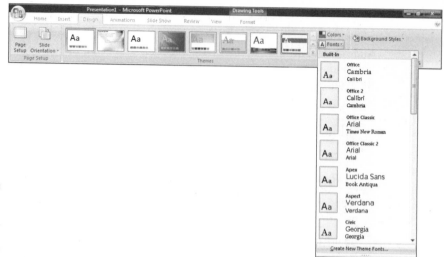

Figure 8-10:
The Fonts
gallery.

Figure 8-11:
Create a
new Theme
Fonts set.

Font guidelines

Follow these font guidelines to ensure that your presentations look sophisticated and cutting edge:

- ✔ **Avoid using more than two font types in a presentation.** I normally
  use just one font type and provide the variation component by using
  different colors, sizes, and formatting attributes like bold and italic.

- ✔ **Using two sans serif styles in a PowerPoint presentation is perfectly
  acceptable.** For instance, your title and body text can each be composed
  in a different sans serif style.

- ✔ **If you can't read the text in your presentation from about two meters
  (about six feet) from your computer, use a larger font size.**

  For most fonts, you want to use a font size of 24 points or larger for
  maximum readability.

Fonts with the same "point size" might be different actual sizes. For
example, 24-point Times New Roman is smaller than 24-point Arial.

✔ **Use fonts that are installed on most systems by default.** Most PowerPoint installations, especially of the last two versions, include these fonts:

- Arial
- Book Antiqua
- Bookman Old Style
- Century Gothic
- Century Schoolbook
- Comic Sans
- Courier New
- Georgia
- Gill Sans MT
- Lucida Sans

- Perpetua
- Rockwell
- Symbol
- Tahoma
- Times New Roman
- Trebuchet MS
- Tw Cen MT
- Verdana
- Wingdings

This list also includes fonts that are part of Microsoft Windows.

In addition, PowerPoint 2007 includes these new fonts as part of the built-in Theme Fonts:

- Calibri
- Cambria
- Corbel
- Consolas
- Constantia

✔ **If you use an uncommon font, consider embedding it in the presentation.**

Only TrueType fonts can be embedded. Find the whole scoop about embedding fonts in the next section.

Embedding TrueType fonts

PowerPoint lets you embed a copy of a font in a presentation. But this isn't a solution to all your font problems. Sometimes, embedding a font creates more problems than solutions. Trust me — you don't want to know more about these problems until you run into them! If that made you more curious, you can find out more at

www.cuttingedgeppt.com/fontembedproblems

Follow these steps to embed a font within a presentation:

1. **Choose Office⇨Save As.**

   You're presented with the Save As dialog box.

2. **In the Save As dialog box, choose Tools⇨Save Options, as shown in Figure 8-12.**

   This opens the Save Options dialog box, as shown in Figure 8-13.

3. **Select the Embed Fonts in the File option.**

   The Save Options dialog box has two other noteworthy options in the embed fonts section:

   • *The Embed Only the Characters Used in the Presentation option* embeds just the font characters you have used in the presentation. This means that if you haven't used the capital letter *Z* anywhere in the presentation, that character isn't embedded.

   • *The Embed All Characters option* embeds the entire font into the PowerPoint presentation.

4. **When you're done, click OK to get back to the Save As dialog box.**

5. **Give the file a new name and then click Save.**

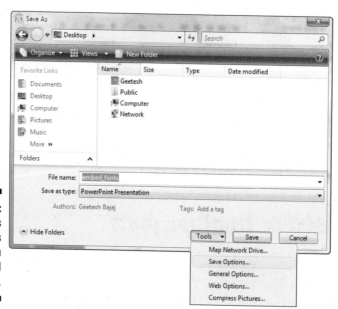

Figure 8-12: The Save As dialog box is where you embed fonts.

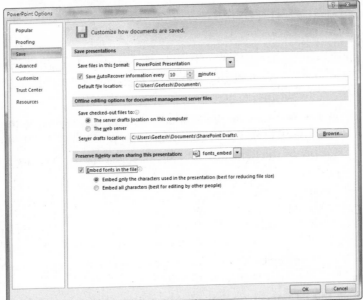

Figure 8-13:
Font
embedding
options.

Font embedding guidelines

Follow these guidelines to make sure that you don't run into any font embedding problems:

- ✔ If a particular font doesn't support embedding, PowerPoint warns you.

  You can't embed Type 1 fonts at all.

- ✔ If your recipients use PowerPoint on the Mac, they can't see embedded fonts.

- ✔ To find out whether a particular font supports embedding, download the free Font Properties Extension from the Microsoft Typography site:

  ```
  www.cuttingedgeppt.com/fontextension
  ```

- ✔ PowerPoint 2003 won't allow you to edit a presentation with embedded fonts that aren't installed on a local machine, even if you replace the font (discussed in the next section). This is important if you have friends or colleagues who still haven't upgraded to PowerPoint 2007. You can find more information at this book's companion site:

  ```
  www.cuttingedgeppt.com/fontembedproblems
  ```

Replacing fonts

You might receive a presentation that uses fonts that would look better on a garage-sale poster, or you might inherit a presentation with a zillion font styles. Luckily, setting the fonts in order is a snap — follow these steps to replace your fonts:

1. **On the Home tab on the Ribbon, click the arrow next to the Replace option in the Editing group and select the Replace Fonts option.**

   This opens the Replace Font dialog box, as shown in Figure 8-14.

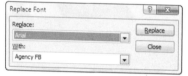

Figure 8-14: Replace fonts.

2. **In the Replace drop-down list box, select the name of the font you want to change; in the With drop-down list, select the name of the font that you want to use.**

3. **Click the Replace button.**

4. **Repeat Steps 2 and 3 to replace more fonts.**

5. **When you're done, click Close.**

If you want to change fonts for the entire presentation, it is best that you choose or create another Theme Fonts set as explained earlier in this chapter. If you replace fonts that are part of an applied Theme Font set to something else, the fonts would become disconnected from the theme.

Inserting symbols

If you're mentioning a product or company name in a presentation, you might need to put in the trademark (™) or registered (®) symbol. At other times, you might require other symbols like copyright (©) or just an infinity symbol (∞, if you're describing the meeting length). Follow these steps to insert a symbol as part of the text:

1. **Click within a text box to create an insertion point.**

2. **Click the Insert tab on the Ribbon, and then click the Symbol button to summon the Symbol dialog box, as shown in Figure 8-15.**

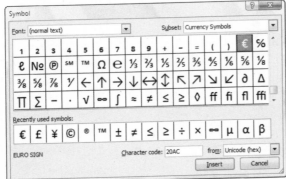

Figure 8-15:
Insert
symbols.

3. **Select the font that contains the symbol from the Font drop-down list.**

   Common symbols for trademarks and copyrights are available in most fonts; you can find more exotic symbols in Dingbat fonts, which I explain earlier in this chapter in the "Font types" section.

4. **For each symbol you want to insert, select the symbol and click the Insert button.**

5. **When you finish inserting symbols, click Close.**

Doing Your Research inside PowerPoint: The World Is Your Oyster!

If you need to make your presentations more authentic, using quotes from sources as diverse as literary luminaries and stock market gurus, look no further than the Research task pane. Imagine looking for a definition, seeking alternative words in a thesaurus, searching the Web, and translating from one language to another — all from within PowerPoint!

You can do all that with the Research pane in PowerPoint 2007, which is shown in Figure 8-16. Access the Research task pane by clicking the Review tab on the Ribbon and then clicking the Research button.

Figure 8-16:
Do research
inside
PowerPoint.

Here's a partial list of some reference sources available within the Research task pane:

- ✔ **Dictionary:** PowerPoint can access dictionaries in several languages.
- ✔ **Thesaurus:** Thesauruses are also available in multiple languages.
- ✔ **Encyclopedia:** Microsoft's award-winning Encarta Encyclopedia is available as part of the Research pane.
- ✔ **Translation:** You can translate text into 12 languages, and you can add more languages. However, because the translation is done entirely by computers, the translations are word-for-word, so you might end up with some hilarious or bewildering results. Have fun!
- ✔ **Stock Quotes:** Yes, you can get stock quotes, change percentages, and charts for the last five years!

The Research task pane is *extensible* — Microsoft and third-party developers can create extensions that allow you to search more reference sources. Most of the reference sources in the Research task pane require an Internet connection to access the content.

> To quickly access the thesaurus and the Research task pane at the same time, right-click any word and choose Synonyms⇨Thesaurus.

WordArt Wonders

WordArt is a text effects component whose *raison d'être* is to create artistic effects with ordinary words. Such words could be anything — an advertising blurb, a headline, or even an entire design all its own.

Creating WordArt

Follow these steps to create WordArt within PowerPoint:

1. **Click the Insert tab on the Ribbon and then click the WordArt button.**

   You come face-to-face with the WordArt Gallery, as shown in Figure 8-17.

2. **Choose a preset style from the gallery.**

   If you can't find something you like, choose something close to your requirements. You can tweak it later.

3. **Type your text right on the slide.**

   You can change the font style and size here. To do that, right-click the WordArt on the slide and you'll see the Mini Toolbar that allows you to do all sorts of font formatting, including changing the font size.

4. **Move or resize the WordArt as required.**

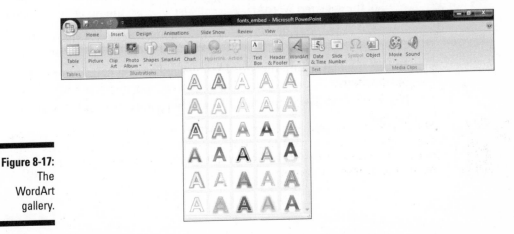

Figure 8-17:
The
WordArt
gallery.

Editing WordArt

Changing the appearance of WordArt text is easy. Follow these steps to change the fills and other frivolities of your WordArt:

1. **Select the WordArt on the slide to activate the Drawing Tools Format tab of the Ribbon.**

2. **Click the Drawing Tools Format tab.**

   The WordArt Styles group, as shown in Figure 8-18, houses several buttons.

Figure 8-18:
The
WordArt
options.

3. **Work with all the buttons in the WordArt Styles group to edit the WordArt as required.**

   - *The leftmost button* allows you to see the WordArt gallery again, and change the overall WordArt style.

     The WordArt styles can be applied to any text in the presentation, not only inserted WordArt objects.

   - *The Text Fill option* allows you to change the fill — options include colors, gradients, textures, and picture fills.

   - *The Text Outline option* allows you to change the outline attributes of the selected WordArt. You can also choose the No Outline option.

   - *The Text Effects option* includes several galleries that allow you to change the shadow, reflection, glow, bevel, and other properties.

4. **To edit the text within the WordArt, just select and retype the text as required.**

5. **Deselect the WordArt by clicking anywhere outside it to get back to the slide.**

Chapter 9

Adding Images to Your Presentations

*I*n this chapter, I show you how to get those gazillion digital-camera images into your presentation in an instant and share that presentation with Grandma or your colleagues at the office. The best part of images is that the content is entirely visual, so they aren't dependent on languages and words. This is perfect for a multilingual audience.

You also find out about resolution, compression, and adding visual effects to images inside PowerPoint, as well as how to do the simple edits outside of PowerPoint in advanced image editors such as Adobe Photoshop.

I use the words *image, photo,* and *picture* interchangeably throughout this chapter.

Parade Your Photos

PowerPoint is often the glue that binds visual content from various sources, such as

✔ An image created or edited in an image-editing program such as Adobe Photoshop or Corel Painter

✔ A scanned picture or document

✔ A photograph from a digital camera

✔ A picture from a clip art collection

✔ A picture saved from the Internet

In every case, you should make sure that the content you're using is copyright-free.

Batch import pictures with Photo Album

PowerPoint lets you insert pictures in numerous ways, but the easiest option is to use the Photo Album feature. Photo Album allows you to batch import tons of photos inside a presentation.

To get started with batch importing pictures into your Photo Album presentation, you need some pictures.

I put some of my favorite pictures on the *Cutting Edge PowerPoint 2007 For Dummies* CD. You can use these pictures to create your Photo Album presentation.

Although they're called Photo Albums, you can use the Photo Album feature to insert any type of graphic for your presentation, whether or not they're photos. This means you can use Photo Album to insert line art, drawings, and illustrations, too, as long as these graphics are in file formats that PowerPoint can recognize.

Follow these steps to get started with Photo Album:

1. **On the Insert tab of the Ribbon, click the Photo Album button. Alternatively, click the small down arrow beneath the Photo Album button and then choose the New Photo Album option.**

    This brings up the Photo Album dialog box, shown in Figure 9-1.

2. **Choose options as required. These options are detailed next.**

Photo Album paraphernalia

When you create an empty photo album, PowerPoint shows you the Photo Album dialog box.

The Photo Album dialog box is crammed with mystifying options you might not always need. In the following two sections, I've organized the options into two groups: frequently used and seldom used.

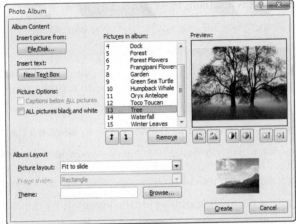

Figure 9-1:
The Photo
Album
interface.

Frequently used options

The following steps describe the Photo Album options that you'll want to use all the time:

1. **Click the File/Disk button to begin inserting the pictures you want to add to the album.**

   This step opens the Insert New Pictures dialog box.

2. **Navigate to the folder that contains all your pictures, select them, and click Insert.**

   The Insert New Pictures dialog box closes.

   If you want to insert pictures from another folder, repeat Steps 1 and 2.

3. **If you don't want to look into other niceties, accept the default options and click the Create button. Alternatively, follow the remaining steps to make your Photo Album more personal.**

4. **(Optional) Select a picture and click the Move Up and Move Down buttons to reorder the sequence in which your pictures are shown.**

   Each picture is previewed when selected. You can

   - *Remove pictures* you don't need or want by selecting the picture and clicking the Remove button.
   - *Rotate a selected picture* in 90-degree increments by using the relevant icons.
   - *Alter the contrast and brightness* values of a picture by clicking the contrast and brightness buttons.

5. **Select a picture layout from the Picture Layout drop-down list.**

   Within the Picture Layout drop-down list, you can select

   - *Layout options for one, two, and four pictures per slide*

     If you need to have a title on each slide, you can choose the layout options for one, two, or four pictures with a single slide title.

   - *The Fit to Slide option to insert full-screen images*

6. **Choose a frame style from the Frame Shape drop-down list.**

   The Frame Shape drop-down list lets you provide specific corner styles to each picture. Choices include rectangle, rounded rectangle, simple frame, compound frame, center shadow rectangle, and soft edge rectangle.

   If you select the Fit to Slide option for the layout, the Frame shape options are grayed out.

7. **Apply a theme.**

   Click the Browse button, and the Choose Theme dialog box opens, showing several themes. You can also navigate to any other folder and choose any other theme or template.

8. **Select a design theme or template and click Select.**

9. **Click the Create button and watch PowerPoint weave its magic.**

The *Cutting Edge PowerPoint 2007 For Dummies* CD contains some PowerPoint templates created especially for Photo Albums. Look in the folder for this chapter.

Seldom used options

Here are some options in the Photo Album dialog box that aren't used most of the time. All these options appear in the dialog box shown earlier in Figure 9-1:

- ✔ The Captions Below ALL Pictures option lets you add a separate caption under each picture.

- ✔ The ALL Pictures Black and White option converts all your pictures to grayscale color mode.

- ✔ You can include a separate text box on each slide by clicking the New Text Box button. Such text boxes can include some tidbits of interesting info or memorabilia and show up within the picture list — so every text box takes the place of one picture.

Most options can be added after your Photo Album is created — just click the down arrow below the Photo Album button on the Insert tab of the Ribbon and choose Edit Photo Album when your Photo Album presentation is open in PowerPoint.

More ideas for Photo Album

Here are a few tips for using Photo Album to its fullest:

✔ Don't just use Photo Album to create family or vacation keepsakes. The same options let you create quick product catalogs and after-conference shows.

✔ Refine the output by adding a continuous musical score to your entire presentation. This is covered in Chapter 11.

✔ If you start with high-resolution images, your Photo Album presentation saves to a huge size — which is impractical if you want to e-mail it to others. By default, PowerPoint 2007 uses some compression, but you might still want to tweak it yourself to get better results. To sidestep this problem, use the picture compression options I explain later in this chapter.

Inserting Pictures

Inserting single pictures in PowerPoint is easy, especially when you follow these steps:

1. **Navigate to the slide where you want the picture inserted.**

2. **Click the Insert tab on the Ribbon and then click the Picture button.**

   This brings up the Insert Picture dialog box.

3. **Navigate to wherever your pictures are saved, select one of the pictures, and click the Insert button.**

PowerPoint lets you insert pictures in several formats, including JPEG, GIF, BMP, WMF, EMF, and PNG.

Between pictures and drawings

Graphics are classified into two types:

✔ **Bitmap graphics** (or just *bitmaps*) are collections of bits (pixels) that form an image. Because bitmaps are composed of pixels, they can't be scaled to more than their original size without visual deterioration (see Figure 9-2).

All photographs are bitmaps. Typical bitmap file formats include JPEG, GIF, BMP, TIFF, PNG, and PCX.

✔ **Vector graphics** contain no pixels — they're created entirely through mathematical coordinates. These mathematical coordinates can easily be scaled to any size without any deterioration in quality (see Figure 9-2).

All line drawings and illustrations are vector graphics. Typical vector graphic file formats include WMF, EMF, EPS, AI, and CDR.

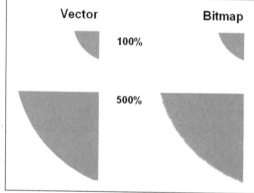

Figure 9-2: Bitmaps and vector graphics.

Design considerations

Inserting a visual on a PowerPoint slide is extremely easy — and because of the amount of clip art that Microsoft provides, everyone seems to be taking advantage of this feature! But don't insert visuals just because they're available, without any consideration of aesthetics or design.

Follow these guidelines to ensure that your visuals look professional:

✔ Don't use visuals at all if you don't have a graphic that adds relevance to the slide content.

✔ Try to use coordinated visuals; all visuals in a presentation should use the same design style.

✔ Experiment with PowerPoint's picture effects. Double-click a picture to bring up the Picture Tools Format tab of the Ribbon. You can find various buttons on this tab that allow you to increase and reduce brightness and contrast. In addition, you can change the picture to grayscale or a watermark, apply Picture Styles, crop it, and resize it.

✔ Sometimes, you might want to show a process, a detail, or an event through a picture. Including captions for such pictures is a good idea (especially if the presentation will be distributed to audiences who are going to view the presentation without a live presenter).

Using PowerPoint's clip art collection

PowerPoint includes an amazing collection of clip art in both bitmap and vector formats. Even more content is available online, and PowerPoint does a great job of accessing the online collections. Needless to say, you have to be connected to the Internet to access them.

Follow these steps to access the Clip Organizer:

1. **On the Insert tab of the Ribbon, click the Clip Art button.**

   This activates the Clip Art task pane, which appears in Figure 9-3.

   If this is the first time that you're using this option, you might be prompted to catalog all the media files on your computer. For now, just click the Later button to get rid of this dialog box.

Figure 9-3:
The Clip Art
task pane.

2. **Set up your search options as follows and then click Go:**

   - In the Search For text box, enter some keywords that describe the type of picture you're looking for. For example, I typed **prism**.

   - In the Search In drop-down list, choose whether you want to search on your system, online, or both (see Figure 9-3).

- In the Results Should Be drop-down list, choose whether you want to search for clip art or photographs.

PowerPoint also allows you to search for movies and sounds through the Clip Art task pane.

All your search results show up as thumbnail-size previews.

3. **To insert the actual clip art, drag a preview thumbnail onto a slide.**

To browse and search for more clip art, click the Clip Art on Office Online button in the Clip Art task pane to access additional content through the Office Online Web site. Obviously, your computer needs to be connected to the Internet to use this option.

All about Resolution and Compression

Because all your visual content can originate from so many disparate sources, you need to know about *resolution* and *compression:*

✔ Knowledge of **resolution** ensures that you bring only optimized visual content into PowerPoint.

✔ Knowledge of **compression** helps you optimize your existing visual content that's already part of a PowerPoint presentation.

The following sections give you the knowledge you need about resolution and compression.

All the dpi/ppi stuff

dpi stands for *dots per inch.* In the print world, dpi reigns supreme for obvious reasons. A higher density of dots per inch translates into sharper, higher-quality prints. Most of the print world uses 300 dpi (dots per inch).

ppi stands for *pixels per inch.* Although there's so much disagreement in this world about the relationship between dpi and ppi, you can assume that a pixel is almost a dot. (It won't hurt to simplify, as long as you don't argue about this with your prepress people!) Most monitors display 96 ppi.

Here's where the difference between print resolution and screen resolution matters: 96 ppi (the typical screen resolution) is about a third of 300 dpi (the most common print resolution). If you use the high-resolution print images in PowerPoint, your presentation file sizes will be bloated. And when PowerPoint brings up and animates these images while presenting, it has to work three times as much, thus putting a drain on your computer's system resources.

PowerPoint delivers only 96 ppi screen resolution images — in the PowerPoint world, only the picture *dimensions* in pixels matter.

Resolution in Photoshop

Here I show you how to set image resolution in Photoshop. Most other image editors work the same way.

Follow these steps to create a new image in Photoshop with a set resolution:

1. **Create a new image by choosing File⇨New.**

   The New dialog box appears, as shown in Figure 9-4.

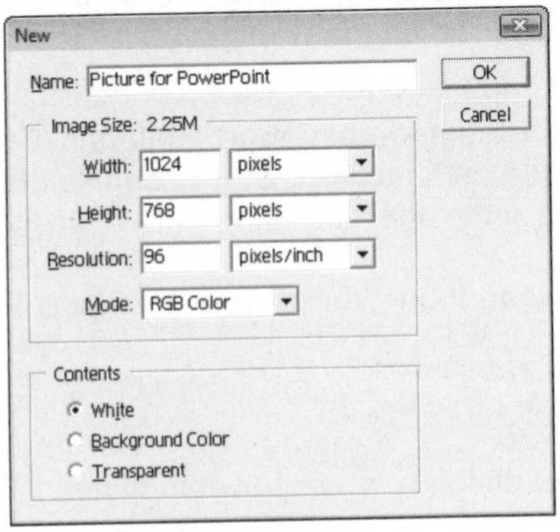

Figure 9-4:
Resolution
for a new
image in
Photoshop.

2. **In the Resolution text box, enter** 96 **and then make sure the drop-down list displays Pixels/Inch.**

3. **Enter the dimensions for your image in the Width and Height text boxes, and then make sure the drop-down lists display Pixels.**

   For example, if you're creating a background for PowerPoint that will take up the entire screen, enter **1024** in the Width text box and **768** in the Height text box. That's the most common screen size.

I don't discuss how you can change the resolution of existing pictures in Photoshop here because that's automatically taken care of when you use Photoshop's Save for Web option, which I discuss next. And if you already inserted some high-resolution images in your presentation, take a look at how to put some pressure on their bulk in the "Put the squeeze on file size" section, later in this chapter.

Other than the procedures that relate to image editing for PowerPoint presentations, I don't discuss Photoshop in too much detail in this book. You might want to look at another book about Photoshop for more detailed instructions — I recommend *Photoshop CS2 All-in-One Desk Reference For Dummies,* by Barbara Obermeier (Wiley).

Exporting formats from Photoshop

Exporting images from Photoshop to a PowerPoint-compatible format is very easy. Consider these three file formats:

- ✔ **JPEG** works best for photographs and any other design composition that includes lots of shaded areas. JPEG files can be quite small.

- ✔ **GIF** works best for images that include large areas of solid color. GIF is limited to 256 colors and supports limited transparency (that is, full or no transparency).

- ✔ **PNG** works best as a GIF alternative — it supports millions of colors as well as *variable transparency,* which means that it supports different levels of transparency in the same image.

Open your graphic in Photoshop and follow these steps to export to one of the three formats.

1. **Choose File⇨Save For Web.**

   This opens the Save For Web dialog box, as shown in Figure 9-5.

2. **In the top-right corner of the dialog box, select the file format and/or export setting.**

   Photoshop shows you a live export preview, allowing you to experiment with settings and file formats. In the bottom-left corner of the dialog box, Photoshop even shows you the file size of the exported graphic.

3. **Click OK to accept the options and export the graphic.**

Put the squeeze on file size

PowerPoint includes a compression feature that *optimizes* all the pictures in a presentation. Optimization essentially deletes the cropped-out areas of pictures and then compresses what's left.

Select JPG, GIF, or PNG

Figure 9-5:
Save For
Web
options in
Photoshop.

Follow these steps to put the squeeze on:

1. **Choose Office⇨Save to create an updated version of your presentation.**

2. **Choose Office⇨Prepare⇨Properties to summon the Document Properties panel.**

   This typically appears below the Ribbon, as shown in Figure 9-6.

3. **Click the Document Properties option in the top-left portion of the panel and choose Advanced Properties to summon the Properties dialog box.**

   The General tab provides information about the file.

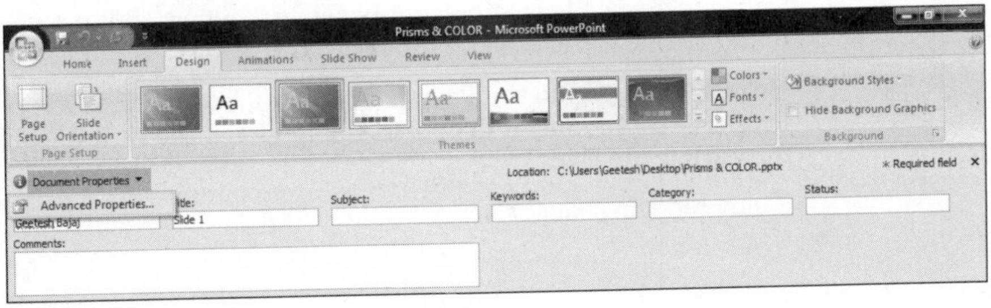

Figure 9-6:
The
Properties
panel.

4. **Make a note of the file size and then click OK to close the Properties dialog box. Close the Document Properties panel, as well.**

5. **Double-click any picture to activate the Picture Tools Format tab of the Ribbon.**

6. **Click the Compress Pictures button on this tab.**

   The Compress Pictures dialog box appears. In this dialog box, select the Apply to Selected Pictures Only check box if you don't want to apply the settings to all the pictures in the presentation. More often than not, you probably want to leave this option deselected.

7. **Click the Options button.**

   The Compression Settings dialog box, shown in Figure 9-7, appears.

Figure 9-7: Compressio n settings for pictures.

8. **Choose your compression options as follows:**

   • Leave the Automatically Perform Basic Compression on Save and the Delete Cropped Areas of Pictures options selected.

   • Select the E-Mail (96 ppi): Minimize Document Size for Sharing option.

9. **Click OK; then click OK again in the successive dialog boxes.**

   PowerPoint might take a while to get responsive again if it has to compress many pictures.

10. **Choose Office⇨Save As to save your presentation to a new file.**

   Saving to a new file is important because it allows you to revert back to the old file if you aren't happy with the results.

11. **Make a trip again to the Properties dialog box (Office⇨Prepare⇨ Properties⇨Advanced Properties) and check the new file size against the earlier file size.**

   If only reducing waist sizes were this easy!

Picture Edits

PowerPoint offers several options that allow you to create coordinated visuals right inside the program. I give you the lowdown in the following sections.

Recoloring pictures

The option to recolor clip art (which was a neat trick in earlier versions of PowerPoint) is no longer available in the 2007 version of PowerPoint. However, if you have an older version of PowerPoint installed, you can still use the recolor clip art trick and then get those recolored graphics into PowerPoint 2007. To find out how you can recolor clip art in older PowerPoint versions, check out the first edition of this book, *Cutting Edge PowerPoint For Dummies,* by yours truly, Geetesh Bajaj (Wiley).

But recoloring photos — that is, bitmaps — in this new version of PowerPoint is easy and intuitive. Not only can you add almost any color variation you want to achieve a duotone-like effect, you can also create quick sepia, grayscale, and washout color effects on any picture. In addition, you can set one color value as transparent, as I explain toward the end of this section.

Follow these steps to start recoloring your pictures:

1. **Double-click the picture you want to recolor so that the Picture Tools Format tab of the Ribbon is activated.**

2. **Click the Recolor button to see the Recolor gallery, shown in Figure 9-8.**

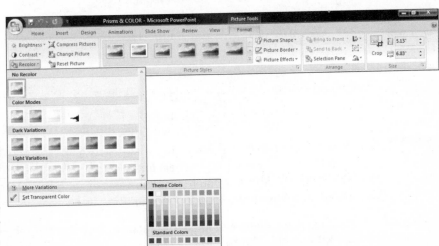

Figure 9-8:
The Recolor gallery lets you play with color variations.

3. **Choose the variation that you like from the gallery.**

   If you have the Live Preview feature enabled, you'll see exactly how the recolored version of your selected picture would look on the slide by hovering over the thumbnails within this gallery. (To find out how you can enable Live Previews, check out Chapter 2.)

   To see more options, click More Variations to bring up the Colors submenu that lets you choose from PowerPoint's standard color offerings. If you can't find the color you need, click the More Colors option to get to choose from any other color.

   Within the Recolor gallery (see Figure 9-8), you'll find a Set Transparent Color option that lets you set any one color value in the selected picture as transparent. As soon as you choose this option, the cursor turns into a picker that lets you click on the exact spot in the selected picture that contains the color you want to turn transparent.

   This works well for pictures that have large, solid blocks of one color such as a company logo. For anything else, including photographs, this can make your picture look ghastly! (But maybe ghastly is what you're looking for?)

TIP

Use a dedicated image editor like Adobe Photoshop to play with transparency in a photograph. I explain more of this in the "PowerPoint and Photoshop" section, later in this chapter.

Crop, adjust, and reset

Whenever you select a picture on a slide, the Picture Tools Format tab in the Ribbon shows up. You can see this tab in Figure 9-9.

Figure 9-9:
The Picture
Tools
Format tab
of the
Ribbon.

The options in this tab allow you to perform basic image-editing tasks with a click or two — follow these steps to perform these tasks:

1. **Double-click a picture to make the Picture Tools Format tab active in the Ribbon (see Figure 9-9).**

2. Perform any of these tasks:

- *Brightness and Contrast:* Click either the Brightness or the Contrast button to open the Brightness or Contrast gallery. These galleries include preset values that let you alter the brightness or contrast within the selected picture with one click.

  In either of the galleries, you can click Picture Correction Options to view the Format Picture dialog box shown in Figure 9-10. This dialog box provides sliders that control the brightness and contrast settings for the selected picture.

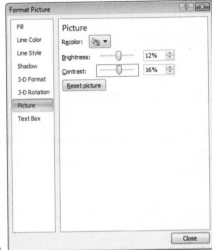

Figure 9-10:
Drag the
sliders to
control
brightness
and
contrast.

You can drag the dialog box away from the selected picture to see how the change in values affects the look of the picture.

- *Change Picture:* Clicking the Change Picture button lets you replace the selected picture with another picture. This can be very useful if you want to change a picture but leave its other properties untouched — for example, any animation settings that you have used for the picture.

- *Arrange:* The Arrange group includes options that let you align pictures, reorder and flip them, and more. These are the same concepts that I explain in Chapter 5 — head there for a refresher if you need it.

- *Crop:* Clip the Crop button to see eight black handles on the edges of the selected picture. Drag these handles into the picture to set your crop area. Then, to actually crop the picture, click anywhere outside the picture area.

- *Reset:* This option can be a lifesaver. Imagine you really did overdo it by going astray with all the cool picture-editing tasks in PowerPoint. Now you want your original picture back! Just click the Reset button to get it back.

WARNING!

If you used the Compress Pictures option, explained earlier in this chapter, the Reset button won't be able to magically get back your original picture.

3. **That's all you need to do — now sit back and enjoy the pictures!**

Picture styles

So what are picture styles? I could explain all those styles in intimate detail, but it'll be easier and clearer if you just take a look at the Picture Styles gallery and the slide shown in Figure 9-11.

Now that you have seen those styles, I show you how you can apply those styles to your pictures easily:

1. **Select a picture and activate the Picture Tools Format tab of the Ribbon.**

2. **Click the down arrow next to the Picture Styles gallery to see the drop-down gallery shown in Figure 9-11.**

Figure 9-11:
The Picture
Styles
gallery.

3. **Hover over any of the thumbnails in the gallery to see a live preview of how it affects the selected picture on the slide.**

4. **Click any of the thumbnails in the gallery to apply the selected picture style.**

If you don't want to use any of the picture styles that you see in the gallery, you can combine a shape, border, and effect to create your own style. These are controlled by the buttons of the same name within the Picture Styles group on the same Ribbon tab (refer to Figure 9-9):

✔ The **Picture Shape** option lets you use any of the shapes that are part of PowerPoint's Shape gallery as a container for the picture.

✔ The **Picture Border** option adds an outline to the selected picture. It works in the same ways as PowerPoint's lines, as explained in Chapter 6.

✔ The **Picture Effects** option provides the same effects that I discuss in Chapter 6.

PowerPoint and Photoshop

You can use Photoshop to create cool graphics for your PowerPoint presentations. That might be an understatement because the gamut of possibilities between the two programs might justify a whole book! On the other hand, this version of PowerPoint includes amazing graphic abilities that might translate into fewer trips to Photoshop.

This section provides guidelines and design ideas for creating graphics for your presentations by using Photoshop.

The companion site to this book has links to tutorials and samples for you:

www.cuttingedgeppt.com/photoshop

Most of the editing concepts I discuss here work with any image editor:

✔ **Shrink your pictures' file sizes.** Don't insert that bloated, 8-*megapixel* (just think of megapixels as lots and lots of pixels!) photo you shot with a digital camera into PowerPoint! Get rid of the bloat as follows:

   1. *Open the photo in Photoshop and resize it to a more realistic size.*

   2. *Use Photoshop's fantastic Save For Web feature, explained earlier in this chapter, to trim the file size.*

✔ **Focus on what's important.** If only a part of your image is required, feel free to use the Crop tool in Photoshop to cut out the remaining areas. If you want to change the background elements, or make them a little out of focus, you can do that in Photoshop, too.

PowerPoint includes a cropping tool as well. Although it doesn't provide the minute level of control that Photoshop affords, it might be all you need. Check out the "Crop, adjust, and reset" section, earlier in this chapter.

✔ **Play with Photoshop *layers*.** Think of them as sheets of transparent acetate placed over each other. When your composition is done, you can *flatten* the layers and export to a graphic file format that PowerPoint can import.

✔ **Experiment with transparency.** Photoshop, in particular, is a great tool for creating transparent graphics that include *alpha channels*. Such compositions, when saved in TIF or PNG formats, can be inserted on a PowerPoint slide with their transparency intact. Don't confuse this with PowerPoint's transparency tool, which I cover in the "Recoloring pictures" section, earlier in this chapter.

You can find more information on alpha channels at

```
www.cuttingedgeppt.com/alpha
```

✔ **Create cool PowerPoint slide backgrounds in Photoshop.** Among the easiest ways to convert a busy photograph to a useable background is to use the Photoshop Blur filter and make everything appear soft and unfocused. Find more information at

```
www.cuttingedgeppt.com/blur
```

Chapter 10

Pulling in SmartArt, Charts, Equations, and Maps

*I*nfo-graphics — the word says it all. *Info-graphics* are more than mere graphics — these intelligent visuals help users comprehend difficult principles like figures, statistics, or even directions easily. Examples include

✔ A map that gives directions to your new office

✔ An organizational chart that explains hierarchies and power levels

✔ A chart that shows your popularity ratings shooting through the roof, or your competitor's ratings plunging

This chapter also explores vistas outside PowerPoint's offerings in programs as diverse as SmartDraw, Visio, and MapPoint.

Delectable Diagrams

Diagrams are drawings that are based entirely on logic — they help convey relationships, hierarchies, and flows through a combination of simple shapes and text. Organization charts and cycle relationship drawings are all examples of diagrams.

PowerPoint 2007 now includes the SmartArt component that includes all sorts of diagram types. There are ten times more diagrams in the SmartArt component than what you can find in the Diagram gallery in PowerPoint 2002 and 2003.

Figure 10-1 shows some SmartArt variants that you can create in PowerPoint 2007.

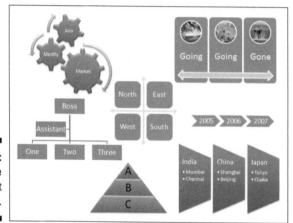

Figure 10-1:
Some
SmartArt
variants.

If you want to create a diagram style that isn't included in the SmartArt gallery, consider creating a diagram by using shapes. I cover shapes in Chapter 5.

Inserting SmartArt

You can insert a SmartArt graphic into a PowerPoint slide in three ways:

- ✔ Insert a new slide with a slide layout that includes a content placeholder. Then, within the content placeholder, click the Insert SmartArt Graphic icon to launch the Choose a SmartArt Graphic dialog box shown in Figure 10-2.

- ✔ Click the Insert tab on the Ribbon and then click the SmartArt button to summon the same dialog box.

- ✔ Select any text placeholder or text box on a slide, right-click, and choose Convert to SmartArt — a submenu shows you previews of some SmartArt graphic variants, as shown in Figure 10-3.

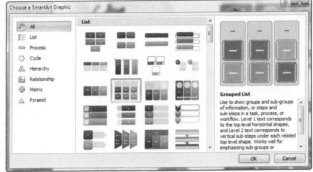

Figure 10-2:
Select the
SmartArt
graphic
variant you
want to
insert.

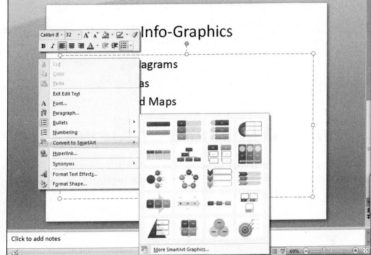

Figure 10-3:
Quickly
convert text
to SmartArt.

If you can't decide which SmartArt variant you want to use or if you don't find something you want, just choose the variant that's closest in style to what you require. Later in this chapter, I show you how you can format your SmartArt graphics and how you can change from one SmartArt variant to another.

SmartArt Ribbon tabs

Two new tabs are activated on the Ribbon whenever you have a SmartArt graphic selected. These tabs are collectively called the SmartArt Tools tabs:

✔ **The SmartArt Tools Design tab,** shown on the top in Figure 10-4, lets you add and reorganize shapes within a SmartArt graphic; change layouts, colors, and styles; and reset a formatted SmartArt graphic to its default state.

✔ **The SmartArt Tools Format tab,** shown on the bottom of Figure 10-4, lets you change, enlarge, or reduce shapes; apply Shape Styles to the shapes; format text with WordArt Styles; and also arrange and resize graphics.

Figure 10-4:
The
SmartArt
Tools Design
tab (top) and
the SmartArt
Tools Format
tab (bottom).

Working with SmartArt shapes

After you place a SmartArt graphic on your slide, you can do a lot more to make it look interesting and relevant. These techniques work with individual shapes within a SmartArt graphic:

✔ To type text in any of the shapes, just select the individual shape and start typing. To edit existing text on a shape, select the text and start typing.

✔ To add an extra shape to the SmartArt — such as adding another circle to a cycle diagram — click the Add Shape button on the SmartArt Tools Design tab of the Ribbon. To add a shape with more control, such as above or after a selected shape, click the down arrow below the Add Shape button to see the menu shown in Figure 10-5, and then make a choice.

✔ Text within a shape can use WordArt Styles that you can find on the SmartArt Tools Format tab of the Ribbon.

✔ To delete a shape you don't need, select the shape within the SmartArt graphic and press Delete.

✔ To add effects to individual shapes, use the Shape Styles options in the SmartArt Tools Format tab — these are preset styles. You can also format the fills, lines, and effects individually — this is explained in more detail in Chapter 6.

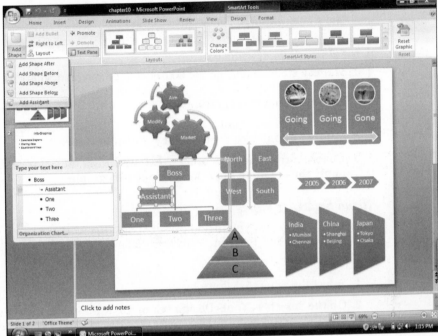

Figure 10-5:
Add more
shapes.

The Text Pane

The Text Pane is visible whenever you select any SmartArt graphic (refer to Figure 10-5). If the Text Pane isn't visible, click the Text Pane button on the SmartArt Tools Design tab of the Ribbon. Remember, this is a toggle option.

When the Text Pane is visible, each line of bulleted text in the Text Pane corresponds to the text on an individual shape within your SmartArt. Add or edit text within the Text Pane, and the changes automatically appear in the SmartArt graphic. The Text Pane can be very useful when you have a complicated SmartArt graphic with many elements and you're having difficulty selecting individual shapes to add or edit text.

Playing with colors and styles

You can metamorphose your SmartArt graphic so that it can spawn thousands of incarnations. Each incarnation can be different, yet perfectly coordinated with your slide design. This is possible because PowerPoint's themes contain color and style variations.

These changes apply to the entire SmartArt graphic, even if you've selected just one shape within the SmartArt graphic.

Changing colors of SmartArt

Follow these steps to change the colors of your selected SmartArt graphic:

1. **Select the SmartArt graphic.**

2. **On the SmartArt Tools Design tab of the Ribbon, click the Change Colors button to view the gallery shown in Figure 10-6.**

3. **Choose any of the thumbnail previews within the color categories to apply the colors to the selected SmartArt graphic.**

Using SmartArt Styles

SmartArt Styles allow you to add preset styles that work well with your overall slide look. Follow these steps to apply a SmartArt Style to your selected SmartArt graphic:

1. **Select the SmartArt graphic.**

2. **On the SmartArt Tools Design tab of the Ribbon, click the downward-pointing arrow within the SmartArt Styles group to view the gallery that you can see in Figure 10-7.**

3. **Choose from any of the thumbnail previews within the categories.** There are essentially two categories:

   • Best Match for Document displays preset styles that work best within the theme on which the presentation is based.

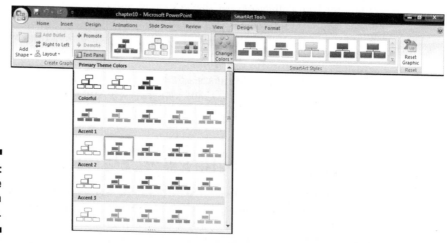

Figure 10-6: Change colors like a chameleon.

You really don't need to know anything about themes to use this feature, but just in case you want to educate yourself, look at Chapter 4.

• *3-D* shows an assortment of 3-D SmartArt Styles to choose from.

4. **Click the thumbnail preview of the style you want to apply to the selected SmartArt graphic.**

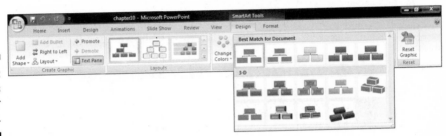

Figure 10-7:
Smart styles for SmartArt.

Change SmartArt variant

Imagine that you have added or edited text and shapes, changed colors, applied styles, and anything else you want to do with a SmartArt graphic. It's just that your boss now likes all the formatting, but he or she wants you to use another SmartArt variant!

Well, you haven't landed yourself in hot water yet because you can change your SmartArt graphic variant with one click while leaving all your other formatting unchanged. Don't do this in front of your boss, though!

1. **Select the SmartArt graphic that you want to change.**

2. **Select the SmartArt Tools Design tab on the Ribbon and click the down-pointing arrow within the Layouts group to see the Layout gallery shown in Figure 10-8.**

3. **Choose from any of the SmartArt variants visible in this gallery.**

   PowerPoint only displays SmartArt variants that are similar to the selected SmartArt graphic.

   If you want to choose some other variant that isn't available in the Layout gallery, click the More Layouts option to summon the Choose a SmartArt Graphic dialog box (refer to Figure 10-2).

   That's all you need to do!

Figure 10-8:
The Layout
gallery
allows you
to change
the SmartArt
variant.

Organization charts

Organization charts, lovingly called *org charts,* are a great way to portray parent-child relationships of all sorts. Examples of org charts include company hierarchies, family trees, and product lines.

Although organization charts are just another SmartArt variant, I still cover them in a separate section because they're such an important element in presentation slides.

To insert an organization chart on your slide, follow the same steps that you use to insert a SmartArt graphic, as I explain earlier in this chapter in the "Inserting SmartArt" section. Just select any of the SmartArt variants in the Hierarchy category (see Figure 10-9).

After you do that, PowerPoint places a sample org chart ready for you to edit and enhance, as shown in Figure 10-10. Thereafter, you can format organization charts in the same way as any other SmartArt graphic.

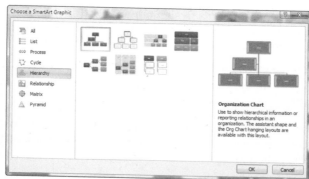

Figure 10-9:
Organization
charts are
in the
Hierarchy
category.

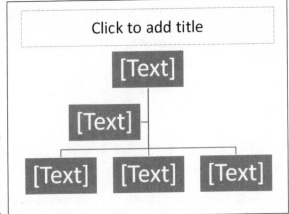

Figure 10-10:
A sample organization chart.

Charting Vistas

The easiest way to get your audience squint-eyed is to put in reams of figures in tables that use 6-point text. Nowadays, audiences are less forgiving and polite — they'll soon fire up their PDAs to check their e-mail or the latest stock quotes instead of paying attention to your presentation. Ouch!

If you show the same figures by using charts and graphs to get your point across, you'll find that the audience is more receptive. Charts make it easy to visualize trends and patterns — and thus prevent people from getting squint-eyed or distracted.

Unlike SmartArt graphics that are based on logical relationships, charts are entirely based on figures. SmartArt graphics are covered earlier in this chapter. The terms *chart* and *graph* are used interchangeably in PowerPoint terminology. More chart terminology can be found in the following section.

Microsoft Graph, the charting application that used to create charts in Excel and PowerPoint since Office 97, takes its leave in Office 2007. Now, Microsoft Excel takes care of most charting options — even in PowerPoint, you'll actually use Excel's new charting components. For the same reason, if you don't have Excel 2007 installed along with PowerPoint 2007, you'll still be using the archaic Microsoft Graph program — this would mean losing out on all the new, cool-looking charts!

Chart elements

Before you get deeper into charts, you must be aware of some of the technical gobbledygook:

✔ **Datasheet mode:** You get into a special datasheet mode whenever you

- Right-click an existing chart on a slide and choose the Edit Data option.

- Insert a chart for the first time.

Essentially, getting into datasheet mode is the same as getting into Microsoft Excel. Your screen will show PowerPoint and Excel tiled up against each other, as shown in Figure 10-11. Close Excel after you make required changes in the datasheet to get back to PowerPoint in maximized mode.

If you need to import data from an existing Excel spreadsheet, just create the chart within Excel and then copy and paste it into a PowerPoint slide. Or paste just the data into the Excel interface when you insert a new chart in PowerPoint.

✔ **Axes:** Most charts have two axes:

- The bottom, horizontal axis (also called the *x-axis* or the *category axis*)

- The left, vertical axis (also called the *y-axis* or the *value axis*)

✔ **Plot area:** The area within the axes is called the *plot area.*

The legend and titles are normally placed outside the plot area.

✔ **Titles:** These include the

- Chart titles (placed by default above the chart)

- Axis titles (placed by default beside the axes)

✔ **Series:** Every column of data that's shown as a component of the chart is a series. However, you can plot rows instead of columns for the series.

✔ **Values:** Values are the individual figures that constitute part of each series.

✔ **Legend:** The legend is a box placed outside the plot area that identifies the series. Legends are automatically created — you can opt to leave them out altogether if needed.

Inserting a chart

Follow these instructions to add a chart within PowerPoint:

1. Click the Insert tab of the Ribbon and then click the Chart option.

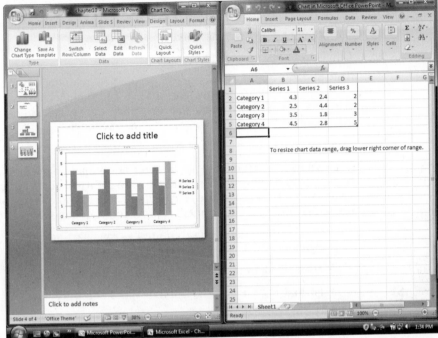

Figure 10-11: PowerPoint and Excel side by side.

You can also insert a slide with a layout that contains a content place-holder and then click the Insert Chart icon.

Either of these options summons the Insert Chart dialog box shown in Figure 10-12.

2. **Select the chart category you want in the left side of the dialog box.**

3. **Select the chart type within the selected category.**

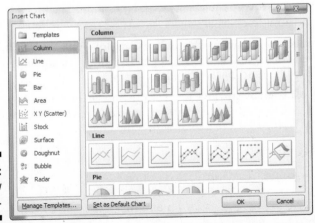

Figure 10-12: Insert a new chart.

Each category has several chart variants — select the one you want. If you can't find a type that you want, choose the one that's closest to your requirement; you can make small changes later.

4. Click OK to insert a chart.

This places a dummy chart, and the datasheet with dummy data opens in Microsoft Excel (refer to Figure 10-11). The sample chart is almost as haggard as a newborn chick, but formatting the design and data of the chart can result in a much better-looking specimen.

5. Edit the chart.

You're now in chart-editing mode; three additional Chart Tools tabs appear on the Ribbon. These tabs provide plenty of chart formatting options that I discuss in the next section. Some simple tasks that you could perform to make your chart more relevant include

- Editing the datasheet as required — the chart updates dynamically

- Formatting the fills and effects for the individual series

- Formatting the font sizes of the values and titles

- Opting to include the legend

6. After you finish editing your chart, just click anywhere outside the chart area to go back to the normal PowerPoint interface without the Chart Tools tabs.

Chart Tools tabs

Whenever you select a chart, PowerPoint displays a set of three extra tabs on the Ribbon — collectively, these are called the Chart Tools tabs:

- **Chart Tools Design tab,** as shown at the top of Figure 10-13, lets you change the chart type, save chart templates, edit data, change the chart layout, and apply a chart style.

- **Chart Tools Layout tab,** as shown in the middle of Figure 10-13, lets you add and edit chart and axis titles, legend, gridlines, trendlines, error bars, and other chart paraphernalia.

- **Chart Tools Format tab,** as shown at the bottom of Figure 10-13, lets you apply graphic styles to your chart, arrange and resize chart elements, and apply WordArt styles to text within the chart.

Change the chart types

PowerPoint has many chart types to play with. Most of the time, the chart type you use is directly related to the type of data you need to portray. Nevertheless, you should experiment with various chart options before you decide what suits your needs best.

Follow these steps to change or preview the chart types.

1. **Select an existing chart and then select the Chart Tools Design tab (refer to Figure 10-13).**

2. **Click the Change Chart Type option to summon the Change Chart Type dialog box, as shown in Figure 10-14.**

   If this dialog box looks familiar, that's because it's almost identical to the Insert Chart dialog box (refer to Figure 10-12).

3. **Preview all the chart types by choosing their categories in the left pane.**

   The thumbnail previews on the right automatically update to show you the options possible in that type.

4. **Click OK to change the chart type.**

Figure 10-13: Chart Tools Design tab (top), Chart Tools Layout tab (middle), and Chart Tools Format tab (bottom).

All the chart types

Although PowerPoint provides many chart types, some charts are used more than others — I've placed them in the "Simple charts" section. The other chart types are mainly used by statisticians and other geeky types — I've placed them in the "Advanced charts" section.

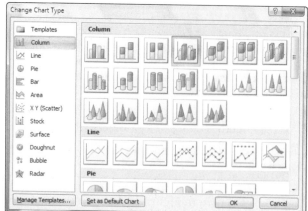

Figure 10-14:
Change
your chart
type.

Simple charts

Here are the chart types you could use in your everyday work life. These are the easy and uncomplicated ones:

 ✔ **Column** charts are used more than any other type because they make it so easy to discern a change in pattern. The columns rise (or dip) from the X-axis. The Y-axis represents the values.

 ✔ **Line** graphs use lines to connect graph points *(vertexes)*. They work best when you want to show trends over time. The 3-D version of this type uses ribbons rather than lines.

 ✔ **Pie** charts work best with percentage values — most of the time, they're used when you have just one series of values that add up to 100%. You can also create multiple pie charts on the same slide to show relationships between two percentage-wise series. Examples include two pie charts for income and expenditure.

 ✔ **Bar** charts work on the same concept as the column charts, but with the axes reversed. You have the values on the X-axis and the categories on the Y-axis.

 ✔ **Area** charts are like stacked line graphs with the gaps filled in with individual colors or patterns. You can use area charts when you don't have too many values — normally four to five values work best.

 ✔ **X Y (Scatter)** charts are used when both the axes have numbers as the underlying data. For this reason, they're also called *XY charts.*

Advanced charts

These are the type of charts you encounter only once or twice a year (unless you have an affinity for math and statistics):

✔ **Stock** charts are meant to portray stock price levels, including the high, low, and closing prices.

✔ **Surface** charts work best to represent the synergistic effects of two values working together. The chart connects values in the data series to create a ribbon-like line graph.

✔ **Doughnut** charts are like pie charts, but unlike pie charts, you can use the same doughnut chart to represent more than one series by using concentric doughnuts. Predictably, doughnut charts work best if you have fewer series — no more than five.

✔ **Bubble** charts might look like the bubbles you blew out of liquid soap, but that's where the similarity ends. They compare sets of three values — it's almost like a Scatter (XY) chart on steroids:

  • Two of the series are represented on the X- and Y-axes.

  • The third series is represented by the size of the bubble.

✔ **Radar** charts work best when you need to compare the total values of data series. If you use a radar chart, you're on your way to becoming a chart geek — most users stay away from this complicated chart type!

Data, thy name is dynamic

Although the purpose of any chart is to portray data in an easy-to-comprehend visual, data still remains more important than the chart. Follow these guidelines to make the most of the underlying data:

✔ **Enter all your data in the Excel datasheet.**

If you can't see the datasheet, select the chart so that the Chart Tools tabs on the Ribbon are visible. Then activate the Chart Tools Design tab and click the Edit Data button. You can also just right-click the chart and choose Edit Data.

✔ **The datasheet works exactly like any other data in an Excel spreadsheet.**

When you first insert a new chart, Excel already fills in some sample data for you — change the data as required, and the chart updates dynamically.

✔ **The rows and the columns in the datasheet typically contain the values of the corresponding X- and Y-axis series.**

Import your data

If I already have all the data I need to use for a chart available in another document, I don't want to type it again! Call me lazy or efficient, whichever you choose.

Follow these steps to import your existing data into the datasheet:

1. **Select the chart, activate the Chart Tools Design tab, and then click the Edit Data button.**

   This step opens the data inside Excel.

2. **Inside Excel, select the Data tab on the Ribbon and click the options in the Get External Data group (see Figure 10-15) that allow you to import data from several data, Web, and spreadsheet formats.**

   You can import data from Microsoft Access databases, Web pages, text files, SQL Server files, and XML files.

Each data import option works differently — you might want to look at another book about Excel for more detailed instructions — I recommend *Excel 2007 For Dummies,* by Greg Harvey (Wiley).

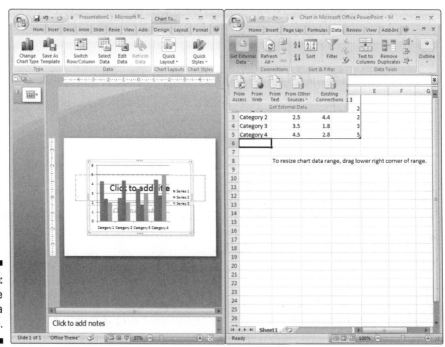

Figure 10-15:
Choose the exact data source.

Extend your chart horizons with Excel

If you already work with Excel, you probably have charts already created on your spreadsheets. Understandably, you don't want to import the same data inside PowerPoint and duplicate the chart creation. All you want to do is reuse the whole chart — lock, stock, and barrel! That makes more sense because PowerPoint uses Microsoft Excel behind the scenes to create its own charts.

Follow these steps to paste your Excel charts inside PowerPoint:

1. **Select the chart inside Excel and click the Copy icon on the Home tab of the Ribbon (or press Ctrl+C).**

2. **Back in PowerPoint, insert a new slide or go to an existing slide where you want to paste the Excel chart.**

3. **Click the Paste icon on the Home tab of the Ribbon to place the chart on the active slide (or press Ctrl+V).**

Charts pasted from Excel 2007 into PowerPoint 2007 work as native PowerPoint charts — you can format them as required and even animate them in PowerPoint. Chapter 12 covers animation.

Make your charts look awesome

PowerPoint 2007 includes a great new graphic engine that can work its magic with charts. The following steps show you how to take a default column chart in PowerPoint and tweak it:

1. **Select your chart and then click the Chart Tools Format tab on the Ribbon.**

2. **Now select any of the individual series within the chart.**

   If you have trouble selecting an individual chart series, just select the series from the Current Selection area on the extreme left of the Chart Tools Format tab in the Ribbon (refer to Figure 10-13).

3. **On the same tab, click the down arrow within the Shape Styles gallery to see more options to change the look of your selected series, as shown in Figure 10-16.**

   You can also individually change the fill, outline, and effects of the selected series by using the options of the same names next to the Shape Styles gallery.

4. **Repeat Steps 2 and 3 as required for all the series in your chart.**

Figure 10-16:
The Shape
Styles
gallery can
provide
quick
makeovers.

5. **(Optional) Select the value labels in your chart and right-click to summon the convenient Mini Toolbar. Format the font face as required.**

   You can do much more to your charts by using the options in the various Chart Tools tabs. Remember, the more you play with these options and experiment, the better and more original your charts will look.

Chart layouts and styles

In the previous section, I show you how you can individually format each series in a chart and make them look awesome. A quicker way to make them look great is to use the new Chart Layouts and Styles galleries in PowerPoint 2007. True, you are using presets that don't allow you to tweak individual elements — but these can be so helpful when you want a quick makeover. And because these layouts and styles are theme-based, your charts will look coordinated with the overall look of your slides.

1. **Select the chart you want to format.**

   The three Chart Tools tabs become visible on the Ribbon (refer to Figure 10-13).

2. **Select the Chart Tools Design tab and change either the layout or style or both:**

   • *Layout:* Click the down arrow in the Chart Layout group to view a drop-down gallery. Click any of the thumbnail previews to apply a new layout to the selected chart.

   • *Styles:* Click the down arrow in the Chart Styles group to view a drop-down gallery. Click any of the thumbnail previews to apply a new chart style to the selected chart.

Neither the Chart Layouts nor Chart Styles drop-down galleries show you a live preview of the selected chart when you hover over the thumbnail previews.

Slide Over to Equations

All versions of PowerPoint include _Equation Editor,_ a small application that lets you insert equations in PowerPoint slides. This can be very helpful if you create lots of slides involving math, chemistry, or statistics.

Follow these steps to insert an equation inside PowerPoint:

1. **Navigate to the slide where you want to insert an equation, click the Insert tab on the Ribbon, and then click the Object button.**

   You see the Insert Object dialog box, shown in Figure 10-17.

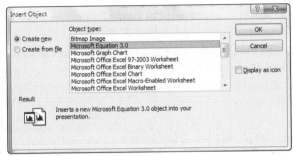

Figure 10-17: Insert objects such as equations.

2. **Scroll down the choices in the Object Type box and select Microsoft Equation 3.0 (or another version) and then click OK to launch the Equation Editor.**

3. **Create your equations inside Equation Editor.**

   More details about creating equations are available on this book's companion site:

   `www.cuttingedgeppt.com/eqeditor`

4. **When the equation has been created, choose File⇨Exit and Return to get back to the PowerPoint slide.**

   PowerPoint inserts the equation on the slide. To edit the equation, double-click the equation on the slide to launch Equation Editor.

If you use Equation Editor often, you might want to take a look at its big brother, MathType, which can do a lot more:

`www.cuttingedgeppt.com/mathtype`

If you just want to use some equation symbols rather than an entire equation, those are available within the new Equations category of the Shapes gallery (see Chapter 5).

Go Cartographic with MapPoint

Microsoft MapPoint is a mapping application that lets you route your journeys and much more. Assuming that you have PowerPoint and MapPoint installed on the same system, follow these steps to insert a map on a slide:

1. **Create a new slide or use an existing one to hold the map.**

2. **Click the Insert tab on the Ribbon and then click the Object button to summon the Insert Object dialog box (refer to Figure 10-17).**

3. **Scroll down the choices within the Object Type list, select Microsoft MapPoint North American Map (or another version of MapPoint), and then click OK to launch MapPoint.**

   MapPoint places a basic map on the PowerPoint slide — which probably isn't what you want.

4. **Double-click the map and watch the magic as it metamorphoses into an active MapPoint instance!**

   Figure 10-18 shows how all the menus and toolbars convert to the MapPoint interface.

5. **Zoom, pan, or search the map by using the toolbar controls as required until the display on the slide looks exactly how you want it.**

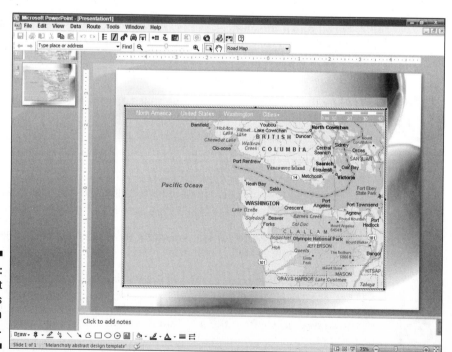

Figure 10-18:
PowerPoint
does maps
with
MapPoint.

6. **Click anywhere outside the map to return to PowerPoint.**

If you want to find out more about MapPoint, check out *MapPoint For Dummies,* by B. J. Holtgrewe and Jill T. Freeze (Wiley).

Beyond PowerPoint

Although PowerPoint provides umpteen ways of inserting info-graphics on a slide, I still like to think of PowerPoint as a glue to hold disparate elements together. That's easy to visualize because PowerPoint can accept visual content from so many other applications. This section shows you how to incorporate content from Microsoft Visio and other applications.

Working with Visio

Microsoft Visio is a diagramming application that's useful for everything from creating small home plans to complex networking prototypes.

You need to use Visio in either of these cases:

- ✔ PowerPoint's diagramming tools aren't sufficient for your needs.
- ✔ You want to reuse someone's Visio diagrams in a PowerPoint presentation.

Visio works in much the same way as PowerPoint because Microsoft has created very similar interfaces for the Office suite of applications.

PowerPoint doesn't support Visio's native drawing format. Either you need to link to an existing or newly created Visio drawing as an object, or you need to export the drawing from Visio to a different graphic format and then import it into PowerPoint. Between the two methods, choose the latter if you want to transport your presentation to a system without Visio installed.

The link option

Follow these steps to link a Visio drawing to a PowerPoint slide:

1. **In PowerPoint, click the Insert tab on the Ribbon and then click the Object button.**

2. **In the opened dialog box, select the Create New radio button.**

3. **Select Microsoft Visio Drawing (or similar, depending on which version of Visio you have installed) from the Object Type list and then click OK.**

   Visio opens and displays the Choose Drawing Type dialog box.

4. **Make your selection from the diagram categories and click OK.**

   Visio prompts you with a dialog box that asks whether you want the Visio shapes to use the PowerPoint color scheme of the host presentation.

   Accepting this option provides you with a coordinated look, so you might want to click Yes in this dialog box.

5. **Create your diagram inside Visio.**

6. **Click anywhere outside the Visio area to get back to your PowerPoint slide.**

The insert option

This method is more straightforward. Although you can't edit the original drawing this way, the resultant presentation is more compact and portable:

1. **Open or create a Visio diagram from within the Visio application.**

2. **Choose File⇨Save As.**

   The Save As dialog box that appears lets you save the diagram in 28 different graphic formats, both vector and raster.

3. **Choose WMF or EMF from the Save as Type drop-down list.**

   WMF and EMF are the best formats to transport line drawings between Microsoft applications.

4. **In PowerPoint, click the Insert tab on the Ribbon and then click the Picture button.**

   The Insert Picture dialog box appears.

5. **Navigate to and choose the WMF/EMF file and then click Insert.**

Info-graphics programs

Although PowerPoint has an impressive repertoire of drawing and diagramming capabilities, you should explore some third-party add-ins and companion programs that allow more possibilities:

- **SmartDraw** is a drawing application that's especially geared toward Microsoft Office users. It includes over 50,000 symbols and templates that you can use within a drag-and-draw interface that require no artistic skill.

- **Crystal Xcelsius** and **rChart** allow you to create Flash-based animated vector charts. You can insert these charts within PowerPoint slides with one click.

You can find out more about these tools at

www.cuttingedgeppt.com/infographics

Part III
Adding Motion, Sound, and Effects

The 5th Wave   By Rich Tennant

"Okay-looks like the 'Dissolve' transition in my presentation needs adjusting."

In this part . . .

This part makes PowerPoint come alive. It's about the audio-video stuff, and the movement. Can you hear the humming and the footsteps?

Chapter 11

Listening and Watching: The Sound and Movie Stuff

- -

In This Chapter

▶ Creating multimedia formats

▶ Sounding off

▶ Spanning your slides with music

▶ Using voice-overs in PowerPoint

▶ Putting movies in slides

▶ Creating Media playlists in PowerPoint

▶ Getting to know codecs, codecs, codecs

▶ Making movies from your PowerPoint presentation

- -

*I*nserting sound and movie clips into PowerPoint slides is usually easy. PowerPoint allows ample control over how they play in Slide Show mode.

Sound and movies come from disparate sources — from camcorders and music CDs to stock footage libraries and in-house rendered content, not to mention downloads from the Internet. An amazing number of sound and movie formats actually are entwined with an even more amazing number of *codecs.* And if you don't know what this format and codec thing means, read on and get PowerPoint to sing and dance! If you just need some quick codec cures, skip to the "Getting Friendly with Codecs" section.

In addition to reviewing the basics of adding multimedia to your PowerPoint presentations, I discuss the nuances of multimedia — such as adding fades to your sounds and using PowerPoint's amazing narration features. Finally, if you want to show DVD movie clips inside PowerPoint or maybe export an entire presentation to a movie, you're reading the right chapter!

All Those Multimedia Formats

Unless you've been living under a rock for the last decade, you have most likely been flabbergasted by the names of all those multimedia formats, such as MP3 and WMA. In this section, I tell you about all those wonderful multimedia formats that PowerPoint loves or hates.

The sound brigade

PowerPoint can accept and play almost all the standard audio formats:

- **WAV:** This is the most common sound file format on Microsoft Windows. PowerPoint works well with this format.

- **MP3:** MP3s can be inserted and played inside PowerPoint but are a no-no for slide transition sounds.

- **WMA, ASF:** The same concepts that apply to MP3s apply to WMA.

  Stay away from WMA and ASF if you must show your presentation using any of the Mac versions of PowerPoint.

- **MID or MIDI:** These are actual music notations that your computer's sound card interprets and plays in real time. To enjoy this type of sound, you should have a high-fidelity sound card that retails for over a hundred dollars. Anything less than that can still do a good job, unless you start comparing the sound outputs!

- **AIFF, AU:** These are the other sound formats that PowerPoint accepts; however, it's best you leave them alone — and they'll probably leave you alone, too!

Wise up to movie formats

PowerPoint can cope with a plethora of movie formats:

- **AVI:** AVI has been around the longest, and PowerPoint is usually happy with this format unless it has been rendered using a nonstandard codec. (You discover more about codecs later in this chapter.)

- **MPG, MPEG:** Conventional MPEG movies, also called MPEG 1 movies, play well in PowerPoint. They're the best option to create a presentation that you want to be able to play on both the Windows and Mac versions of PowerPoint.

  MPEG 2 movies are DVD-quality but aren't too PowerPoint-friendly — they're extremely reliant on both hardware and software and usually don't play in PowerPoint, even if they do play well in Windows Media Player.

- ✔ **WMV, ASF:** WMV (Windows Media Video) works great inside PowerPoint, but stay away from it if your presentations must be Mac friendly. ASF is the older name for Windows Media files.

  For all practical purposes, WMV and ASF are identical. When Microsoft introduced the Windows Media format, both audio and movie files used the .asf extension. Later, Microsoft started using the .wmv and .wma extensions for video (movies) and audio, respectively.

- ✔ **Flash:** Flash isn't actually a movie format. It's a vector format that supports animation. PowerPoint (and Windows itself) doesn't consider Flash a native movie format. However, Flash movies can be played within PowerPoint. You can find more information about inserting Flash within PowerPoint in the Bonus Chapter on the CD.

- ✔ **VCD:** VCD, or *Video CD,* files usually have the .dat extension. For all practical purposes, they're MPEG 1 videos, and several tools, including freeware applications, can convert VCD DAT movies to MPEG files without any problem. An online search for "VCD to MPEG converter" should result in several hits.

- ✔ **DVD:** Some third-party tools let you play DVD movies right inside PowerPoint — I cover those tools toward the end of this chapter.

Inserting Sounds

Even before you insert a sound on a slide, you must make two decisions:

- ✔ **Do you want the sound to play automatically as soon as the slide is shown?**

  Most of the time you want to do this.

- ✔ **Do you want the sound to play across multiple slides?**

  This is the way to go if you want to insert a background music track. Check out the upcoming section, "Sound across slides," for the lowdown.

After you answer these questions, follow these steps to insert the sounds:

1. **Navigate to the slide where you want the sound to be inserted.**

2. **On the Insert tab of the Ribbon, choose Sound⇨Sound from File.**

   This summons the Insert Sound dialog box, shown in Figure 11-1.

3. **Choose a sound in any of the formats that PowerPoint accepts and click OK.**

   PowerPoint asks you whether you want the sound to play automatically in the slide show or when clicked, as shown in Figure 11-2.

Figure 11-1:
Get some
sound into
PowerPoint.

Figure 11-2:
Do you want
PowerPoint
to play
the sound
automat-
ically?

**4. Click the Automatically button if you want the sound to play automati-
cally; otherwise, click the When Clicked button to play the sound
when you choose to.**

PowerPoint places a sound icon in the middle of the slide. If you chose
to play the sound automatically in the previous step, you might want to
make this icon invisible. To do that, just drag it off the slide area; it will
still play just fine within the presentation.

Sound across slides

Mainstream corporate presentations don't normally include a musical score
that spans the entire slide presentation. However, a musical background
score can be a pleasing accompaniment to a lunch-hour or tea-break presentation, especially at a convention. For example, a product photo-album presentation can benefit from an upbeat music score. Also, when the music
stops, the audience members know it's time to get back to their seats.

Turning off the music in any presentation can be as easy as setting the volume bar to mute in Windows, so there's no harm in including music in any presentation (as long as the presentation doesn't include narration!).

Assemble your sound files in the same folder as the presentation, even before you insert the music into a saved presentation. This ensures that PowerPoint doesn't lose its links if you move the presentation to another system — you can just copy the entire folder to another machine.

The following instructions show you how to insert a musical score that spans multiple slides in PowerPoint:

1. **Open a new or existing presentation in PowerPoint and navigate to the first slide.**

2. **On the Insert tab of the Ribbon, choose Sound⇨Sound from File.**

   The Insert Sound dialog box opens (refer to Figure 11-1).

3. **Navigate to and select the sound file that you want to use and then click OK.**

   PowerPoint asks how you want the sound to play. Click the Automatically button (refer to Figure 11-2).

   This places a sound icon on your slide.

4. **Select the sound icon so that the Sound Tools Options tab of the Ribbon gets activated, as you can see in Figure 11-3.**

5. **In the Sound Options group, click the Play Sound drop-down list and choose Play across Slides.**

6. **Select the Loop Until Stopped option on the Sound Tools Options tab.**

   Thereafter, you can drag the sound icon off the slide if you don't want the icon to be visible while you play the presentation.

7. **Save your presentation!**

Figure 11-3:
The Sound
Tools
Options tab
allows you
to play
sound
across
slides.

The accompanying CD contains several music loops from the Liquid Cabaret and Opuzz collections. Any of the loops can play continuously across multiple slides.

The sound-across-multiple-slides feature isn't well-suited for all types of presentations:

✔ Avoid including a background musical score in a corporate presentation that has a presenter discussing issues before an audience.

✔ Unless you're a professional presentation designer or an audio-video person who is certain about the entire concept, never use a background score in a presentation that includes narration.

Watch for these opportunities to use music in presentations:

✔ You can use the sound feature in presentations that don't have a live presenter — although you should choose a soft, understated background score.

✔ For trade shows and exhibition kiosks, try to use upbeat and optimistic music instead of monotonous, weary tunes.

✔ You can use music to great advantage within presentations that are distributed on CD.

If you want your sound to play across just a few slides within a presentation, you can do that by using transition sounds. They are discussed next.

Transition sounds

Transition sounds play with slide transitions. If the sound is longer than the transition, it continues to play beyond the actual transition. In fact, transition sounds can loop and play continuously across *several* slides. You can find more about transitions in Chapter 12.

Follow these steps to add transition sounds that play over one or more slides:

1. **Navigate to the slide where you want the sound to begin.**

2. **Click the Animations tab on the Ribbon, and from the Transition Sound drop-down list, select Other Sound. (See Figure 11-4.)**

   You can also select any of the built-in sounds that PowerPoint provides, but because most of the offerings are rather comic, I just stay away from them! Imagine the sound of clapping hands every time you transition from one slide to the other and you'll understand what I'm talking about.

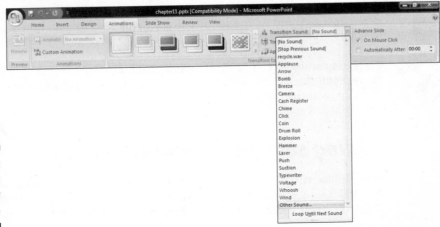

Figure 11-4:
Inserting
sounds in
transitions.

3. **From the Add Sound dialog box that appears, browse to and select any WAV file.**

   This technique doesn't work with MP3, WMA, or MIDI files.

4. **Again, revisit the Transition Sound drop-down list and select the Loop Until Next Sound option, as shown in Figure 11-5.**

   This option makes the transition sound continue to play across the consecutive slides. If you don't select this option, the sound will play just once.

5. **Navigate to the slide where you want the sound to stop playing.**

6. **In the Transition Sound drop-down list on the Animations tab, select the [Stop Previous Sound] option.**

Figure 11-5:
Loop your
transition
sound.

The biggest advantage to using transition sounds in a looping background score (instead of inserting sounds into the slides) is that all transition sounds are embedded as part of the presentation.

Transition sounds over 50MB are *neither embedded nor linked* — and PowerPoint doesn't even warn you, so make sure that your transition sounds don't go over that limit!

Fading sounds in an audio editor

Many times, you don't want a sound to start playing at full volume — a sound that fades into a presentation is usually much more interesting. In the same way, you might want to end your presentation with a sound that fades out.

PowerPoint by itself has no sound-fading mechanism — you must use an external sound editor to do the fades. Plenty of good sound editors are available. My favorites are

✔ Sony Sound Forge

✔ Adobe Audition

✔ Audacity (freeware)

For this tutorial, I use Audacity because it is simple and free — download a free copy of the product from

```
www.cuttingedgeppt.com/audacity
```

Follow these steps to fade your sounds in and out in Audacity:

1. **Choose File⇨Open and navigate to wherever you have saved a sound file.**

   If you don't have a sample sound file, use one of the samples on this book's CD.

   The sound opens in a waveform view similar to the one shown in Figure 11-6.

   Stereo sounds display two waveforms; mono sounds display a single waveform.

2. **Select a part of the waveform.**

   Drag over the waveform area to select as required:

   • *For a fade-in effect,* select a small part of the beginning of the waveform.

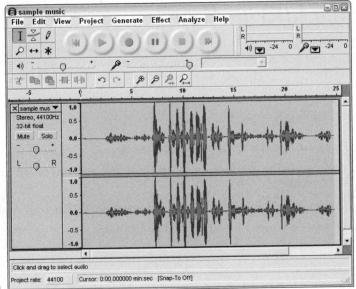

Figure 11-6: Waveform view in Audacity.

Fade-in sounds are ideally inserted in the first slide of the presentation.

- *For a fade-out effect,* select a small part of the end of the waveform.

Fade-out sounds are ideally inserted in the last slide of the presentation.

3. **Apply the fade effect:**

- *For a fade-in effect,* choose Effect⇨Fade In.
- *For a fade-out effect,* choose Effect⇨Fade Out.

4. **Listen to the faded sound by clicking the big Play icon on the toolbar.**

If you aren't satisfied with the fade effect, choose Edit⇨Undo and select a smaller or larger area of the waveform.

5. **After the fade effect is to your liking, choose File⇨Export as WAV or one of the other export options to save the sound to a new file.**

A similar tutorial for Sony Sound Forge can be found on this book's Web site:

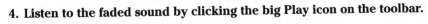

```
www.cuttingedgeppt.com/sforgefades
```

A trial version of Sony Sound Forge can be found on the CD attached to this book.

Add a CD soundtrack

A CD soundtrack is great accompaniment to a picture collage or photo album–style presentation for anything from a reunion to a keepsake. And if you restrict yourself to instrumental music tracks, there's no reason why you can't use a CD soundtrack in corporate presentations.

Here's how you get PowerPoint to play CD tracks:

1. **Put your favorite CD in your CD-ROM drive.**

2. **Open a new or existing presentation in PowerPoint and navigate to the first slide.**

3. **On the Insert tab of the Ribbon, choose Sound⇨Play CD Audio Track.**

   This summons the Insert CD Audio dialog box, shown in Figure 11-7.

Figure 11-7: Insert CD audio tracks in PowerPoint.

4. **Choose both a start track and an end track on the CD.**

   You can start or stop in the middle of a track by providing specific timings. In addition, you can loop the sound continuously.

5. **Click OK when you're done.**

   PowerPoint asks you how you want the sound to start (refer to Figure 11-2). Accept the Automatically button, or click the When Clicked button if you want the tracks to play on click while you're presenting.

   A CD icon appears on the slide. If you choose the option to play the tracks automatically, you can drag the icon off the slide area if you don't want it to be visible while you're playing the presentation.

After you have inserted the CD track, you can adjust it to play across slides by following these steps:

1. **Click the CD icon on the slide so that the CD Audio Tools Options tab of the Ribbon gets activated, as shown in Figure 11-8.**

2. **From the Play Track drop-down list, select the Play Across Slides option.**

Did you spot that prominent Slide Show Volume button in Figure 11-8? Actually, stay away from it; it doesn't apply to CD audio tracks at all. you can find more info at

```
www.cuttingedgeppt.com/volumeissue
```

Figure 11-8:
A whole tab
of options to
tweak your
audio CD
tracks in
PowerPoint.

Playing CD tracks: Guidelines

Follow these guidelines to avoid problems with CD tracks playing in PowerPoint:

✔ CD tracks are never saved with a presentation.

PowerPoint refers to tracks via track numbers — so if you choose to play tracks 2 through 5 using a particular CD and then replace that CD with another, PowerPoint plays tracks 2 through 5 from the new CD. This can be a blessing or a curse — whichever way you want to look at it!

✔ If your computer has more than one CD drive, use the same CD drive both when you add the CD track and when you show the presentation. While your audio CD is in one drive, PowerPoint might be looking for it on the other drive!

✔ Rip the CD tracks as WAV, MP3, or WMA files (use MP3 if you're working between both the Mac and Windows versions of PowerPoint) that can be inserted as normal sounds in the presentation. (See the "Converting CD tracks" section, later in this chapter, to find out how to rip CD audio tracks.)

✔ Be aware of copyright regulations, especially if you're distributing presentations. More or less, all music is copyrighted, and the music business has an extremely negative opinion of illegal copying and sharing of its work.

Converting Sound Formats

Many times, the sound you want isn't in a format you need. At other times, the *sampling rate* of a sound needs to be changed.

Sounds that have higher sampling rates have a higher fidelity. They can also be huge files — and putting those high-fidelity sounds inside a PowerPoint slide might make the presentation slow and unresponsive.

Fortunately, converting between sound formats and sampling rates is easy. In this section, you find out more about tools and procedures for conversion.

Converting CD tracks

Ripping is the process of converting CD audio tracks to other formats like WAV, MP3, and WMA. Several shareware and freeware CD-ripping programs are available. You can also use Windows Media Player, an application that's part of Microsoft Windows.

The following instructions are based on Windows Media Player 11 on Windows Vista. If you're using a different version, there might be slight differences in the dialog boxes and options.

Follow these steps to rip a CD audio track with Windows Media Player:

1. **Make sure that you have an audio CD in your CD drive; then launch Windows Media Player.**

2. **Click the small down arrow below the Now Playing tab and choose More Options. Or, if you're using an older version of Windows Media Player, you can choose Tools⇨Options.**

   This summons the multi-tabbed Options dialog box, shown in Figure 11-9.

3. **Click the Rip Music tab to find several options:**

   • Click the Change button to change the location of the folder where all your ripped music is saved.

   • Select the format for ripping from the Format drop-down list — options include MP3 and WMA.

4. **When you have chosen your options, click OK to exit this dialog box.**

   This gets you back to Windows Media Player.

5. **Click the Rip tab in the Player to see all your CD tracks listed.**

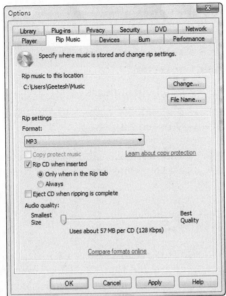

Figure 11-9:
Options in
Windows
Media
Player.

6. **Select the track(s) you want to rip and then click the Rip Music icon (or the Start Rip button) to start the ripping process.**

   Be patient. Ripping might take some time depending upon your computer speed and processor.

Converting between MP3, WMA, and WAV

Converting between MP3, WMA, and WAV formats is something you might often want to do. For instance, you might want to

- ✓ **Use an MP3 track as a transition sound.** You have to convert it to a WAV because only WAVs can be used as transition sounds.

- ✓ **Convert WAV or MP3 to WMA to take advantage of the superior compression so that the sounds take even less space.** This is even more important if you intend to e-mail your presentation.

The people at Illustrate offer an inexpensive program called dBpowerAMP Music Converter to help you convert sound files. You can download a trial version of dBpowerAMP from

www.cuttingedgeppt.com/dbpoweramp

dBpowerAMP also lets you rip CDs to WAV files.

Follow these guidelines to convert between file formats with dBpowerAMP:

1. **Start dBpowerAMP Music Converter.**

   An Open dialog box (see Figure 11-10) appears.

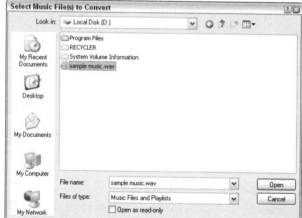

Figure 11-10:
Convert
sound
formats with
dBpowerA
MP.

2. **Choose a file you want to convert.**

   You see the dialog box shown in Figure 11-11.

   This dialog box lets you choose the destination format and save location for the converted file.

3. **Choose these options as required.**

4. **Click the Convert button and you're done!**

Figure 11-11:
Choose the
sound
format and
other
attributes.

Converting MIDI to WAV

MIDI files need a fairly high-level sound card to play with full fidelity. Thus, depending on your sound card, your MIDI might sound heavenly or clunky inside your PowerPoint presentation.

✔ If you're happy with the way the MIDI sounds inside PowerPoint, don't bother with the conversion.

✔ If you aren't sure of your delivery machine, or if the MIDI doesn't sound too good on your system, consider converting it to a WAV file.

Several programs can do the conversion — this book's companion site has more details and download links to such programs:

```
www.cuttingedgeppt.com/midi2wav
```

You can find 100 free MIDI samples on the CD for your use.

Converting sampling rates

The *sampling rate* loosely translates to the fidelity of the sound.

The version of Sound Recorder bundled with Windows Vista is not as full-featured as earlier versions, so these instructions work only with Windows XP and earlier versions of Windows.

The following steps show you how to convert the sampling rate for a WAV file by using the Sound Recorder applet:

1. **Launch Sound Recorder by choosing Start⇨Run and typing** sndrec32 **in the dialog box that appears.**

2. **In Sound Recorder, choose File⇨Open.**

3. **Select a high-quality WAV file and click Open.**

4. **Choose File⇨Properties to summon the Properties dialog box, shown in Figure 11-12.**

   In the Format Conversion area, make sure the Choose From drop-down list shows All Formats.

5. **Click the Convert Now button to view the Sound Selection dialog box, shown in Figure 11-13.**

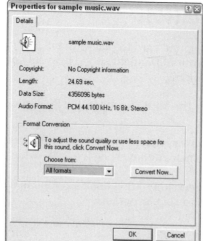

Figure 11-12:
Sound
properties.

Figure 11-13:
Converting
sampling
rates.

You can choose your own format and attributes or just make it a whole lot simpler and choose any of the three default options available in the Name drop-down list:

- CD Quality

- Radio Quality

- Telephone Quality

For most PowerPoint work, Radio Quality offers a nice balance between file size and sound quality.

6. **Click OK to begin the conversion.**

   If this is a large file, Sound Recorder might take a while.

7. **Click OK again to exit the Properties dialog box.**

8. **Choose File➪Save As and save the file under a new name so that the original file doesn't get overwritten.**

Recording Narration

To record narration from within PowerPoint, all you need is a sound card and a decent microphone. Yet, narration is one of PowerPoint's least-used and most misunderstood aspects. Many people try it out, get frustrated, and give up.

Microphone setup

Most narration problems stem from conditions not related to PowerPoint, ranging from incompatible sound cards to loose microphone cables to messed-up multimedia settings.

Before you start recording, install your microphone and test it. The following sections show you how.

Installation

If your microphone isn't already installed, follow the instructions included with your microphone. Most of the time, all you do is plug your microphone into a sound card or a USB port.

Make sure that the microphone is selected as the default recording device in Microsoft Windows. Follow these steps to access your computer's audio settings — the steps might differ depending upon the version of Windows that you are using.

Windows XP

Follow these steps if you are using Windows XP:

1. **Open the Control Panel.**

   Depending on your Windows configuration, choose either

   - Start➪Control Panel
   - Start➪Settings➪Control Panel

2. **In the Control Panel, click the audio icon.**

   Depending on your Windows version, it's called either

   - Sounds and Audio Devices
   - Sound, Speech, and Audio Devices

   This opens the Sounds and Audio Devices Properties dialog box, shown in Figure 11-14.

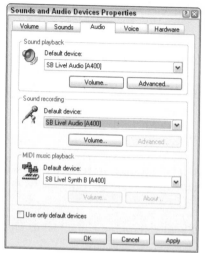

Figure 11-14:
Sound and
Audio
Devices
properties.

3. Set these properties on the Audio tab:

- Select your microphone in the Default Device drop-down list.
- Click the Volume button to access the Record volume slider and make sure the volume slider is around ¾ of the way up.

Windows Vista

Follow these steps if you are using Windows Vista:

1. Open the Control Panel by choosing Start➪Control Panel.

2. In the Control Panel, access the sound settings.

Depending on your configuration, this is either

- Hardware and Sound, Sound, Recording
- Sound, Recording

This opens the Recording tab in the Sound dialog box, as shown in Figure 11-15.

3. Set these properties:

- Select your microphone and click the Set Default button if it is not already set as the default sound recording device.
- Make sure your microphone is still selected and then click the Properties button to summon the Microphone Properties dialog box.
- In the Levels tab, make sure the volume slider is around ¾ of the way up.

Figure 11-15:
Recording
properties.

Testing

If Sound Recorder can record your voice, you shouldn't have any problems recording your narrations in PowerPoint.

Follow these steps to do a test recording in Sound Recorder:

1. **Launch Sound Recorder.**

   - Windows XP users can choose Start➪Run, type **sndrec32**, and click OK.

   - Windows Vista users can choose Start➪All Programs➪ Accessories➪Sound Recorder.

   This launches the Sound Recorder applet, shown in Figure 11-16. This is a very simple, intuitive applet that looks and functions like a tape recorder.

2. **Click the round, red Record button to begin recording narration through the microphone.**

3. **Speak a sentence or two before clicking the Stop button.**

   In Windows XP, the Stop button is the second button from the right.

   In Windows Vista, the Start Recording button acts as a toggle and changes to Stop Recording button.

4. **Play the recorded narration.**

   In Windows XP, click the Play button.

   In Windows Vista, save the recorded narration and then double-click the saved file to play it in an associated application.

Figure 11-16:
Sound
Recorder in
Windows
XP (top) and
in Windows
Vista
(bottom).

Preparation

Your PowerPoint narration depends on

✔ **A good script**

Make sure your script is ready — practice it aloud several times.

In your script, avoid words with these sounds:

- *Popping P,* such as *pack* and *topped*
- *Hissing S,* such as *send* and *central*

✔ **Confidence**

- Try for the exact nuance you need and experiment with speaking slowly in the parts where you want to provide more impact.
- Practice your narration by running the presentation in Slide Show mode and narrating along with the slides without recording anything.

At the end of this practice, you might want to make some changes in your script.

Be sure that you have enough light so that you can read your script clearly.

Recording

When your microphone is connected and the script is ready, you can record your narration. Follow these steps:

1. **In PowerPoint, go to Slide Sorter view.**

2. **Select the slide where you would like to begin narration.**

3. **Click the Slide Show tab on the Ribbon and then click the Record Narration option.**

   This opens the Record Narration dialog box, shown in Figure 11-17.

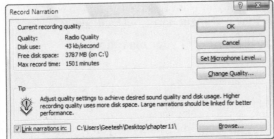

Figure 11-17:
Record
narration.

Before you click OK to start the recording, check out some options:

- *Set Microphone Level:* Click the Set Microphone Level button, and you're presented with a Microphone Check dialog box. Use this dialog box to ensure that your microphone is working properly.

- *Change Quality:* This option lets you change the quality of the sound recorded. The three preset options, from highest to lowest quality, are CD Quality, Radio Quality, and Telephone Quality.

  Radio Quality provides the best balance between quality and file size in PowerPoint.

- *Link Narrations In:* Select this check box if you want to link your sound files instead of embedding them as part of the presentation. Enabling this option also lets you later directly open the recorded sound files and edit them in a sound-editing application such as Sony Sound Forge, Adobe Audition, or Audacity.

4. **Click OK to start recording the narration.**

5. **Choose the starting location you want.**

   Unless the active slide is the first slide, PowerPoint pops up the Record Narration dialog box that asks you to choose whether to begin narration from

   - The present slide (selected at the start of this list)
   - The first slide of the presentation

6. **Record the narration for each slide.**

   When you finish recording a slide:

   a. Leave a two-second pause.

   b. Either click your mouse button or press the spacebar to go to the next slide. If your mouse makes a click sound whenever you click, it's better to use the spacebar.

7. **Press Esc when you finish recording the narration for all your slides.**

PowerPoint asks you if you want to save the *timing* with each slide (the duration of time that you spent narrating each slide).

8. Click Yes to save the timing of your narration.

Editing

You don't have to use your narration exactly as you record it. PowerPoint lets you edit your recordings.

Rough cuts

Often, you can just record your narration into PowerPoint as a "rough cut," choosing an option to link instead of embedding the narration sequences. Save these linked files in the same folder as the actual presentation because keeping all elements of the presentation in a single folder is very helpful when you want to transport the presentation to another system.

Replacing narrations

If you're unhappy with the way your narration sounds, or if you used your narration as a stop-gap or temporary measure, you can replace the narration files with edited or new sound files:

- ✔ If you opted to link the narrations in the same folder as the presentation, you find them as a bunch of WAV files. These WAV files can be opened in a sound editor, where you can clean all the hiss and click sounds. Or you might want to hand over these WAV files to a sound technician to get them *cleaned.* Good sound technicians can also add reverb to your narration so that it sounds more impressive. They can also *normalize* your narrations so that all narrations play at the same volume.

- ✔ After you have edited or cleaned the narrations, just place them in the same folder as the original narrations. This overwrites your old narrations, and PowerPoint won't even know that you have worked all that magic into the voices.

- ✔ You must be certain that the new narration files are exactly the same length as the original ones. Also, the new files must have the same names as the original files.

Other significant aspects are related to narration. Take a look at the "Sounding super!" sidebar to find out about them.

TIP

Sounding super!

Sound quality is influenced by many very subtle properties. Follow these guidelines to record great narration:

✔ Speak normally; don't be overly loud.

✔ Start by placing the microphone around four inches away from your mouth and then adjust the distance as needed to prevent breathing noises, hissing, and popping in the recording.

Getting the microphone positioned correctly will help prevent words with an *s*

sound from having an elongated *sss* sound and *p* sounds from popping.

Rodney Saulsberry has written an amazing book on voice-overs called *You Can Bank on Your Voice* (Tomdor Publishing). He has provided a free excerpt on my site:

    www.indezine.com/products/
       powerpoint/books/
       bankonyourvoice.html

Inserting Movies

Normally, you insert movie clips into PowerPoint by using the options on the Insert tab of the Ribbon, as explained in the following steps. This works best for movie files in the formats that PowerPoint understands, such as AVI, MPEG, and WMV. For unsupported formats, take a look at the "Link movies" section, later in this chapter.

Follow these steps to insert a movie on a PowerPoint slide:

1. **Navigate to the slide where you want the movie inserted in a new or existing presentation.**

2. **Click the Insert tab on the Ribbon and choose Movie⇨Movie from File.**

   This brings up the Insert Movie dialog box, shown in Figure 11-18.

3. **Select a movie clip.**

   The movie file must be in a file format that PowerPoint accepts, such as AVI, MPEG, or WMV.

4. **PowerPoint asks you whether you want the movie to play automatically or only when clicked — choose your option.**

TIP

   Click the Automatically button if you aren't sure because

   • *Removing* that behavior later is a simple, one-click operation.

   • *Adding* that behavior later takes several steps.

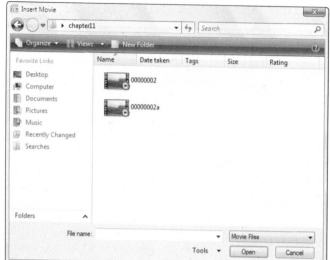

Figure 11-18:
Inserting
movies.

Resize the movie clip

You can resize your movie clip after it's inserted in a slide. If you select the clip, you see eight handles around it — four on the corners and four between the corners (on the sides).

- Press the Shift key and drag a corner handle to resize the movie clip without altering its proportions.

- Drag a side handle to resize it without maintaining proportions. (Note that doing this will make the movie appear distorted.)

- Drag the corner or sides with both the Ctrl and Shift keys pressed to resize it from the center while maintaining the movie clip's proportions.

While downsizing a movie works well, making it larger is not necessarily a good idea. Movie clips taken from the Internet or from digital cameras and video phones are small to start with, and making them fill up more screen space will make them look very grainy.

Add a border

You can also add a nice border to your movie clip in PowerPoint. This often ends up looking like a frame. Just follow these steps:

1. **Right-click the movie clip on the slide and choose Format Picture from the contextual menu that appears.**

This opens the Format Picture dialog box.

2. **Within the Line Color tab, choose either the Solid line or Gradient line option.**

   You can also alter the line weight, style, and dashed attributes of the line (border) by choosing the options in the Line Style tab of the same dialog box.

3. **Click Close to get back to the slide.**

For an interesting effect, choose a weight of at least 10 points and then choose the Gradient Line option on the Line Color tab. Use restrained gradient colors for the line border so the border isn't more attractive than the movie clip itself! You can find out more about gradient lines in Chapter 6.

When you select a movie, the Picture Tools Format tab appears on the Ribbon, and you can add interesting frames from the Picture Styles gallery to the movie. However, some video graphic cards might not be capable of playing these movies well. Many times, your movie can end up as a black silhouette instead of a playing video!

Link movies

For unsupported movie formats, such as RealVideo and QuickTime, the only route open is to create a hyperlink on the slide to the movie clips. You can then click the hyperlink in Slide Show mode to play the clip in the appropriate player (RealPlayer or QuickTime, for example).

Follow these steps to link a movie clip from a PowerPoint slide:

1. **Create an anchor.**

   To link a movie clip, you need an *anchor* to link from. This can be any PowerPoint object, such as text or a shape.

   Type something like **Click here to play movie** or something descriptive within the text box or the shape.

2. **Select the anchor, click the Insert tab on the Ribbon, and then click the Action option.**

   The Action Settings dialog box opens (see Figure 11-19).

3. **On the Mouse Click tab, choose Other File from the Hyperlink To drop-down list.**

4. **Navigate to and select the movie clip that you want to play and then click OK.**

Figure 11-19:
Anchor a
hyperlink to
a movie clip.

If you link to a RealVideo movie, clicking the hyperlink initiates RealPlayer; the QuickTime player opens if you link to a QuickTime movie. In all cases, you must close the video clip independently after it finishes playing.

You can use this linking technique to initiate any associated program from within PowerPoint — even nonmovie files.

Full-screen movies

PowerPoint lets you play full-screen movies in a presentation. After you place a movie in a presentation (see the previous "Inserting Movies" section), follow these steps to make it a full-screen playback:

1. **Select the movie clip.**

   The Movie Tools Options tab (see Figure 11-20) appears on the Ribbon. Select this tab.

2. **Select the Play Full Screen check box.**

3. **Select any other playback options you want in the Movie Options group of the Movie Tools Options tab:**

   • To loop the movie's playback, select the Loop until Stopped check box.

   • To rewind the movie after it plays, select the Rewind Movie after Playing check box.

Figure 11-20: The Movie Tools Options tab.

Links and link problems

Whenever you insert a movie within PowerPoint, it's invariably linked to the presentation. In fact, PowerPoint can't embed any movies within the presentation — sound reasoning considering how embedded movies would balloon PowerPoint file sizes like nothing else!

Now for the bad news — PowerPoint isn't too good at remembering link locations. If the presentation and the movie clips are on the same system, you shouldn't face any problems. However, if you decide to move or copy the presentation to another system, PowerPoint can't locate the movie clips — it won't even offer to find the links for you.

The solution is quite simple: Assemble all your movie clips in the same folder as your presentation even before you insert them into PowerPoint. And yes, insert the movie clips into a presentation only after the presentation itself has been saved at least once.

Finding Sources for Movie Clips

Finding good sources of movie clips is more of a challenge than inserting them in PowerPoint. The following list describes some possible sources:

- ✔ **Digital camcorders and cameras:** Digital camcorders record straight to a digital video format that can be transferred to your computer through a special cable and saved to a PowerPoint-friendly movie format like AVI, MPG, or WMV. Many digital cameras (as opposed to digital *video* cameras) also let you shoot short movie clips. Digital camcorders start at around $500, and a good digital camera that can also record movie clips costs less than that.

- ✔ **Webcams:** Webcams attached to your computer let you record live video while you sit in front of your PC. Most Webcams include a built-in microphone. Webcams cost between $50 and $150.

✔ **Movie stock libraries:** Many a time, you want to add movie clips to the beginning of a presentation to create a splash slide. For instance, you might want to show a collage of medical movie clips before you speak to an audience about medicine. Luckily, locating stock movie footage for most subjects is easy nowadays. Stock movie footage is indeed more expensive than stock images, but prices are coming down.

Most clips are usually available in both WMV and MOV formats for use in PowerPoint for Windows and Mac, respectively.

A few royalty-free movie clips can be found on the *Cutting Edge PowerPoint 2007 For Dummies* CD.

✔ **Video capture devices:** Various video capture devices let you digitize existing VHS or analog camcorder content to a format that PowerPoint can understand. Costs vary between $200 and $1,000, depending upon the video capture quality and features.

Movie Playlists in PowerPoint

You can create a playlist of your movie clips in Windows Media Player and get PowerPoint to play the entire sequence of movies — an invaluable technique if you want to play a series of movie clips within a presentation seamlessly and don't have the time to get them rendered together in a video-editing package.

Creating a movie playlist

Windows Media Player enables you to create a movie playlist. To start with, you need some movie clips in the type of formats that Windows Media Player can play — these include AVI, WMV, and MPEG files. You also need a copy of Windows Media Player 10 or higher — you can download a free copy of Windows Media Player from

```
www.microsoft.com/windows/windowsmedia/download
```

Follow these steps to create a video playlist in Windows Media Player:

1. **Place all the video files in the same folder and select them all.**

2. **With all files selected, right-click and choose the Add to Now Playing List (or Add to Windows Media Player List) option.**

   This opens all the videos as part of a new playlist in Windows Media Player.

3. **Save this playlist by choosing either of these options, depending on your version of Windows Media Player:**

   • If you have version 10, choose File⇨Save Now Playing List As.

   • If you have version 11, click the arrow under the Now Playing option in the playlist (see Figure 11-21) and choose Save Playlist As.

4. **Save the playlist as a Windows Media Playlist file (*.WPL) in the same folder as the movie clips.**

Inserting a movie playlist

Follow these steps to insert your movie playlist on a PowerPoint slide:

1. **In PowerPoint, create or open an existing presentation and go to the slide where you want to begin playing the videos.**

2. **Click the Insert tab and then click the Movie button.**

   This summons the Insert dialog box.

3. **Navigate to the folder that contains the playlist (*.WPL) file.**

   You might need to change the option shown in the Files of Type drop-down list to All Files (*.*).

Figure 11-21:
Saving your
playlist file.

4. Select the WPL playlist and click OK.

PowerPoint asks you whether you want the movie to start automatically or when clicked; click the Automatically button.

PowerPoint places a rectangle representing the playlist on the slide. This rectangle is the same area where the videos will actually be played.

5. Resize the playlist rectangle as required.

You can also create a playlist that contains both movie and sound clips. In such a case, the videos play normally and the sounds display Windows Media visualizations. Try this; it looks cool.

The DVD Factor

Lots of people want to play DVD clips inside PowerPoint, but most commercial DVDs are encrypted, and the studios and companies that own rights to these DVDs aren't too happy to allow their DVDs to be played within your presentation.

On the other hand, many users just archive all their camcorder footage to DVDs — and then they suddenly discover that there's no easy way to use their own, non-commercial movie footage within their presentations!

Another issue is entirely hardware-based — you probably don't want to play the clip straight off a DVD because you might not have the same DVD spinning in your drive all the time. That translates to saving a part of the DVD as a movie clip on your hard drive. Again, that won't make too many of those movie studios happy.

Not surprisingly, Microsoft has steered away from directly supporting the playing of DVDs in PowerPoint. But lots of people nowadays create home DVDs with their camcorder footage. Such DVDs aren't encrypted, and clips from these sources can be easily inserted into a PowerPoint slide by using third-party products:

- ✔ A company called Visible Light creates a product called Onstage DVD ($89) for PowerPoint that lets you insert and play DVD content within PowerPoint. It's available for download at

    www.cuttingedgeppt.com/onstage

    As of this writing, this tool isn't yet compatible with PowerPoint 2007.

- ✔ PFCMedia ($50) is another product that plays your DVD content. It also inserts the clips inside PowerPoint for you. You can find it at:

    www.cuttingedgeppt.com/pfcmedia

    As of this writing, this tool isn't yet compatible with PowerPoint 2007.

✔ Cinematize is another product that lets you extract footage from non-encrypted DVDs to movie clips. You can find it at:

`www.cuttingedgeppt.com/cinematize`

One factor can never be stressed enough: copyright. Never assume that you can use a movie or sound clip in a presentation if it's neither yours nor licensed to you. To use a movie clip that is or contains copyrighted work, you need explicit permission in writing from the owner of that content. For more info, see this site:

`www.indezine.com/ideas/copyright.html`

Running Smooth Videos

What do you do if your movie clips don't run well within PowerPoint?

Movies require more system resources than most other media, and taking some steps can go a long way in helping you run smoother videos. Here's some help:

✔ **Don't run any programs in the background that can be avoided.** These include instant messengers, camera or Webcam software, and your PDA connectivity application, among others. Also, it's a good idea to disable your screen saver.

✔ **Close all open programs except PowerPoint.**

✔ **Defragment your hard drive often so that it can function optimally.**

✔ **Upgrade your video RAM if possible.** Also upgrade your system RAM.

Getting Friendly with Codecs

Codecs can be scary — unless you make friends with them. After you've broken the ice, you'll wonder why you were ever scared of codecs. If you're already convinced that codecs are a piece of cake, then you have enough time to go for a swim and become really cool! For everyone else, I have answers for two questions:

✔ Why should you know more about codecs?

✔ So, what's a codec, anyway?

And here are the answers!

Sound and movie files can be huge — a dozen songs can fill an entire audio CD. Music and movie buffs have always needed some technology that can squeeze such files down to size without deteriorating the quality. This entails both coding and decoding. Codecs take care of the coding and decoding — if that sounded too geeky, let me give you an example.

I just recorded a five-minute movie clip with my digital camcorder. Its size leaves a lot to be desired, so I use a coding algorithm to compress it. Later, when I want to play it back, I use a similar decoding algorithm. Now, what I am essentially doing is coding and decoding — in other words, I am using a codec. The term *codec* is an abbreviation for *coder/decoder*.

Most multimedia problems in PowerPoint stem from *codecs*. Changing the codec or format of a multimedia file can provide a solution.

Different codecs use different coding and decoding algorithms. At last count, more than 100 unique codecs were available for the AVI video format alone!

Which codecs are installed?

You can convert only between the codecs that are installed on your system.

Although you can view which codecs are installed on your system by using the options in the Windows Control Panel, specialized applications like AVICodec and GSpot provide much more information more easily. Both are freeware and can be downloaded from

```
www.cuttingedgeppt.com/codecapp
```

Converting the codecs

Converting codecs is almost like converting a file format. Providing the details here is beyond the scope of this book. However, you can find instructions on converting codecs on my site:

```
www.indezine.com/products/video/virtualdub.html
```

Export Your Presentation to a Movie

This is among the most frequently requested features for PowerPoint. Maybe Microsoft will include it in a future version. Until then, you must use third-party software to create a movie from a PowerPoint presentation. Nothing is as easy and straightforward as a solution called Camtasia Studio, from TechSmith Corporation.

Actually, Camtasia Studio is a full-blown application that can capture all your on-screen activity and save it as a movie. These captured movies can then be further enriched with hot spots, narrations, and transitions. In addition, Camtasia Studio installs a new toolbar within your PowerPoint interface, as you can see in Figure 11-22.

Record audio (on/off)

Figure 11-22:
Camtasia
toolbar in
PowerPoint.

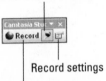

Record settings

Start presentation
and record to video

The screenshot in Figure 11-22 shows the Camtasia Studio toolbar in an older version of PowerPoint; an updated PowerPoint 2007–compatible version of Camtasia Studio was not available at the time of this writing. TechSmith has confirmed that it is updating Camtasia Studio to run within PowerPoint 2007.

Just click the Record icon, and Camtasia Studio starts capturing the entire live presentation to a video. Apart from the presentation, Camtasia Studio also captures your voice-over if you simultaneously narrate with a microphone. You have to set these options before you begin capturing.

Captured videos can be output to a multitude of video formats, including AVI, WMV, and QuickTime. In addition, you can also convert to Flash-based online rich content or record the captured video to create VCDs and DVDs. Finally, you can also export in an iPod-ready format that works with the new video iPods from Apple.

You can find more information on this book's companion site:

`www.cuttingedgeppt.com/camtasia`

You can find a full version of Camtasia 3 (the precursor of Camtasia Studio) for free on the CD attached to this book!

Chapter 12

Moving On with Animations and Transitions

In This Chapter

▶ Adding movement with animations and transitions

▶ Pulling out all the animation tricks

▶ Moving down motion paths and using trigger animations

▶ Putting animations in order with the timeline

▶ Flowing along with transitions

*M*ovement beckons vision like nothing else can. Movement also takes PowerPoint presentations to a level that can never be attained by mere paper handouts.

PowerPoint allows two types of movement:

> ✔ **Custom animations:** Slide elements like text, shapes, and pictures are animated via the Custom Animation feature.
>
> ✔ **Slide transitions:** Slides themselves use slide transitions to move and flow from one slide to the next.

"Everything in moderation" definitely applies to movements inside PowerPoint presentations. If you have seen, presented, or created your share of PowerPoint presentations, you know what I'm talking about — those classic over-the-top presentations in which every line of text flies onto the slide with a swishy sound. Those presentations are so loaded with special effects that you wonder what new effect you'll see on the next slide instead of paying any attention to the actual content of the presentation. How can you remember the presenter's point when you have this circus to watch?!

In this chapter, I describe how to add movements to your presentation by using custom animations and slide transitions. I also provide you with guidelines to keep your presentations from getting overloaded with movement.

Understanding Animation

Every element on a PowerPoint slide can be animated, although you don't have to animate them all in the same way. For each element that you animate, consider experimenting with various animation types, *builds*, and *events*. Most of these terms might be familiar to you if you have used a multimedia or animation program. If you have never used an animation program before, don't worry: I explain all the concepts relevant to PowerPoint here.

Animation has its own terminology. Knowing these terms can help you grasp the concepts of animation.

Build and sequence

Builds are series of animations played one after the other to portray a logical *sequence* of happenings. Here are some example builds:

- ✔ The charts for the previous year animate before the charts of the present year.
- ✔ The bulleted text on a slide builds one bullet point at a time.

These builds are created by using *animation events*.

Animation events

PowerPoint gives you three types of animation events that determine the *happening* (or starting) of an animation in relation to any other animation or event:

- ✔ **On Click** is the default animation event that occurs after a mouse click. Although it's called On Click, it also activates when the spacebar is pressed or when a specific button on a presentation remote control is pressed.

   On Click events require some user input, such as a mouse click or a key press.

- ✔ **With Previous** is an animation event that plays simultaneously with the previous animation.

   Think of this as two or more animations happening at the same time on a slide.

- ✔ **After Previous** events begin automatically after the previous animation has concluded.

Think of this as one animation waiting to play automatically after the previous animation has ended.

Both With Previous and After Previous events happen without any user interaction.

In addition, you can use *trigger animations,* which occur when the user clicks one object, and another object displays an animation. Trigger animations are discussed in more detail later in this chapter in the "Trigger animations" section.

Animation speed

PowerPoint includes a few speed presets that determine how long an animation takes to complete:

- ✔ Very Slow (5 seconds)
- ✔ Slow (3 seconds)
- ✔ Medium (2 seconds)
- ✔ Fast (1 second)
- ✔ Very Fast (0.5 seconds)

In addition, you can change the time to any duration you want by using the *Timeline.* You find out more about the Timeline later in this chapter in the "Timing Animations with the Advanced Timeline" section.

Animation types

PowerPoint lets you insert four types of animations via the Custom Animation pane:

- ✔ **Entrance animations** are used when an object appears for the first time on a slide.
- ✔ **Emphasis animations** influence the animation of an object while it's on the slide between its entry and exit.
- ✔ **Exit animations** are associated with an object's departure from the slide area.
- ✔ **Motion paths** let you move an object along a path set either by PowerPoint defaults or by a path that you draw on the slide.

Adding an Animation

In PowerPoint, you can add animation to any object on a slide.

This book's CD has sample presentations that show every single PowerPoint animation. It's a great reference to use when you want to look for that wonderful (but unnamed) animation you saw last week.

Follow these steps to animate an object in PowerPoint:

1. **Select an object and click the Animation tab on the Ribbon so that it is visible (see Figure 12-1).**

2. **Click the Custom Animation button on the Animation tab.**

   This opens the Custom Animation pane, as shown in Figure 12-2.

3. **Click the Add Effect button to reveal a menu with four options (shown in Figure 12-2).**

   The four options are Entrance, Emphasis, Exit, and Motion Paths — an explanation of these animation types is covered in the preceding section.

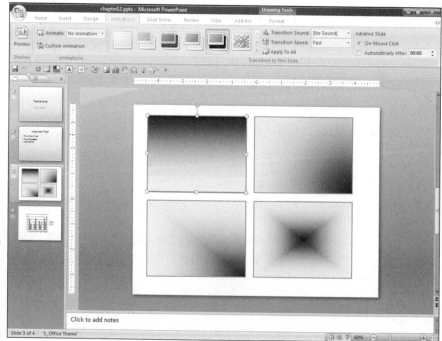

Figure 12-1:
The
Animation
tab on the
Ribbon.

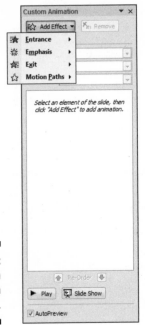

Figure 12-2:
The Custom
Animation
pane.

4. **Select one of the options from the menu.**

   You see another flyout menu that lets you choose one of the more frequently used animation styles, as shown in Figure 12-3.

5. **If you want to see more choices or preview the animations, click the More Effects option.**

   A dialog box similar to the one shown in Figure 12-4 appears. This figure shows you the options for the Entrance animations, but the choices for Emphasis and Exit animations work in the same way.

6. **Move this dialog box off the slide area and make sure that the Preview Effect option is selected.**

7. **Click an effect to preview the animation of the selected object on the slide.**

8. **When you decide which effect you want, click OK to accept; click Cancel to exit the dialog box without making any changes.**

A single object can have all animation types — Entrance, Emphasis, Exit, and Motion Paths — applied. This means that the selected object:

- ✔ Appears on the slide with one animation type (entrance animation).
- ✔ Stays on the slide with another animation type (emphasis animation).
- ✔ Moves out of the slide area with a third animation type (exit animation).

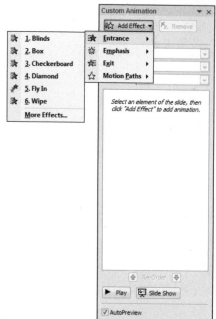

In addition, the object can move on the slide on a motion path.

You can also apply multiple animations of the same type. You discover how
to fade and move text at the same time in Chapter 16.

Managing Animations

PowerPoint provides numerous options for controlling the appearance and behavior of animations.

More movement in the Custom Animation pane

After you've added an animation to an object, you can change the timing and speed of the animation by using the Custom Animation pane. This pane is the nerve center of all animation activity in a presentation.

Follow these steps to view this task pane and make any changes:

1. **Select the object with animation already applied.**

   If the animation attribute hasn't been applied yet, read the "Adding an Animation" section earlier in this chapter to apply an animation.

2. **Click the Animation tab on the Ribbon and then click the Custom Animation button to reveal the Custom Animation pane, shown in Figure 12-5.**

3. **The animation for the selected object is highlighted within the task pane (see Figure 12-5).**

   The task pane lets you change several attributes of the animation:

   - *Start:* You can change the animation event to On Click, With Previous, or After Previous. For an explanation of these terms, refer to the "Animation events" section, earlier in this chapter.

   - *Direction:* If you're using an animation that has no Direction attribute, this option might be grayed out. For an animation like Wipe that supports direction of the animation, you find choices like From Bottom, From Left, From Right, and From Top. Experiment to figure out what works best for your presentation.

   - *Speed:* This is the time required for the animation to play — predefined choices range from Very Slow to Very Fast, but these can be tweaked in the Animation Timeline. (The Timeline is covered later in this chapter in the "Timing Animations with the Advanced Timeline" section.)

4. **When you're done tweaking the settings, click the Play button to preview the slide with the animations.**

Figure 12-5:
Working
with the
Custom
Animation
pane.

Changing, removing, and reordering animations

At times, you might want to do some housekeeping with the animations already applied — for instance, you might want to change an animation. The process to change, remove, and reorder animations is simple:

1. **If the Custom Animation pane isn't visible, click the Custom Animation button (found on the Animation tab of the Ribbon).**

2. **In the Custom Animation pane, select the animation to be changed.**

   This causes the Add Effect button to metamorphose into the Change button (refer to Figure 12-5).

3. **Change, remove, or reorder the animation.**

   • Click the Change button to open a flyout menu with Entry, Emphasis, Exit, and Motion Paths options. Choose any of the animations within these categories as explained in the preceding section.

   • To remove an existing animation, just select it in the Custom Animation pane and click the Remove button.

   • To reorder the sequence of animations on a slide, select any of the animations in the Custom Animation pane and then click either of the Re-Order arrow buttons below the animation listing. Of course, this works only if you have more than one animated object on a slide.

4. **When you're done with all the changes, click Play to preview the slide with the animations.**

Animating charts and text

PowerPoint provides options for animating charts and bulleted text — for example, you can have the series of the chart animate in sequence, and bullets can appear one at a time.

Text animation

PowerPoint provides umpteen text animation possibilities — you can animate by words, by letters, and by paragraphs.

Follow these steps to tweak the text animation options in PowerPoint:

1. **Select part of the text or the entire placeholder with bulleted text.**

2. **Click the Animation tab on the Ribbon and then click the Custom Animation button to activate the Custom Animation pane (refer to Figure 12-2).**

3. **Add an Entry animation to the text if it isn't already done.**

   Refer to the detailed instructions in the "Adding an Animation" section, earlier in this chapter.

4. **Double-click the animation within the task pane to summon the dialog box shown in Figure 12-6.**

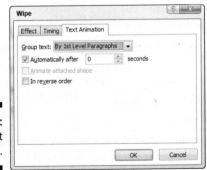

Figure 12-6:
Text
animation.

5. **Select the Text Animation tab and change settings as required:**

- The Group Text drop-down list lets you choose how to animate the bulleted text in consecutive builds. The By 1st Level Paragraphs option is selected by default; you can experiment with other options.

- If you want to synch the time more evenly, select the time span after which the next bullet animation occurs by selecting the Automatically After check box and entering a time in the Seconds text box.

- If required, change the sequence of bullets by selecting the In Reverse Order check box.

6. **Click OK to apply the animation.**

You can individually animate each line of bulleted text. To do that, click the downward-pointing chevron below a selected text object within the Custom Animation pane to view all the text lines; then select each individual line and change the animation settings as required.

Chart animation

It's nice to see all your columns rise up one at a time. You can do this and more with PowerPoint's chart animation capabilities.

Follow these steps to tweak the chart animation options in PowerPoint:

1. **Select the chart.**

2. **Click the Animation tab on the Ribbon and then click the Custom Animation button to activate the Custom Animation pane (refer to Figure 12-2).**

   The Custom Animation button is a toggle button — so if your Custom Animation pane is already visible, clicking the button again makes it disappear.

3. **Add an animation to the chart if it isn't already applied.**

   You can find detailed instructions in the "Adding an Animation" section, earlier in this chapter.

4. **Double-click the animation listed for the chart within the Custom Animation pane to summon the dialog box shown in Figure 12-7.**

5. **Click the Chart Animation tab.**

6. **Click the Group Chart drop-down list, which provides you with several animation options.**

   The By Series option works well, but you might want to experiment with the other alternatives. The alternative you use depends on the type of chart and data being animated.

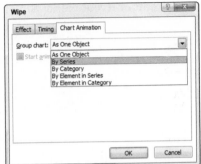

Figure 12-7:
Chart
animation.

7. Select the Start Animation by Drawing the Chart option, if required. This option lets you begin the animation by filling in the chart background.

You can find out more about chart terminology in Chapter 10.

8. Click OK to apply the animation.

After you finish tweaking the animations for the chart, preview them by clicking the Play button on the Custom Animation pane. If you aren't happy with the animations, return to the Custom Animation pane and change the settings. If the listing for the chart animation in the pane has a downward-pointing arrow, you can click the arrow to select individual chart elements and then time their animations differently.

Motion paths

Motion path animations enable objects to move along a preset or custom path — this path can be a straight line, a curve, a preset path, or any path you draw yourself.

A presentation that shows all motion path preset animations in PowerPoint is included on this book's CD.

Follow these steps to create motion path animations:

1. Select an object on a slide that you want to animate on a motion path.

You can open one of the sample presentations on the CD attached to this book and select an object on one of the slides.

2. Click the Animation tab on the Ribbon and then click the Custom Animation button to activate the Custom Animation pane (refer to Figure 12-2).

3. Click the Add Effect button on the task pane to reveal a flyout menu.

4. Choose Motion Paths to reveal another flyout menu, shown in Figure 12-8.

Figure 12-8:
Motion
Paths get
your objects
moving.

5. Choose any of the options, or choose More Motion Paths to open the Add Motion Path dialog box (see Figure 12-9)

You can find 64 motion path presets — choose any of them and you see a preview of the effect on the slide if the Preview Effect option is checked. All these motion paths are previewed in a sample presentation on the *Cutting Edge PowerPoint 2007 For Dummies* CD.

6. Click OK when you're done.

If none of the 64 preset motion paths appeals to you, choose Add Effect➪Motion Path➪Draw Custom Path in the Custom Animation pane. You can use any of PowerPoint's line tools (such as Line, Curve, Freeform, and Scribble) to draw your own motion path. You can find out more about line tools in Chapter 6.

Here are few techniques for working with motion paths:

✔ After you draw a motion path, you can resize and move it.

✔ Preset motion paths always start from the exact center of the selected object that is being animated over the path. Custom paths can start wherever you want, but if you start drawing them close enough to the center of the selected object, PowerPoint will helpfully snap it right to the center of the object.

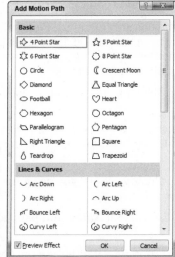

Figure 12-9:
How do I
move you?
Choose
from 64
options.

✔ By default, motion paths are unlocked. This means that the motion path moves if you move the slide object to which they are applied. You can change this to locked within the Custom Animation pane, which "locks" the motion path to its placement on the slide.

✔ You'll find a green back end of an arrow at the starting point of a motion path, and a red arrow pointer at the end.

You can find more information and resources for motion paths on this book's companion Web site:

```
www.cuttingedgeppt.com/motionpaths
```

Trigger animations

Trigger animations work with On Click animation events. In this case, the object being clicked doesn't perform the trigger animation; instead, it triggers another object on the slide to animate — hence the name *trigger animation*.

Make sure you have two images available to create a trigger animation — several sample images are available on the CD attached to this book. Then follow these steps to create a simple trigger animation sequence:

1. **Insert two images of the same size within a blank slide in a new presentation; make sure you place the two images in different areas of the slide.**

   To insert an image, click the Insert tab on the Ribbon, click the Picture button, and navigate your folders to choose a picture.

2. (Optional) Add more descriptive names to the pictures.

By default, PowerPoint names the pictures Picture 1, Picture 2, and so on. It's a good idea to access the Selection and Visibility task pane and then rename the pictures to something more descriptive. For example, **canyonpicture** is easier to remember than **Picture 4**!

You can find out more about the Selection and Visibility task pane in Chapter 5.

3. Select one of the images and activate the Custom Animation pane by clicking the Animation tab on the Ribbon and then clicking the Custom Animation button.

If the Custom Animation pane is already visible, you can ignore this step, but make sure that the picture is selected.

4. Click the Add Effect button in the Custom Animation pane and then choose an Entrance animation.

You could use any Entrance animation type, but for the purpose of this tutorial, I like the Appear animation because it happens almost instantly — that seems like a trigger. By default, PowerPoint chooses an On Click animation event for the Start options, which is what you should use for this example.

5. Select the animation in the Custom Animation pane and click the down arrow to reveal a drop-down list.

6. Select the Timing option in that menu, as shown in Figure 12-10.

This opens the Timing tab in the Appear dialog box, as shown in Figure 12-11.

7. Click the Triggers button to reveal more options:

a. Choose Start Effect on Click Of.

b. Choose the name of the second image you inserted on the slide.

c. Click OK.

8. Play the presentation. Clicking the visible image triggers the visibility of the other image.

A sample trigger presentation can be found on the CD.

You can find more resources on trigger animations on the companion Web site:

    www.cuttingedgeppt.com/triggeranimations

When choosing which type of animation you want to use, remember that animation effects that aren't commonly used are listed under the More Effects option.

Figure 12-10:
Timing
triggers.

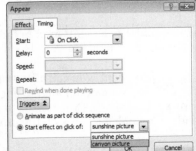

Figure 12-11:
Set the
trigger
action.

Timing Animations with the Advanced Timeline

Let me start with these questions:

✔ What happens when you want your animation to be a little faster or slower and the speed presets don't work for you?

✔ What do you do when you want two animations to start at the same time, but you want one of them to end two seconds before the other?

That sort of ultimate animation control in PowerPoint is possible through the *Advanced Timeline*.

Follow these steps to access the Advanced Timeline:

1. **Add an animation to any object on a slide by**

   • Following the instructions provided in the "Adding an Animation" section, earlier in this chapter.

   • Opening any sample presentation from the CD included with this book and selecting an animated object.

2. **Activate the Custom Animation pane if it is not already visible.**

   To activate this task pane, click the Custom Animation button found on the Animation tab of the Ribbon.

3. **Select any object in the task pane and click the down arrow next to it to reveal a flyout menu.**

4. **Choose the Show Advanced Timeline option in the flyout menu (refer to Figure 12-10).**

   The task pane changes to show the timeline.

5. **To work more effectively with the Timeline, move it below the slide by dragging the title bar of the task pane to the bottom of the screen, as shown in Figure 12-12.**

6. **Edit the animation by using the guidelines mentioned in the following section, "Using the timeline."**

If you are working in a dual monitor environment, you can also drag the entire Advanced Timeline (and the Custom Animation pane) to another monitor. This gives you much more working space. Drag it back to the edge of the PowerPoint application window to dock it again with the program.

When you're done editing timings in the timeline, you can get back to the normal Custom Animation pane by following these steps:

1. **Select any object in the timeline.**

2. **Click the down-arrow to the right of the object listing to reveal a flyout menu.**

3. **Choose Hide Advanced Timeline.**

Using the timeline

The Advanced Timeline is fairly easy to use, and these guidelines ensure that you get it right the first time:

✔ The main advantage of using the Advanced Timeline is that you can control the time factor to the most minute level — you aren't limited to the time/speed presets that PowerPoint provides. Thus, you can create a very, very slow animation that spans a whole minute or more by just dragging the start and end points for any animation in the timeline.

✔ The timeline provides a more intuitive look at which events happen at the same time or overlap — again, changing those timings is as easy as pulling the start and end points, or dragging the whole animation bar to a different place in the timeline.

✔ You can zoom in and out of the timeline. Just click the Seconds button below the timeline to open a flyout menu with the Zoom In and Zoom Out options.

✔ After you select an animation in the timeline, right-click it to access several logical options. These same options are visible when you aren't viewing the Advanced Timeline. The one difference is that you now see a Hide Advanced Timeline option that lets you get back to the normal Custom Animation pane.

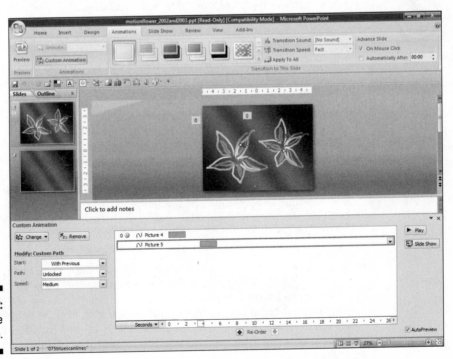

Figure 12-12:
Relocate
the timeline.

If you don't want a graphical representation of how your animation will work in relation to other animated objects on the slide, you can double-click any animation within the Custom Animation pane, click the Timing tab in the resultant dialog box (refer to Figure 12-11), and type in the number of seconds you require within the delay and speed boxes, and a number in the repeat box if you wish.

Animation guidelines

Here are some guidelines to help you use animation more optimally in your presentations:

- **Emphasize, don't distract.** You probably see presentations that flout this rule all the time — these presentations use every animation option available in PowerPoint and needlessly bury the actual message in a heap of effects.

  If you're working on a presentation, I have a simple suggestion: Use one or two common animation styles, such as fades and wipes. Then, when you need to emphasize an object or text on a few slides, use an animation effect that grabs attention and sets that slide apart from the others. By using this technique, you can ensure that your audience focuses on the important points. More important, your presentation appears professional and elegant — the fades and wipes ensure that your content flows smoothly from one concept to the next.

- **Use builds to get the message across.** *Animation builds* are the result of playing one animation after the other in a logical sequence so that the audience can grasp the content more easily. For instance, you might want the figures for the last year to be entirely visible in a chart before the present year's figures appear so you can follow them with next year's forecasts. Because all these figures are animated (and thus become visible) one at a time in sequence, the audience has a better understanding of both the figures and their relationship to the previous year's figures. This technique is even more effective when a narrative accompanies the slide: The builds appear along with the relevant voice-over.

- **Think of animation from the beginning.** Animation can be an aid to delivering content right from the conceptualization stage of the presentation. Presentation creators often insert animation as an afterthought. This lessens the creative opportunities you gain from animation by relegating it to the mundane (such as merely adding bullets to a slide) instead of using it for more interesting output. For instance, you can use animation to

  - Create effective builds in charts and graphs.

  - Show part of a diagram and then follow it up with builds to show remaining parts of the same diagram.

- Create info-graphics with PowerPoint's shapes and text boxes and then reveal each part of the info-graphic sequentially.

- Create a timeline using PowerPoint's shapes and then show logical parts of the timeline one after the other.

Animation is best used to emphasize content — this translates to using it sparingly. If you use too much animation, the audience quickly becomes distracted from the primary focus of your presentation — something you should avoid at all costs.

Saving and sharing animations

Imagine that you just spent the greater part of an hour fine-tuning an animation sequence for a single object. Your boss likes it so much that he expects you to use that style on all the slides. The only problem is that those animation settings take a long time to apply. PowerPoint can't save the animation sequences you so painstakingly created.

Thankfully, two PowerPoint add-ins let you reuse your animations:

✔ **Animation Carbon,** from Shyam Pillai, lets you save your animation styles in libraries. Thereafter, you can apply the same animations to other objects on the same presentation or even in other presentations. You can also share your animation libraries with friends and colleagues if they have a copy of Animation Carbon.

```
www.cuttingedgeppt.com/animationcarbon
```

✔ **Effects Library,** from pptXTREME, lets you work in the same way as Animation Carbon but uses menus and submenus to organize your animation sequences into easily accessed libraries.

```
www.cuttingedgeppt.com/effectslibrary
```

At the time of this writing, neither of these add-ins were yet compatible with PowerPoint 2007.

Making the Transition

The term *transition* refers to the movement (or lack of movement) that occurs when you change from one slide to another. Movement in the transition period can add interest and flow to a presentation, and you should explore these options instead of accepting PowerPoint's default, boring, movement-free transition in which one slide just rudely disappears to allow another slide to be visible.

However, don't go crazy with the numerous transitions that PowerPoint includes. The People for the Ethical Treatment of Transitions will be very angry if you use a zillion transition styles in one presentation! Try to use the same transition style for all the slides in a presentation. If that sounds like a punishment, use one or two of those showy transitions for the really important parts of the presentation.

Transition concepts

Not surprisingly, transitions have their own terminology. Here are some of the transitions options PowerPoint offers on the Animation tab of the Ribbon:

- **Transition Type:** PowerPoint ships with several built-in transitions, such as Wipes, Fades, Cut, Comb, and Dissolve.

- **Transition Speed:** Transitions happen at three speeds: Slow, Medium, and Fast.

- **Transition Sound:** You can play a sound along with a transition. If the sound is longer than the transition, it continues playing on a slide after the transition is over.

   Read Chapter 11 to find out how to use this to your advantage.

- **Advance Slide:** You can advance slides either by using the On Mouse Click event or automatically after a given period of time.

Adding transitions to slides

Follow these steps to add transitions to your slides in PowerPoint:

1. **To view the slides in Slide Sorter view, click the View tab on the Ribbon and then click the Slide Sorter button.**

   Viewing the slides in Slide Sorter view makes it easier to add transitions, especially if you want to add the same transition to multiple slides.

2. **Select one or more slides to apply the animation to.**

3. **Activate the Animations tab on the Ribbon (refer to Figure 12-1).**

4. **Click the down arrow on the bottom right of the gallery to see many more transition types in the Transitions gallery (shown in Figure 12-13); choose any of the transitions by clicking its icon.**

   PowerPoint shows you a preview of the transitions on the selected slides.

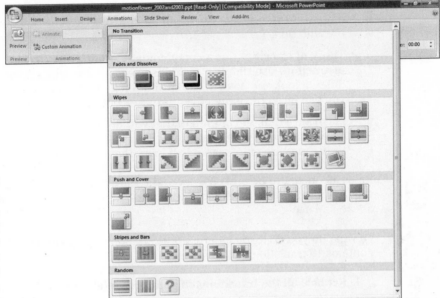

Figure 12-13:
The
Transitions
gallery
in all its
resplendent
glory.

5. **From the Transition Speed drop-down list on the Animation tab, select Slow, Medium, or Fast.**

6. **From the Transition Sound drop-down list on the Animation tab, select a sound — select No Sound if you want a silent transition.**

   This option is best left unused unless you want to use transition sounds to play or loop across slides, as explained in Chapter 11.

7. **Choose an Advance Slide option on the Animation tab by either**

   • Selecting the On Mouse Click check box to transition the slide when you click

   • Selecting the Automatically After check box and typing a time in the text box

8. **If you want to apply the transition to all slides in the presentation, click the Apply to All button on the Animation tab.**

   To apply the animation only to the selected slides, do nothing else.

Transition guidelines

Follow these transition guidelines to ensure that your transitions serve your presentation well:

✔ **Restrict your presentation to one or two transitions.** If you use more transition types, you might end up interrupting the flow of the presentation.

✔ **Think of transitions as a complement to your presentation instead of a distraction.** Use simple transitions like fades and wipes if your slides differ in look and color. If all the slides follow the same visual pattern, you can be a little more adventurous — but don't overdo it.

✔ **Make sure that all computers that will deliver the presentations you create can cope with transitions.** Transitions are resource hogs. Fancier transitions are more resource-hungry than the simpler ones.

Rules are meant to be broken — even the rules in this book. If you believe that a particular transition effect is apt for a particular presentation, go ahead and use it.

So what do you do if you inherit a presentation of a hundred slides that contains 16 transition styles? Here's help:

1. **Replace all the transitions in your presentation with fades or wipes.**

2. **Add those special transitions to one or more slides.**

3. **Play the presentation to make sure that the presentation flow isn't interrupted by the special transitions.**

Part IV

Communicating Beyond the PowerPoint Program

The 5th Wave   By Rich Tennant

CAUTION
LIVE SNAKES

So old Dave's presentations are boring? They're dull, huh? "Add some dynamic content," they said. I'll give you dynamic content...

In this part . . .

This part is about doing more with your created presentations. From interactivity and quizzes to sharing and delivering, this part has it all.

Chapter 13

Interactivity and Linking

In This Chapter

▶ Discovering anchors, hyperlinks, and targets

▶ Putting Action Buttons into action

▶ Creating links that take you wherever you want to go

▶ Getting rid of link problems

▶ Becoming a quiz master

*L*inking (or *hyperlinking*) is connecting one object to another object or an action. In PowerPoint, linking is much like networking a few computers — the value of the whole is always greater than the sum of the parts.

Interactivity is the result of linking and raises PowerPoint presentations to a whole new level. With interactivity, you can link to slides on the same or another presentation. In fact, you can even link to another document on your computer or on the Internet. Take interactivity to its extremes, and you can even create an interactive quiz inside PowerPoint, as I show you in this chapter. And yes, you can also link an object to an action, such as ending a presentation with a click.

All this interactivity might lead you to believe that PowerPoint is a great tool for creating multimedia demos and CBTs (Computer Based Training). However, that's not the entire truth: Although it's possible to create multimedia demos and CBTs using PowerPoint, they tend to be fairly basic.

Linking All the Stuff

Linking has three distinct ingredients:

> ✔ **Anchor:** The object that contains the hyperlink. Any object on a PowerPoint slide can be an anchor. Typical anchors include Action Buttons or other shapes, images, and text. (I show you more about Action Buttons later in this chapter.)

   ✔ **Hyperlink:** The address of the target contained within the anchor — for example, the path to a document on your computer or a Web site's URL. It's the functionality that links the anchor to the target.

   ✔ **Target:** The object or information that launches as the result of clicking the anchor and causing the hyperlink to activate. Such targets can be another slide within the same presentation or a Web site that opens in your browser.

All about Action Buttons

Action Buttons are special types of shapes that are meant to be used exclusively as anchors for links. They contain overlaid symbols (such as common icons for Home, Back, and Forward) so users understand what action clicking an Action Button will cause. Figure 13-1 shows a sample of the Action Button types that PowerPoint provides.

Action Buttons share almost all the same attributes as other shapes in PowerPoint, including versatile fills, lines, and effects. To discover more about fills and lines for shapes, refer to Chapter 6.

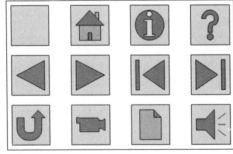

Figure 13-1:
Action
Buttons on
display!

Follow these steps to insert an Action Button on your slide:

   1. **Select the Insert or Home tab on the Ribbon and then click the Shapes button to view the Shapes gallery.**

   2. **Scroll down to see a category called Action Buttons.**

   3. **Select any of the Action Buttons and click once on the slide to create an instance of the Action Button.**

      When you create an Action Button, PowerPoint brings up the two-tabbed Action Settings dialog box, as shown in Figure 13-2.

Figure 13-2:
The Action
Settings
dialog box.

If you want to create a hyperlink, you can now use any of the options available on the Mouse Click tab to link to a slide in an existing presentation or to another presentation, document, or Web URL. I explain these options in upcoming sections of this chapter.

After you close the Action Settings dialog box, you can resize the Action Button to your liking by dragging one of its corners.

You can summon the Action Settings dialog box for any object on a slide by selecting the object and clicking the Action button on the Insert tab of the Ribbon.

Linking within the same presentation

Follow these steps to link any PowerPoint object to a slide in the same presentation:

1. **Select the anchor.**

   This could be any PowerPoint object, such as text, an Action Button, another shape, or an image.

2. **Click the Insert tab on the Ribbon and then click the Action button, as shown in Figure 13-3.**

   This brings up the Action Settings dialog box (refer to Figure 13-2). Make sure you select the Mouse Click tab of the dialog box.

3. Click the Hyperlink To drop-down list to find several options.

The following are some of the options that let you link to another slide within the same presentation:

- *Next Slide* links to the next slide in the presentation.

- *Previous Slide* links to the previous slide in the presentation.

- *First Slide* links to the first slide of the presentation.

- *Last Slide* links to the last slide of the presentation.

- *Last Slide Viewed* links to the slide viewed before the current slide. For instance, if you move from slide 7 to the first slide of the presentation, the Last Slide Viewed option takes you back to slide 7.

- *Slide* summons the Hyperlink to Slide dialog box, shown in Figure 13-4, which lets you link to any specific slide in the presentation.

Figure 13-3: Change the Action Settings.

Figure 13-4: Hyperlink to any slide you fancy!

4. **After you have chosen which slide you want to link to, click OK to apply this interactivity option.**

Linking to other presentations

Instead of creating presentations with hundreds of slides that are a mess to navigate, you might prefer to create multiple presentations with fewer slides and then link between slides of different presentations.

Presentations with fewer slides play more smoothly and are snappier with animation timings when compared with presentations with more slides.

Follow these steps to link to another presentation:

1. **Navigate to the slide from which you want to link to another PowerPoint presentation and select the anchor.**

   This could be any PowerPoint object such as text, an Action Button, another shape, or an image.

2. **Click the Insert tab on the Ribbon and then click the Action button to come face-to-face with the Action Settings dialog box (refer to Figure 13-2).**

3. **Select the Mouse Click tab in the Action Settings dialog box.**

4. **From the Hyperlink To drop-down list, select Other PowerPoint Presentation.**

   This opens the Hyperlink to Other PowerPoint Presentation dialog box shown in Figure 13-5.

Mouse Click and Mouse Over

The Action Settings dialog box has two tabs:

✔ **Mouse Click:** By default, the active tab is always Mouse Click. Any action that you choose on this tab is initiated by a mouse click.

✔ **Mouse Over:** On this tab, the actions work in the same way, but merely moving the

cursor over the anchor object triggers the actions. Be careful about using this or you'll wonder why mysterious things happen while your presentation plays!

5. Browse to the presentation that you want to link to and click OK.

A new dialog box (similar to the dialog box in Figure 13-4) will pop up with a list of slides in the presentation you linked to in the preceding step.

6. Select the slide in the second presentation that you want to link to and click OK.

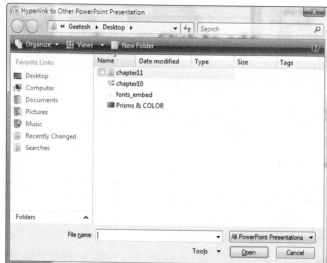

Figure 13-5:
Link to another presentation.

By default, the first slide is selected, but you can choose any other appropriate slide.

7. Click OK again in the Action Settings dialog box to apply the link to the anchor.

You can create a menu slide presentation that links to all your other presentations. Just place all presentations in a single folder and then create a new single-slide presentation in that folder with links to all the presentations. If you need to share these presentations along with the menu presentation, just copy the entire folder!

Always place all linked presentations within the same folder before creating the links. This advice is invaluable if you need to move the presentations to another computer.

Linking to other documents and Web URLs

PowerPoint's linking capabilities let you link an object on a slide to almost any document on your computer — and even on the Internet. Follow these steps to link to other documents and Web URLs:

1. **Select any object on a slide that you want to use as an anchor for your link.**

2. **Click the Insert tab on the Ribbon and then click the Action button to come face-to-face with the Action Settings dialog box (refer to Figure 13-2).**

3. **Select the Mouse Click tab of the Action Settings dialog box.**

4. **From the Hyperlink To drop-down list, select one of the following options:**

    • *Other File* lets you link to any other file or document on your computer.

      This option spawns the Hyperlink to Other File dialog box. You navigate to and select the file or document that you want to link to.

    • *URL* lets you link to any Web URL or e-mail address.

      For a Web URL, just type the address in the Hyperlink to URL dialog box (see Figure 13-6).

      If you want to use the link to create an e-mail, type **mailto:** and the e-mail address in the Hyperlink to URL dialog box, like this:

      ```
      mailto:name@domain.com
      ```

      When you click a live e-mail link, your default e-mail application opens with a new, blank e-mail message window, with the address that follows `mailto:` in the To box.

Figure 13-6:
Connect your presentations to Web URLs!

Hyperlink To URL
URL:
http://www.cuttingedgeppt.com
OK   Cancel

5. **Click OK to apply the link to the anchor.**

In the next chapter, you can find more information about linking to specific bookmarks in Microsoft Word files or to specific cells of Microsoft Excel spreadsheets.

Transparent hot spots make great links

When you create a link anchor from text, you normally end up with underlined text that looks like a conventional hyperlink, as shown in Figure 13-7.

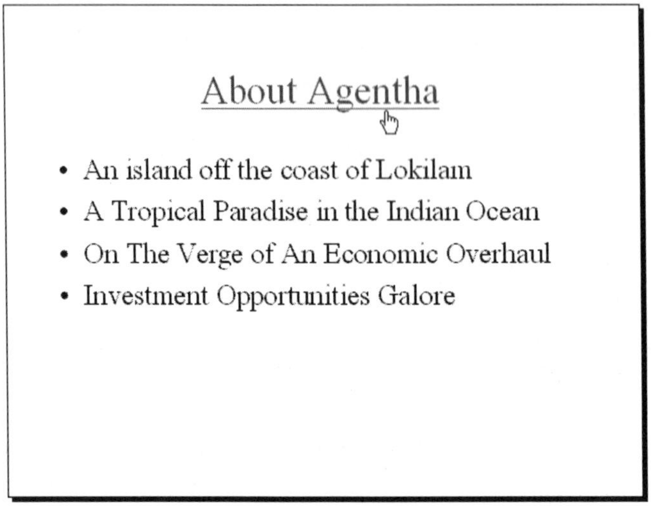

About Agentha

- An island off the coast of Lokilam
- A Tropical Paradise in the Indian Ocean
- On The Verge of An Economic Overhaul
- Investment Opportunities Galore

Figure 13-7:
A conventional text hyperlink.

Most of the time, this won't bother you. But sometimes you don't want the text to be underlined. This might be because you want the slide to have a clean look, or maybe you want to click that hyperlink only if necessary, and so you prefer that the audience not be aware of the hyperlink.

Follow these steps to create transparent hyperlinks without the underlines:

1. **Type some text in a text placeholder or text box and position it exactly as you want it on the slide.**

2. **On the Insert tab of the Ribbon, select the Shapes option to see the Shapes gallery. Select the Rectangle tool and draw a rectangle over the text you want to hyperlink.**

   Make sure that the rectangle covers the entire hyperlink area.

3. **With the rectangle selected, assign a hyperlink to the rectangle by clicking the Action button on the Insert tab of the Ribbon.**

   This opens the Action Settings dialog box (refer to Figure 13-2).

4. **Hyperlink to wherever you want.**

   You can find more details about your linking options in previous sections of this chapter.

5. **After you have created the hyperlink, select the rectangle, right-click, and choose Format↪Shape.**

   This brings up the Format Shape dialog box.

6. **In the Fill tab, set the Transparency attribute to 100%. In the Line Color tab, again set the Transparency attribute to 100%.**

7. **Click Close to get back to the slide.**

Another option for creating a transparent text link is to apply the Action Settings to the entire text box and not to just a part of the text. Select the entire text box (while making sure that no individual text is selected) and then apply the links.

Overcoming Link Problems

If you ever wondered why PowerPoint is unable find the link to your spreadsheet or video file, you aren't alone. These link problems happen because remembering links isn't PowerPoint's strong point. Perhaps you always just blamed yourself for what wasn't your fault!

The solution is actually simpler than the problem: PowerPoint isn't too good at remembering links, which saves you the trouble of understanding *absolute* and *relative* links.

The easiest link option is to place all the content for a presentation in a single folder even before you create the presentation or start inserting links. Follow this rule and you'll be happy:

> *Think about folders that contain presentations; don't just think about presentations.*

If you flout this rule, you might run into all sorts of link problems.

If you don't have time for link problems, follow these guidelines:

- ✓ **Conceptualize your presentation.** *Conceptualize* is a very impressive-sounding verb, but in this case, it simply means that you start by creating an empty folder for each of your presentations.

- ✓ **Before you link any sound or video files or other documents, copy all these files to the same folder and then link to them in your PowerPoint slide.**

  Don't even create subfolders within that folder — keep all the files loose in the same folder!

- ✓ **For other PowerPoint presentations that you need to link to, copy the presentation with all linked files to the same folder and then link them.** Also ensure that all the links in the copied presentation are working!

- ✓ **When you finish creating the presentation and all its links, just copy the entire folder to your laptop or anybody else's computer if required, and you will have no link problems.**

- ✓ **If you need to e-mail the folder, just archive the entire folder into a Zip file and e-mail it as an attachment.**

Even if you take every precaution, you can still run into link problems. Or maybe you receive someone else's presentations, and that person was not half as good as you with links. I recommend that you download a copy of FixLinks Pro, a PowerPoint add-in that fixes or re-links missing links.

FixLinks Pro also copies all linked files to the same folder. This can be very helpful if you didn't place all files in the same folder before you linked to them from within the presentation.

You can download a trial version of FixLinks Pro from

`www.cuttingedgeppt.com/fixlinkspro`

At the time of this writing, FixLinks Pro was not yet compatible with PowerPoint 2007.

Create a Simple Quiz

Quizzes are so much fun — especially if you win prizes for the right answers. I show you how to create a quiz in PowerPoint that you can

✔ Show after a business presentation as an excuse to give away corporate gifts.

✔ Use in a school environment after a lesson to ascertain how much the students understand.

✔ Use in a fund-raising event or anywhere else.

Regardless of why you need a quiz, creating it inside PowerPoint is easy and intuitive. In this tutorial, I show you how to create a multiple-choice quiz. The best part is that you don't need to use any programming at all!

You can find a sample quiz presentation on the CD attached to this book.

Quiz material

Quiz slides require *questions* and *visuals:*

✔ Choose questions that can each have only one correct answer.

Five questions is a good number to start with.

✔ Use visuals to make the slides look interesting.

Defining *interesting* is up to you. Perfect quiz presentations can be created without pictures, too, but where's the fun in that?!

Presentation steps

When you have your quiz material, you're ready to create a quiz presentation in PowerPoint. First, create a new PowerPoint presentation. Next, create your question slides and then link your questions into a quiz.

Creating the question slides

Each question requires a set of three slides:

✔ The question slide

✔ The slide with the correct answer and a congratulatory note

✔ The slide that says that the answer is incorrect and prompts the participant to try again

Create a new PowerPoint presentation for your quiz and then follow these steps for each question in your quiz:

1. **Insert a new slide that uses the Title Only slide layout by clicking the Home tab and then clicking the arrow below the New Slide button.**

2. **In the Layout gallery that appears, select the Title Only layout.**

3. **Type a question in the Title placeholder.**

   If you have any pictures, add them to the slide.

4. **Add the answers to the slide.**

   a. Add a text box on the slide for each possible answer.

   b. Type each possible answer into a separate text box, as shown in Figure 13-8.

   Only one of the answers should be correct.

Three is a nice number of answers — one right answer and two wrong answers make a good combination so the slide doesn't look crowded with answer choices.

Figure 13-8: What's the right answer?

5. **Create a *correct* slide.**

   Type the correct answer on the *correct* slide, as shown in Figure 13-9.

   You can also include inspirational quotations, words of wisdom, or embarrassing pictures of your coworkers on the slide. Be creative!

6. Create an *incorrect* slide.

On the *incorrect* slide, I suggest that users go back to the question slide again and make another choice, as you can see in Figure 13-10.

You can also offer words of encouragement, silly pictures, or embarrassing pictures of your coworkers (especially if they are part of the audience!).

7. **Return to the question slide.**

8. **Link from each answer on the question slide to either the *correct* or *incorrect* slide as follows:**

   a. *Select an answer text box on the question slide.*

   Select the text box, not the actual text.

   b. *Click the Insert tab on the Ribbon and then click the Action button to summon the Action Settings dialog box. (Refer to Figure 13-2.)*

   c. *Select the Mouse Click tab in the Action Settings dialog box and then choose the Slide option from the Hyperlink To drop-down list.*

   This summons the Hyperlink to Slide dialog box (refer to Figure 13-4).

   d. *Create a hyperlink to the* correct *or* incorrect *answer slide.*

Linking the answer slides to the original or next question slides

When you have a presentation with all the necessary slides, you're ready to link the questions into a quiz:

✔ For each *incorrect* answer slide, create a link that enables the viewer to see the question again and attempt to answer it correctly. Add a link to the actual question slide so that users can attempt to answer the question again.

✔ On all the *correct* answer slides, provide a link to the next question slide.

Save your presentation!

Chapter 14

Preparing and Delivering Your Awesome Presentation

. . . .

In This Chapter

▶ Checking that presentation again

▶ Setting up a show

▶ Protecting your slides from prying eyes

▶ Creating Custom Shows within your presentation

▶ Printing your presentation

▶ Making your handouts compelling

. . . .

*Y*our presentation flows smoothly from slide to slide. Every slide is perfect, the animations enhance the concept and visualization of the presentation, and the message has been fine-tuned. When you have finished creating your presentation, it's show time! It's time to get ready to give your presentation.

Don't plug in the projectors just yet. It's time for testing and rethinking — subjects I discuss in this chapter.

I also discuss how to set up your shows and create custom presentations. Then I proceed to the holy grail of PowerPoint — password protection — and end with information about printing your presentation and making compelling and effective handouts to complement your presentation.

Test and Retest Your Presentation

Finding and correcting your own mistakes is one thing. It's an altogether different experience to see them in 32-point Arial with the rest of your audience. Mistakes happen, and it is far better to find and correct them *before* you're presenting.

Awesome delivery ideas for the presenter

After you have taken all precautions and tested your presentation a zillion times, it's time for the showing. Here are some awesome delivery ideas that will ensure that your presentation is a huge success:

✔ **Be sincere.** All the other tricks come to naught if you don't follow the simple principle of being sincere. By *being sincere*, I mean that you should never discuss a topic that you don't know thoroughly. It also means that you don't try to mislead or divert the audience from the truth. Audiences are very perceptive and can recognize a lack of sincerity within moments.

✔ **Be humble.** Even if you are the expert, you don't have to rule over your audience. In many cultures, a person who is not humble is as good as a closed door. And if you are presenting, you most certainly want to come across as open and ready to hear.

✔ **Wear understated clothing and jewelry.** Restrain the urge to wear brightly colored clothes or too much jewelry; your presentation, not you, should be the focus of attention.

Take care to ensure that your clothing is appropriate for the audience and location. A business-casual look should work in most situations, although there are exceptions where you'll need to wear formal attire (a suit), such as for a company board meeting, or more casual wear (jeans), such as for a neighborhood community meeting.

✔ **Don't put junk in your pockets.** I remember a presenter who had so much loose change or keys in his trouser pockets that the constant jingling drowned out his presentation!

✔ **Identify with your audience.** Make sure that you greet anyone you recognize in the audience before you begin. This helps break the ice and involves the audience.

But don't just focus on those familiar people all through the presentation — there are others in the audience too!

✔ **Weave some humor into your narrative.** However, don't carry this too far, and stay away from any humor that might be considered inappropriate for any reason.

✔ **Encourage the audience to ask questions.** If you're discussing multiple topics, you might want to ask for questions often during the presentation. Alternatively, you might want to reserve some time for questions at the end of the presentation.

✔ **Try to weave in some audience activity during or after the presentation.** For example, give the audience a brief quiz, or ask them to play a short game. Audiences love interactivity.

Follow these guidelines to iron out all the wrinkles in your presentation:

✔ **Practice your presentations out loud.** You don't need an audience for this testing. You can also speak out loud along with your slides and simultaneously record your narration on a voice recorder. Then, listen to your recording and pay attention to any areas that require improvement in wording, delivery, or timing.

✔ **Show your slides to a colleague or family member and ask for an honest opinion.** You will be surprised to find the improvements that you can make when you view your presentation from another perspective.

✔ **Test your presentation at the venue a day or several hours before the showing.**

- *Make sure that the projector is in working order.* The projector might display colors a little differently than the monitor on your computer or laptop, so check to make sure your presentation looks just as good projected on the big screen as it does on your computer.

- *If you're using a remote control device to advance slides, make sure that it works.* Also make sure that you have extra batteries for the remote control close by!

- *Make sure that the text is readable from a distance.* If possible, project your presentation in the venue and then go sit in the last row to make certain that everyone in the audience will be able to read the text.

✔ **If you're working in a cross-platform environment, make sure that you test the presentation on both Windows and Mac computers.**

✔ **Don't change any settings on your laptop at the last minute.** Software and hardware configurations differ from system to system and can wreak havoc with your carefully fine-tuned timings.

✔ **Keep a backup copy of your presentation on a USB drive or CD just in case.** For the same reason, keep a printed copy of your presentation with you at all times.

✔ **Call me paranoid, but I suggest that you e-mail a copy of the presentation to your Web e-mail account so that you can access it in an emergency.** It doesn't hurt to be safe!

Setting Up Your Presentation

You have more than one way to set up your PowerPoint show — and most of these options stem from the fact that presenting situations differ all the time. For instance, you might want to present

✔ A conventional presentation in which you move from slide to slide and speak to the audience

✔ A slide show presentation that includes many pictures along with a background music score

✔ A pre-narrated presentation for those times when you can't make it to an event

✔ A kiosk-style presentation that runs unattended at exhibitions

✔ A touch-screen–style presentation that moves to another slide only at the click of an Action Button.

Whichever type of show you present, your first stop has to be the Set Up Show dialog box, shown in Figure 14-1. You access this dialog box by clicking the Slide Show tab on the Ribbon and then clicking the Set Up Slide Show button.

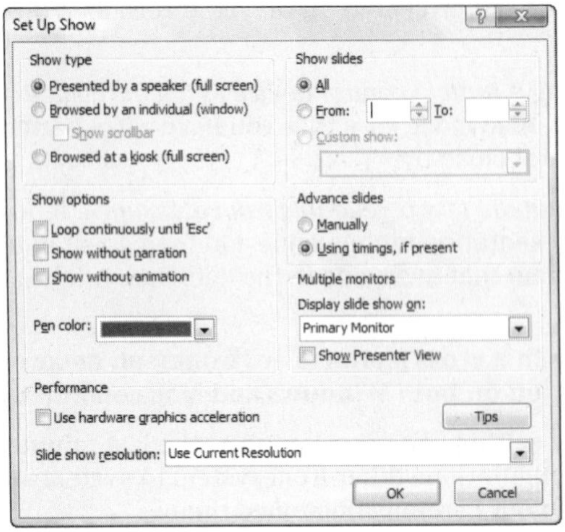

Figure 14-1:
Make your
PowerPoint
shows
behave
themselves!

You have many options in the Set Up Show dialog box. Just select or change the options to your liking, click OK, and you're good to go.

  ✔ **Show Type:**

    • *Presented by a Speaker (Full Screen):* This is the default choice and relates to the conventional use of a live speaker in attendance during the presentation. The presentation plays full screen. All keyboard shortcuts work, and you can use either a mouse, keyboard, or a presentation remote control to navigate between slides.

    • *Browsed by an Individual (Window):* This option (see Figure 14-2) doesn't play the presentation full screen. This mode is best suited for quick edits and reviews or for an in-house presentation.

      You can also select the Show Scrollbar option, which displays the scroll bar toward the right of the slide.

    • *Browsed at a Kiosk (Full Screen):* Use this mode in a trade fair or exhibition. This mode automatically loops the entire presentation. The cursor is also visible all the time so that the audience can move between slides easily. For this mode to be effective, make sure you've put in automatic transition times for each slide in the presentation or that you've provided Action buttons on each slide so that users can navigate between slides.

      Transitions are covered in Chapter 12, andAction buttons are explained in Chapter 13.

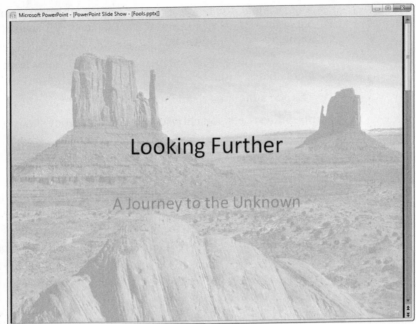

Microsoft PowerPoint - [PowerPoint Slide Show - [Fools.pptx]]

Looking Further

A Journey to the Unknown

Figure 14-2:
Individual
browsing in
PowerPoint.

✔ **Show Slides:**

- *All:* This option shows all the slides in your presentation except the *hidden slides.* See the section, "Slides behind Veils," later in this chapter, for the lowdown on hidden slides.

- *From* and *To:* These options allow you to choose a series of slide numbers that you want to display.

- *Custom Show:* This option lets you play a custom show you've created within the active presentation. If this option is grayed out, you have no custom shows created. See the "Custom Shows" section, later in this chapter, for more information.

✔ **Show Options:** These options allow you to choose specific viewing options. Some of these might be grayed out depending on the Show type you choose.

- *Loop Continuously until 'Esc':* This option is selected by default if you selected the Browsed at Kiosk option. For all show types, selecting this option loops the presentation continuously until you press the Escape key.

- *Show without Narration:* Select this option to play the presentation without any added narration. This works only if you have used PowerPoint's own Record Narration feature — if you have inserted narratives through recordings made outside PowerPoint, this feature won't work.

- *Show without Animation:* This option plays the presentation without animation — all slides that contain animated elements appear in the post-animation stage.

- *Pen Color:* This setting lets you choose a pen color from a convenient color swatch box.

  The *pen* annotates a slide while it is being shown (or projected).

✔ **Advance Slides:** Lets you choose how you want your slides to progress one after the other.

- *Manually:* Select this option to advance slides manually — this overrides any set transition times within the slides.

- *Using Timings, If Present:* The default option, selecting this tells PowerPoint to follow the slide timings set in the Slide Transition properties.

✔ **Multiple monitors:** If you don't have a multiple-monitor setup, this option is grayed out.

- *Display Slide Show On:* This drop-down list lets you choose the monitor for the presentation.

- *Show Presenter View:* Selecting this check box enables the Presenter View, a special multi-monitor viewing mode that shows you thumbnails of slides and previews the next slide that's coming up after the one being shown. It also shows the elapsed time since the presentation started and provides a convenient End Show button.

✔ **Performance:**

- *Use Hardware Graphics Acceleration:* This option turns on graphic acceleration if your computer has the capability. If you notice more sluggish performance with PowerPoint shows after you select this option, deselect the check box.

- *Slide Show Resolution:* This drop-down list lets you change the resolution of the presentation playback — if your presentation is running smoothly, don't change the default settings.

If you're up to it, experiment with all the settings to figure out which works best for you.

Slides behind Veils

PowerPoint slides can hide behind veils — but they can also decide to come out of hiding if the situation demands. No, this isn't some soap opera plot; PowerPoint provides an option to hide some slides that contain information not suitable for all eyes. These slides are visible in editing mode; they just decide to play the invisible game when the show is playing.

You may decide to use the hidden slides feature if

✔ You want to include some backup slides in the presentation, which you can unhide if the situation demands.

✔ Your boss surprises you with an announcement you that you have to give a presentation in 15 minutes. You already have a presentation that's fairly suitable for the occasion, but it contains some unnecessary or off-topic slides. You decide that hiding a few unsuitable slides seems like a better idea than creating an entirely new presentation.

✔ You need to remove some slides but you don't want to delete them because you might regret that later — so hiding them is a better idea!

If any of these tricks sound like something you want up your sleeve, follow these steps to hide one or more slides in your presentation:

1. **Click the the View tab on the Ribbon and then click the Slide Sorter option to view thumbnails of all slides in the presentation.**

2. **Select one or more slides in the presentation.**

   You can select multiple consecutive slides by clicking the first slide and then Shift+clicking the last slide in the series.

   You can select multiple, nonconsecutive slides by clicking the first slide and then Ctrl+clicking each additional slide you want to select.

3. **Click the Slide Show tab on the Ribbon and then click the Hide Slide option to hide the selected slides.**

   This is a toggle option — you select the same slides and click the Hide Slide button again to unhide the slides.

   You can also right-click a slide thumbnail in Slide Show view (or in the Slides pane in Normal view), and choose the Hide Slide option from the context menu (see Figure 14-3).

Figure 14-3:
Shhh! Hide those slides.

Custom Shows

A *custom show* is a set of slides chosen within a presentation that acts like another presentation. Why would you want your presentation to have a dual side of its existence?

✔ You need to create umpteen versions of the same presentation, each containing a subset of that hundred-slide presentation that was created many moons ago. Do you find yourself creating 25- and 40-slide abridged or specialized versions of the same presentation?

✔ You need to insert the same slide multiple times within the same presentation — for example, you might want the Agenda slide to show up after each section in a long presentation.

✔ Just for once, you need to rearrange a few slides.

✔ You don't want to create multiple presentations that contain the same slides — it's such a blessing not to edit those charts in multiple presentations!

Creating custom shows

Follow these steps to create a custom show:

1. **Select the Slide Show tab on the Ribbon and choose Custom Slide Show⇨Custom Shows to summon the Custom Shows dialog box, shown in Figure 14-4.**

Figure 14-4: Custom shows for all occasions.

2. **Click New to bring up the Define Custom Show dialog box, shown in Figure 14-5.**

3. **Give your custom show a name.**

   By default, PowerPoint just calls it *Custom Show 1,* but you can call it *My Marketing Slides* or *Employee Orientation* or something that you can remember easily.

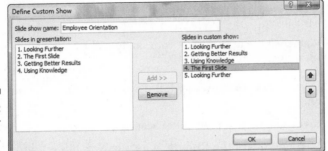

Figure 14-5:
Make your
own shows.

4. Add the slides you want to include in the custom show.

- To add a slide, select the slide in the Slides in Presentation box and click the Add button; the slide appears in the Slides in Custom Show box.

  You can add the same slide more than once.

- To remove added slides, just select them in the Slides in Custom Show box and click the Remove button.

- You can also reorder the sequence of the slides, by selecting the slide within the Slides in Custom Show box, and then using the arrow buttons towards the right of the dialog box.

5. Click OK to create the custom show or click Cancel to exit without changes.

This brings you back to the Custom Shows dialog box. If you have already created some custom shows, you'll find them all listed here.

To view any of the custom shows, just select them in the list and click the Show button. You can also select a custom show and click the Remove, Edit, or Copy button to remove, edit, or copy the selected show.

If you want one of your custom shows to run as the default presentation, just change the settings in the Set Up Show dialog box, accessed by clicking the Set Up Slide Show option (found on the Slide Show tab of the Ribbon). I discuss this in more detail earlier in this chapter.

You might change the default show to one of your custom shows and forget all about it. And you know what happens when you play that presentation six months later — you end up with an audience that isn't too amused. Head to the Slide Show tab of the Ribbon and click the Set Up Slide Show option. Change the play settings and breathe a sigh of relief! Even better, link to your custom shows rather than setting them as default shows — I show you how to do that next.

Linking to custom shows

If you want an easier way to access your custom shows, follow these steps to create a link slide in your presentation:

1. **Create your custom shows by following the steps in the preceding section.**

   Test them all and give them nice, descriptive names.

2. **On the Home tab of the Ribbon, click the New Slide button to add a new slide in your presentation.**

   Change your slide layout if required by clicking the Layout button (found on the Home tab) — this brings up the Layout gallery.

3. **Add anchors for links to custom shows.**

   These anchors could be any PowerPoint object, such as text boxes, shapes (including Action Buttons), and pictures. Figure 14-6 shows a sample link slide I created.

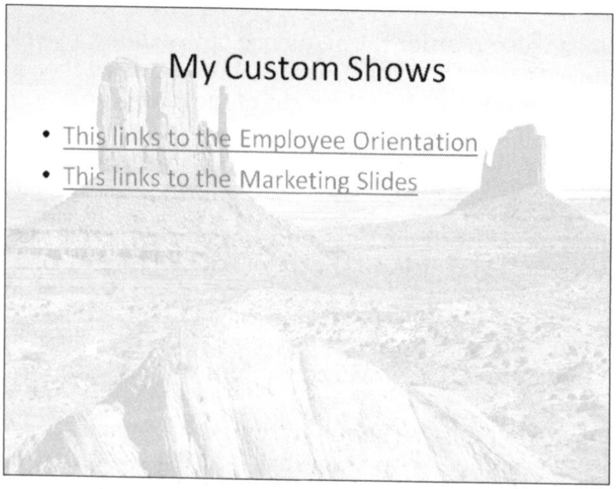

Figure 14-6: Create a link-head-quarters slide!

4. **Select one of the anchors, and on the Insert tab of the Ribbon, click the Action option to bring up the Action Settings dialog box shown in Figure 14-7.**

5. **In the Hyperlink To drop-down list, choose the Custom Show option to summon the Link To Custom Show dialog box, revealed in Figure 14-8.**

6. **All your custom shows are listed here — just select the one you want to link to and click OK.**

   Select the Show and Return option in the Link To Custom Show dialog box to return to the link slide after the custom show has finished playing.

If no custom shows are listed here, that means you haven't created any custom shows in the presentation — trek back to the earlier section, "Creating custom shows," to discover how you create custom shows.

7. Click OK in the Action Settings dialog box to get back to your presentation.

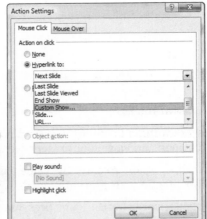

Figure 14-7: Action settings link to custom shows!

Figure 14-8: Choose your custom show.

Password Options in PowerPoint

In today's world, it's perfectly acceptable to be paranoid and safe. PowerPoint helps you protect the information in your presentations by providing password protection options.

Follow these steps to password protect a presentation:

1. Choose Office➪Save As to bring up the Save As dialog box.

2. Choose Tools➪General Options in the Save As dialog box.

The General Options dialog box appears, as shown in Figure 14-9.

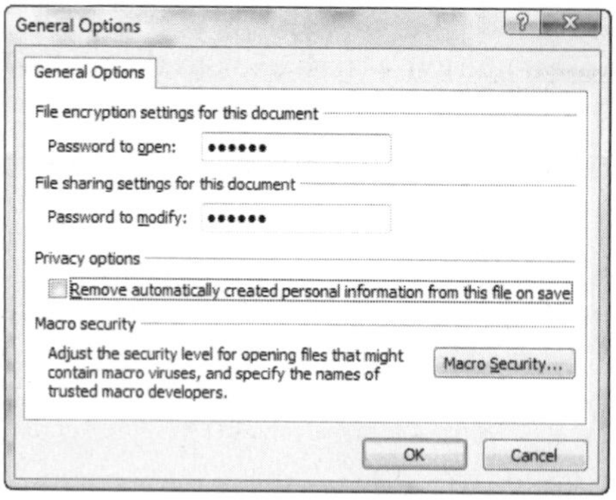

General Options

General Options

File encryption settings for this document

Password to open: ••••••

File sharing settings for this document

Password to modify: ••••••

Privacy options

☐ Remove automatically created personal information from this file on save

Macro security

Adjust the security level for opening files that might contain macro viruses, and specify the names of trusted macro developers.

Macro Security...

OK   Cancel

Figure 14-9:
Access
General
Options.

2. You can set two different passwords here:

- *Password to Open* requires others to enter the same password you type in this text box to open and view your presentation.

- *Password to Modify* requires others to enter the same password you type in this text box to edit your presentation.

You can enter both types of passwords for the same presentation; they're intended for different access permissions.

You can also enter a password just for Modify and leave out the password for Open. This allows anyone to see your presentation, but only those who know the password can edit the presentation.

3. Click OK to apply the changes or click Cancel to dismiss the dialog box.

If recipients of your password-protected presentation are using a version of PowerPoint that is older than PowerPoint 2002, they will be unable to open the presentation, even if they know the password. They will see an error message that offers no explanation about the problem because older versions don't know what a password is! For the same reason, Mac versions of PowerPoint can't open password-protected presentations.

These open and modify passwords for PowerPoint aren't intended to be completely secure. If you need that level of protection, you need to investigate Information Rights Management. I explain more about Information Rights Management on this book's companion site:

`www.cuttingedgeppt.com/irm`

More password options

The following options are for you if you need to distribute your presentations to others who use older versions of PowerPoint that don't support passwords. Here are the options:

✔ You can zip up a PowerPoint presentation and password protect the zip archive. This, however, provides full edit permissions to anyone who can provide the unzip password and view the presentation. This solution works for both Windows and Mac users.

✔ You can create an Acrobat PDF file from a PowerPoint presentation. If you have the full version of Adobe Acrobat, you can require users to enter a password to edit or even print the PDF. Recipients, however, need only the free Acrobat Reader to view the presentation. Discover more information about PDFs in the Bonus Chapter on the CD.

✔ Convert your presentation to rich media by using a rich media product like Articulate Presenter, PointeCast, or Adobe Presenter. These output options don't require passwords, but they do output to formats that cannot be edited.

PowerPoint Printing

Many PowerPoint presentations never travel the distance from the screen to the printer. But many other presentations make that trip and imprint their impressions on papyrus.

Whichever journey your presentation is destined to make, you can't deny that printing PowerPoint slides involves a hundred nuances — from choosing whether to print in color, black and white, or grayscale, to deciding on the dozens of options for printing handouts, slides, and outlines. If all those terms make you dizzy, rejoice in the fact that the following paragraphs present no new riddles, only solutions.

The headquarters of PowerPoint's print capabilities is the multifaceted Print dialog box, shown in all its glory in Figure 14-10.

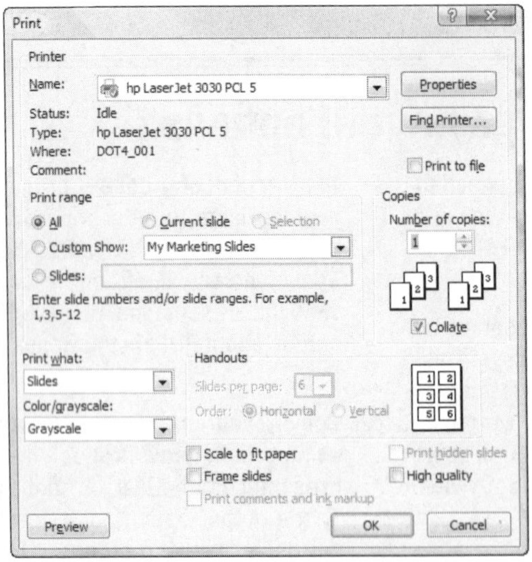

Figure 14-10:
The friendly
Print dialog
box.

Follow these steps to access and use the print options:

1. **If you made any last-minute edits, save your presentation so that all changes are committed.**

2. **Choose Office⇨Print to bring up the Print dialog box (see Figure 14-10).**

3. **Change settings as required.**

   For more information on these settings, check out the next section in this chapter.

4. **Click Preview to bring up the Print Preview window, shown in Figure 14-11, to see how your presentation will look when printed.**

   You need to have a local printer installed for the Print Preview function to work — head to Chapter 2 for more on this option.

5. **Click Print to get back to the Print dialog box, or click Close PrintPreview to get back to PowerPoint, and start all over again.**

6. **Change settings again as required. When you're done, click OK to print the presentation.**

   You can also click Cancel to dismiss the dialog box and go back to the presentation without printing.

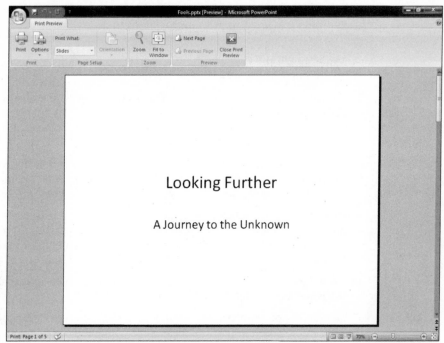

Figure 14-11:
The Print
Preview
mode.

All the print stuff

Here's a rundown of all the printing options in the Print dialog box:

✔ **Printer:** The Printer Name drop-down list lets you choose from a list of physical and virtual printers installed on your system.

- *Physical printers* include normal inkjets, laser printers, and printing devices that are connected to your computer (or network).

- *Virtual printers* are actually printer drivers that output to file formats rather than to paper. Examples include Adobe PDF, Microsoft Office Document Image Writer, and the TechSmith SnagIt printer driver.

Whichever printer you choose, make sure that you click the Properties button next to the printer drop-down list. This presents you with options specific to your printer.

✔ **Print Range:** Choose the All or Current Slide option, or type the slide numbers you want to print in the Slides text box.

You can also choose to print all slides contained in a custom show — remember, if the Custom Show option is grayed out, that's because there are no custom shows in the presentation.

You also see a Selection option. This option is grayed out unless you select one or more slides in the Slide Sorter view (on the View tab, click the Slide Sorter button) before clicking the Print option. The Selection option prints only the selected slides.

✔ **Copies:** Enter the number of copies you want to print in the Number of Copies text box or use the up and down arrows to select a number. Select the Collate check box if you want to collate your copies.

✔ **Print What:** This lets you choose from Slides, Handouts, Notes Pages, and Outline View. If you choose Handouts, you find even more options for the number of slides you want printed on each handout page. Handouts are covered in more detail later in this chapter.

✔ **Color/grayscale:** This lets you choose between color, grayscale, and pure black and white.

Depending on your printer settings, the default color mode might be either color or grayscale — make sure you make the changes to the color mode before you print. Even better, print a test page to see which mode works best for you.

Printing perils

Everyone has a few questions about printing — and here are workarounds for the most frequent printing perils.

Print proofs for free!

Depending on whether you're printing to an inkjet or laser printer, you might end up wasting tons of ink or toner if you don't create proofs before printing a hundred copies of hundred-slide presentations. If you do create a proof, one mistake might send a hundred sheets of paper to the recycle bin, rather than a thousand.

If you love to save trees and protect the environment, print your slides to a PDF first. This gives you an accurate impression of how your slides will look when printed on paper.

PowerPoint now includes PDF output capabilities with a free add-in that you can download from the Microsoft site — see the Bonus Chapter on the CD for more info.

Printing animations

In the last few versions of PowerPoint, Microsoft removed the capability to print slides in different stages of animation. This was done primarily because the new animation engine is so advanced with its new motion paths and trigger animations. If users could print these animations, most of them would end up with flipbooks rather than three or four stages per slide!

However, there's still hope. Shyam Pillai's free PowerPoint add-in, Capture Show, lets you print animated stages of a slide from PowerPoint. In addition, it can also output slide builds as images to a specified folder.

```
www.cuttingedgeppt.com/captureshow
```

The add-in wasn't PowerPoint 2007 compatible at the time of writing.

Printing for prepress

Are you asked to create posters from your PowerPoint slides? Do you need to send high-resolution slide images to a prepress agency? If you need to output something suitable for prepress usage, PowerPoint probably isn't the right tool for the job.

But that's something your boss might not know much about, and he or she doesn't understand that the wonderful pie chart you created in PowerPoint isn't appropriate for a 300 dpi, poster-size image to send to the design agency! (To find out more about dpi and resolution, check out Chapter 9.)

I could tell you about increasing the resolution output and other tedious image manipulations, but I normally just use a PowerPoint add-in from Steve Rindsberg called *PPTools Image Exporter*. You can download a demo version from this site:

```
www.cuttingedgeppt.com/imageexporter
```

Helpful Handouts

Handouts are normally sent for review to those who matter before an actual presentation is shown to an audience. They can also be provided as takeaways after the presentation.

Normally, these sheets have thumbnails of slides. You can opt to include 1, 2, 3, 4, 6, or 9 slide thumbnails per handout page. Some layouts, such as the one for 3 thumbnails, also provide some lines next to the thumbnail for notes. Figure 14-12 shows you a sample handout.

Figure 14-12:
A sample
handout.

Most of the layout options in handouts are directly influenced by the Handout Master. Thus, if you position any logo in the Handout Master, you can be reasonably sure that all handouts printed from that particular presentation will contain the logo.

Unlike slides, handouts are almost always intended for print, so it might be a good idea to edit the Handout Master based on that assumption. You need to be sure to use content that prints well to both grayscale and colored output. You can learn more about the Handout Master in Chapter 4.

Printing handouts works the same way as printing anything else in PowerPoint — refer to the section "PowerPoint Printing" for more information.

Chapter 15

Distributing, Repurposing, and Extending

*A*fter you create your presentation, print handouts, master delivery skills, and do a thousand other chores, your goal is to share your presentations with others — your mother would approve of the sharing part. To keep her happy, this chapter is about sharing.

I also discuss how to repurpose your existing PowerPoint content and how you can put your bank of thousands of PowerPoint presentations to more effective use with the new Reuse Slides feature.

Creating an Autorun CD

It wasn't until PowerPoint 2003 that Microsoft gave in to user opinion and created the autorun CD option. And that decision was very logical because PowerPoint and autorun go hand-in-hand — almost as if they were made for each other. In this section, I show you how to use this amazing feature.

An autorun PowerPoint CD contains everything — the presentation, all linked files, and a runtime version of PowerPoint. It's autorun, meaning it starts up by itself. A user just inserts it in the CD drive, and the presentation plays instantly — even on systems that don't have PowerPoint installed!

By default, all Windows installations are autorun enabled — this allows CDs that contain autorun information to splash a screen or play an EXE. For security reasons, your system administrator (or even you) might have disabled the autorun feature. In that case, the CDs you create will not autorun. Don't worry, though — you can still play the presentations by manually opening the autorun file.

Before you begin, make sure you have a CD burner attached to your computer. And yes, you also need a blank CD! Follow these steps to save an autorun version of your presentation(s) to CD:

1. **Save your presentation and then choose Office⇨Publish⇨Package for CD.**

   This summons a warning dialog box shown in Figure 15-1. Essentially, it warns you that your presentations will be saved in a format compatible with the older PowerPoint 2003 Viewer. Click OK to dismiss the warning.

Figure 15-1:
The Viewer
warning
looks stern.
You have to
accept to
continue.

You next see the Package for CD dialog box, shown in Figure 15-2.

2. **Give your CD a name in the Name the CD text box.**

Figure 15-2:
The
Package for
CD dialog
box.

3. **Click the Add Files button to add more PowerPoint files to the CD.**

You need not add the active PowerPoint presentation because that is already part of the compilation. You also don't have to worry about including any linked PowerPoint presentations or any other linked files because the Package for CD feature takes care of those for you.

Add as many presentations as you need to fit on the CD. All are listed in a sequence in the Package for CD dialog box, as you can see in Figure 15-3. The order in which the presentations appear in this box is the default sequence in which your presentations will run, one after the other, from the autorun CD.

You don't need to add files linked to the presentation (such as sound or video files) because the Package for CD option automatically includes all linked content.

Figure 15-3:
Sequence
your
presen-
tations.

4. **Reorder the sequence of presentations as required by selecting a presentation in the list and clicking the up- and down-arrow buttons.**

5. **Click the Options button to bring up the Options dialog box shown in
Figure 15-4.**

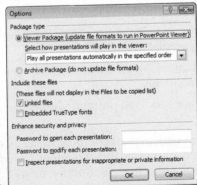

Figure 15-4:
Package for
CD options.

The Options dialog box provides these choices:

- *Viewer Package:* The first option lets you choose whether you want to include the PowerPoint Viewer on the CD. Most of the time, you want to leave this option selected. Remember that there's no updated PowerPoint 2007 Viewer — so all your presentations are made compatible with the older PowerPoint 2003 Viewer.

- *Select How Presentations Will Play:* By default, the Play All Presentations in the Specified Order option is selected — this plays the presentations in the sequence listed in the Package for CD dialog box.

  To specify another option, choose any of the other variants in the drop-down list:

  Play Only the First Presentation Automatically plays the first presentation only; recipients can open other presentations manually.

  Let the User Select Which Presentation to View enables the recipients select any presentation from the autorun CD.

  Don't Play the CD Automatically creates a CD that doesn't autorun, but includes all the presentations and linked files.

- *Archive Package:* This option doesn't include the Viewer. Because the Viewer isn't included, the presentations don't have to be made compatible with the older PowerPoint 2003 format.

- *Linked Files:* This option is selected by default — don't alter this one! If you deselect this option, none of the files that you link to in your presentation are saved on the CD.

- *Embedded TrueType Fonts:* This option lets you embed the TrueType fonts included within the presentation. However, this doesn't work all the time because many fonts don't support embedding. Chapter 8 has more information about font embedding guidelines.

- *Enhance security and privacy:* This option protects your presentations at two levels:

  Password to Open requires that the user enter the password to open and view your presentation.

  Password to Modify requires that the user enter the password in order to edit your presentation.

  These passwords are applied to all presentations burned on the CD.

- *Inspect presentations for inappropriate or private information:* This option determines if any part of the presentations includes private info that should be removed before distribution on a CD.

6. **When you're done changing the options, click OK to return to the Package for CD dialog box (refer to Figure 15-3).**

7. **Now click the Copy to CD button and be done with it.**

   If you don't have a blank CD-R or CD-RW inserted in your recordable drive, PowerPoint asks you to insert one.

   If you have more than one recordable drive, insert the blank recordable CD in another drive until PowerPoint stops whining about the missing CD.

   If PowerPoint still pesters you about a missing CD, click the Cancel button and move to the next step!

   If PowerPoint behaves itself and continues working on the CD, wait patiently. Making the copy might take a while, especially if you have put tons of stuff on the CD. It's a good time for a cup of coffee. After PowerPoint has finished creating the CD, it asks you if you want to burn another CD. Burn as many copies as you need.

8. **If the Copy to CD option doesn't work or if it's grayed out, that might be because PowerPoint relies on the built-in CD burning capability within Windows. I don't teach you how to set that right here, but here's an alternative option: Click the Copy to Folder button, which summons the similar-sounding Copy to Folder dialog box that you see in Figure 15-5.**

Figure 15-5:
The Copy to
Folder
dialog box.

9. **Provide a name and location for the folder and click OK.**

   PowerPoint copies all the contents to the folder.

10. **Copy the entire contents of the folder to a CD using your favorite CD-burning application.**

    Make sure that you copy the entire contents of the folder exactly as created to the CD. Don't copy the folder itself!

If you look beyond the obvious, you discover that the Copy to Folder option can be used for more than merely creating folders to be burned to CDs. You can use this option to assemble your presentations and their linked files within a single folder.

All autorun CDs created run only on systems that have Windows 98 SE or higher installed. In other words, the autorun CD does not run on Windows 95 and the first release of Windows 98 — and please don't tell me that you're still running Windows 3.1!

Sending Presentations by E-Mail

In this section, I show you the best way to e-mail a PowerPoint presentation. Just follow these simple steps to ensure that your recipients are able to view your presentations as you intended:

1. **Make sure that all files linked from your presentation, such as movies and sounds, are placed in the same folder as the presentation (even before you insert them into the presentation).**

   More information on overcoming link problems can be found in Chapter 17.

   You can use the Copy to Folder trick that I explained in the previous section to get all your files in one folder.

2. **Compress the entire folder into a single Zip archive by right-clicking the folder and selecting Send To⇨Compressed (Zipped) Folder, as shown in Figure 15-6.**

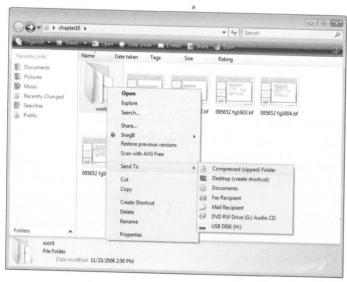

Figure 15-6: Zip your folders.

3. **To make sure that your recipients are aware of how zipped files are unarchived, provide them with links to unzipping applications for Windows and Mac:**

   - WinZip: www.cuttingedgeppt.com/winzip (Windows only)
   - StuffIt: www.cuttingedgeppt.com/stuffit (Windows and Mac)

4. **Attach the Zip file to your e-mail message.**

   If it is a large attachment, consider asking the recipient's permission beforehand. You might also consider uploading your zipped presentation online and including the download URL with the file size in the body of the e-mail.

5. **Provide links to the free PowerPoint Viewer for users who don't have PowerPoint installed on their systems:**

   - PowerPoint Viewer for Windows: www.cuttingedgeppt.com/ppview2007
   - PowerPoint Viewer for Mac: www.cuttingedgeppt.com/ppview98

Reuse All Your Slides

Among the most fascinating features in this new version of PowerPoint is the option that lets you reuse slides from old, long-forgotten presentations so that you don't have to recreate something that already exists. If you find yourself frequently reusing old slides to make slight changes, you'll love this feature.

This feature also lets you (or your company) set up an online *Slide Library* from which you can select slides to reuse — so if you want that elusive slide while you're on a business trip to Singapore, you can access it online at any time. That way you won't run into time zone difference problems and have to wait for your colleagues back home in Chicago to get to the office and send you the slides you need.

For more on the Slide Library feature, take a look at the sidebar with the same name.

For those who worked with earlier PowerPoint versions, this feature might remind you of the Insert Slides dialog box. Well, the Reuse Slides feature is much more than that, as you will soon discover.

Follow these steps to get started with the Reuse Slides feature:

1. **Create a new presentation or open an existing one.**

   Make sure that the active slide is the one after which you want to insert new slides.

2. **Click the Home tab on the Ribbon and then click the down arrow below New Slide. Choose the Reuse Slides option, as shown in Figure 15-7.**

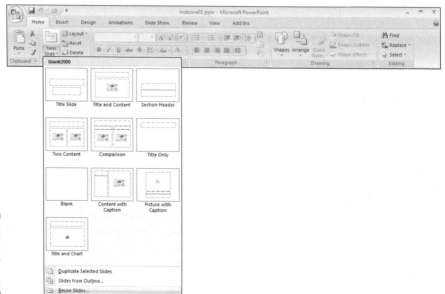

Figure 15-7:
Get ready to reuse your slides.

This activates the Reuse Slides pane, as shown in Figure 15-8.

3. **Open an existing presentation or a slide library as follows:**

   • To access a slide library, you need to have access to a Microsoft Office SharePoint Slide Library — that's something I explain in the sidebar, "What's a slide library?"

   • To access an existing presentation, click the Open a PowerPoint File link in the Reuse Slides pane to bring up a Browse dialog box that lets you choose a file on your computer.

   You now see several slides in the Reuse Slides pane, as shown in Figure 15-9.

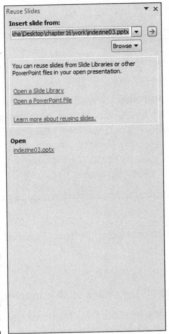

Figure 15-8:
The Reuse
Slides task
pane.

Figure 15-9:
The Reuse
Slides pane
is now
populated
with slides.

What's a slide library?

A *slide library* is not something you will normally set up yourself — rather it is a server-based repository of slides that is set up for you by the system administrator or some other resident geek in your company or organization.

After it is set up, you need not be aware of what's happening behind the scenes. A simple interface lets you and other colleagues publish slides to the slide library and access those slides to reuse as required.

The slide library itself is hosted on a Microsoft Office SharePoint Server (often abbreviated as MOSS) and is, therefore, called the SharePoint Slide Library. As this concept gains popularity, you can expect to see third-party providers of online slide libraries.

6. **Right-click a slide, and in the shortcut menu, choose one of these options:**

   • *Insert Slide:* This inserts the selected slide.

   • *Insert All Slides:* This inserts all the slides visible in the pane.

   • *Apply Theme to All Slides:* This applies the theme of the slide in the task pane to all slides in the active presentation.

   • *Apply Theme to Selected Slides:* This applies the theme of the slide in the task pane to the active slide. If you are in Slide Sorter view, this relates to selected slides. You can also individually select slides in the Slides pane in Normal view.

7. **If you want to retain the source formatting of the slides that you insert through the Reuse Slides pane, make sure that you check the Keep Source Formatting option.**

PowerPoint Add-Ins

Not many PowerPoint users are aware of the concept of PowerPoint add-ins — small programs that can be run only from within PowerPoint. More often than not, they add new buttons on the tabs on the Ribbon in the PowerPoint interface.

Not surprisingly, these add-ins do tasks that PowerPoint can't do by itself, or they perform complicated and repetitive tasks with one click. Here are some of the best PowerPoint add-ins:

✔ **Color Picker (www.cuttingedgeppt.com/colorpicker):** PowerPoint has no built-in Color Picker to help you pick the color on one rectangle and apply it to others — so how do you get a color picker inside PowerPoint? The answer is pptXTREME's Color Picker add-in for PowerPoint.

✔ **CrystalGraphics PowerPlugs (www.cuttingedgeppt.com/power plugs):** This isn't one, or two, or three add-ins — it's actually a suite of more than ten full-featured add-ins for PowerPoint. They do everything from creating better charts and adding more transitions to inserting Flash movies and more. One of the tools lets you insert a quotation from a library of thousands of quotations with just one click!

✔ **Graphicae (www.cuttingedgeppt.com/graphicae):** This is among the most well-conceived PowerPoint add-ins. It contains an entire library of flowcharts and diagram styles that you can adapt to your requirements. In addition, it comes with a library of maps. A Table Editor provides much more control than PowerPoint's default table implementation.

✔ **OfficeFX (www.cuttingedgeppt.com/officefx):** If you imagine your-self creating a presentation with television-style moving backgrounds and lots of other visually stunning elements, such as 3-D bullets, you'll love the OfficeFX add-in from Instant Effects.

✔ **Perspector (www.cuttingedgeppt.com/perspector):** Perspector adds an entire 3-D environment to PowerPoint. With Perspector, you can insert simple 3-D shapes inside PowerPoint slides by using a convenient pane that includes a library of basic 3-D shapes.

✔ **PPTools Starter Set (www.cuttingedgeppt.com/starterset):** This small collection of editing and programming tools from PowerPoint MVPs Steve Rindsberg and Brian Reilly provides several viewing and editing utilities.

✔ **Presentation Librarian (www.cuttingedgeppt.com/librarian):** Your company already has 10,000 slides created across hundreds of pre-sentations — and now your boss expects you to magically find that elu-sive chart slide for tomorrow's board meeting. Wouldn't it be great if you had a searchable index of all your presentations, right up to the slide level?

Take a look at Accent Technologies' Presentation Librarian. This company also creates a simpler search tool, called *PowerSearch,* for PowerPoint presentations.

✔ **PresentationPoint DataPoint (www.cuttingedgeppt.com/ datapoint):** If you've ever wanted to connect PowerPoint to a data-base, look at DataPoint from PresentationPoint. DataPoint lets you create PowerPoint slides on the fly to show data linked from Excel spreadsheets or full-fledged databases. Sample uses include airline schedules, upcoming events in conference halls and theaters, or an instant presentation with a database backend.

- ✔ **Shyam's Toolbox (`www.cuttingedgeppt.com/toolbox`):** Do you think you're becoming a PowerPoint geek? Are you looking for a toolbox to help you become more PowerPoint savvy? If that's the case, look at Shyam's Toolbox, a collection of PowerPoint utilities that probably didn't fit anywhere else! The Toolbox also includes a helpful Insert⇨Flash option for adding Flash animations to your PowerPoint presentation.

- ✔ **Thermometer (`www.cuttingedgeppt.com/thermometer`):** Thermometer is a free add-in that shows a thermometer-like indicator bar in the bottom area of the slide, indicating how much of a presentation has progressed and how much more remains.

- ✔ **Vox Proxy (`www.cuttingedgeppt.com/voxproxy`):** Vox Proxy, from Right Seat Software, is a PowerPoint add-in that uses Microsoft Agent technology to bring talking, animated characters into PowerPoint.

Most of these add-ins weren't updated for PowerPoint 2007 at the time of publishing this book.

Many more add-ins are available — I mention others elsewhere in this book. Myriad great (and not-so-great) PowerPoint add-ins are available to you online . . . but I have to stop somewhere!

Rich Media and LMS

Rich Media is the online delivery of synchronized rich media content, such as visuals, voice-overs, and animations. These features are very similar to what might be contained in your PowerPoint presentations! Rather than reinvent the wheel, companies all around the world are in a rush to create products that convert PowerPoint content into Rich Media.

LMS stands for Learning Management System — several industry standard Learning Management Systems are available. Most of the PowerPoint-to-rich media converter products include LMS capabilities.

Beyond rich media and LMS, the world of presentations is evolving. Presentations aren't just for conference rooms and board meetings anymore. In fact, audience members don't all have to be physically present in a single geographic location to view presentations. The Internet makes it possible for your audience to view the same presentation in different time zones at different times. You can also collaborate in either real time or otherwise.

Rich media formats

Every rich media output from PowerPoint must be exported to a format that can be streamed over the Web. Although you have a large array of exotic output routes, the bulk of PowerPoint rich media programs appear in one of these three output formats:

- ✔ Flash
- ✔ Video formats
- ✔ Java

I explain more about these output formats when I discuss the individual rich media tools in the following section.

PowerPoint to rich media add-ins

Here's a list of some PowerPoint add-ins that convert your presentations to rich media:

- ✔ **Articulate Presenter** (`www.cuttingedgeppt.com/articulate`): Articulate Presenter first converts your entire PowerPoint presentation into sequenced Flash movies, and then it packages the rich media in a highly customizable interface that is equipped with narration. Articulate also creates the QuizMaker and Engage products that work seamlessly with Articulate Presenter.

- ✔ **Impatica** (`www.cuttingedgeppt.com/impatica`): Impatica is possibly the only converter product that converts presentations into Java-based rich media files. Impatica does manage to create super-slim output and actually lets you convert your presentation to file formats that will show on a variety of mobile phones, including the Blackberry. Impatica also creates the ShowMate, a small device that lets you project your converted presentations straight from the BlackBerry without a laptop.

- ✔ **Adobe Presenter** (`www.cuttingedgeppt.com/breeze`): Adobe Presenter has evolved into a family of products that does nearly everything, including creating Flash movies from PowerPoint presentations. That's just the beginning, however; Adobe's related products allow Web conferencing clients and collaborative tools to work with other technologies, including Captivate and PDF. This one is truly for the enterprise-level clients.

✔ **PointeCast** (`www.cuttingedgeppt.com/pointecast`): PointeCast is another offering in the same class as Articulate and Adobe PresenterBreeze — it's more focused toward rich media output geared for e-learning systems.

✔ **PowerCONVERTER** (`www.cuttingedgeppt.com/powerconverter`): PowerCONVERTER, from PresentationPro, converts your PowerPoint presentations to the Flash format. Unlike other similar products, PowerCONVERTER doesn't provide you with capabilities you don't need — so you can choose from a range of PowerCONVERTER products to suit your requirements and cost.

✔ **TechSmith Camtasia** (`www.cuttingedgeppt.com/camtasia`): It's almost an insult to call this venerable capture program a mere PowerPoint add-in because it also works independently of PowerPoint. As an add-in, Camtasia works right inside PowerPoint to allow you to capture your presentations to video files that can be output later in a range of video formats, including Flash.

Part V
The Part of Tens

The 5th Wave   By Rich Tennant

"Well, here's your problem. You only have half the ram you need."

In this part . . .

1've been reading the *For Dummies* books for a decade, and I always read this part first. May you enjoy these tips as much as I enjoyed compiling them for you!

Chapter 16

My Ten Favorite PowerPoint Tips

This chapter is all about my favorite PowerPoint tips. I decided to include tips that are quick and easy so that you can get almost instant results.

I start by showing you how to create PowerPoint presentations without PowerPoint! Then, you find out how to put a picture inside a star or any other shape. I then move on to help you add pizzazz to your presentation titles in a *Star Wars*–style moving, fading crawl.

There's more — see how to create a countdown timer and add ready-made frames to your pictures. I finish the chapter with a discussion on PowerPoint's glue-like capabilities.

Create a Simple Presentation in Notepad

You really can create a PowerPoint presentation in Notepad! That statement renders many people speechless, but the technique really isn't all that difficult:

1. **Choose Start⇨(All) Programs⇨Accessories⇨Notepad to fire up the Notepad application.**

2. Type some text for your presentation — this might help you get started:

```
Indezine for PowerPoint
Why, How and Everything Else
The PowerPoint Blog
What's New
PowerPoint Tips
Fresh Template Designs
More Stuff
PowerPoint Ezine
Sample Presentations
Interviews
```

If you would rather not type all this stuff, just open the sample text file, `notepad.txt`, which I have included on the CD.

3. Choose File⇨Save to open the Save As dialog box. Save the file with a `.txt` extension by typing notepad.txt **in the File Name text box.**

Even if you don't include the `.txt` extension on the filename, Notepad saves the file with a `.txt` extension by default.

4. Launch PowerPoint, and choose Office⇨Open to summon the Open dialog box that you see in Figure 16-1.

5. Choose All Outlines in the File Type drop-down list, and then navigate to and select the TXT file.

You see that each line in the text file is now the title of a new slide.

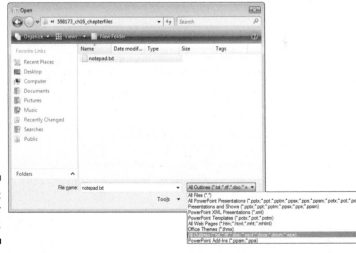

Figure 16-1:
Import your
text outline.

Create a Bulleted Presentation in Notepad

The preceding section shows you how to type some text into Notepad and import it into PowerPoint as the basis of a presentation. The problem is that the text you type into Notepad is imported into PowerPoint as slide title — and slide titles don't make a presentation.

Follow these steps to create the presentation text in Notepad, complete with slide titles and bullets:

1. **Open Notepad and add the basic text for your presentation.**

   Alternatively, if you already created a TXT file, double-click the saved TXT file to fire up Notepad.

2. **Add tabs wherever you need bulleted text. For instance, your text might now look like this:**

   ```
   Indezine for PowerPoint
       Why, How and Everything Else
   The PowerPoint Blog
       What's New
       PowerPoint Tips
       Fresh Template Designs
   More Stuff
       PowerPoint Ezine
       Sample Presentations
       Interviews
   ```

3. **Save the TXT file.**

4. **Create a new presentation (as detailed in Steps 4 and 5 in the previous section) and then open this text file in PowerPoint.**

   Every tabbed line becomes a bullet! You can see how this looks in Figure 16-2.

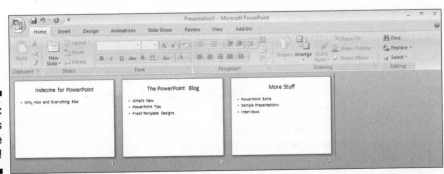

Figure 16-2: Tabs become bullets!

So what happens when you want a sub-bullet of a bullet? That's easy — just press Tab twice at the beginning of a line to create a second-level bullet. Similarly, press Tab three times to create a third-level bullet . . . you get the idea!

You can create presentations with only text-like titles and bullets using this technique — however, no images, sound, or video can be added with this process.

This is a great way to create an outline of a presentation when you have some free time — most PDAs and even mobile phones nowadays allow you to create text files. The next time you're waiting to see a doctor or to catch a plane, you can create the skeleton of your next presentation!

Such presentations normally end up as black text on white slides — you can instantly make over a presentation created this way by applying a template or theme.

Templates are covered in Chapter 4, and you find tons of free templates on the companion CD.

Put a Picture in a Star

Imagine a rectangle on the slide — now imagine that this rectangle is actually a picture. Now, what's so imaginative about a picture that's a rectangle? Almost all pictures are rectangles, but they don't have to be! You just have to use a little imagination.

You can use any PowerPoint shape as a container for a picture. (For the skinny on shapes, refer to Chapter 5.) The following steps show you how to put your image in a star, but you can use any of the shapes available:

1. **Access the Shapes gallery by clicking the Insert or Home tab on the Ribbon and then clicking the Shapes button.**

2. **Select any of the star types in the Stars and Banners category.**

   The five-point star works best for this technique, but you can choose any shape.

3. **Draw the star shape on the slide. Resize the star as required.**

4. **Select the shape, right-click, and choose Format⇨Shape to open the Format Shape dialog box.**

5. **In the Format Shape dialog box, select the Fill tab and choose the Picture or Texture Fill option.**

6. **Click the File button, and in the Insert Picture dialog box that appears, navigate to and select a picture on your hard drive.**

   Alternatively, you can use one of PowerPoint's built-in textures.

7. **Click Insert and Close in successive dialog boxes to get back to your slide.**

   Figure 16-3 shows how your picture might look within the star.

I showed how you how to add a picture fill to a shape. In PowerPoint 2007, you can also go the other way and add a shape to a picture. To do that, double-click any picture to access the Picture Tools Format tab of the Ribbon, click the Picture Shapes button to access the Shapes gallery, and choose your shape.

Figure 16-3:
A beautiful
evening
star.

Jazz Up Picture-Filled Shapes

Using a picture as the fill for a shape is pretty cool. Try out some of the following ideas to do even more with this technique:

 ✔ Even after you contain the picture in a star, you can change the star shape to something else. To change the shape, select the star so that the Drawing Tools Format tab is visible on the Ribbon. Select this Ribbon tab and choose Edit Shape⇨Change Shape to access a variation of the Shapes gallery, as shown in Figure 16-4. Now select the new shape.

 ✔ To draw a set of similar picture-filled shapes, create the first one and then duplicate it any number of times. Thereafter, edit (resize) the duplicated shapes as required.

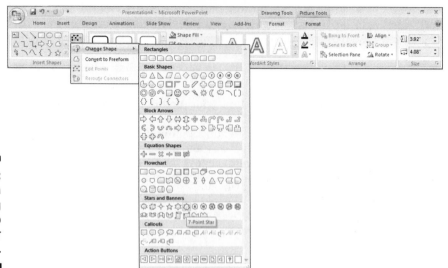

Figure 16-4:
Change an
existing
shape to
another
shape.

✔ Picture fills in shapes can be transparent. You can fill a shape with a picture, right-click the picture inside the shape, and then choose the Format Picture option. On the Fill tab of the resultant Format Picture dialog box, apply a Transparency value from 0 to 100 percent. (The higher the percentage is, the more transparent the picture fill will be.)

✔ Play with shadows and other effects to add more impact to picture-filled shapes. Refer to Chapter 6 to find out more about effects in PowerPoint.

✔ Use a slide with a dark blue background and draw a hundred tiny stars on the slide. Fill them all with a blue-white picture fill. Then, set the stars to animate one after the other. Animation is covered in Chapter 12. This makes a great intermission slide.

You find a sample presentation (`starfield.pptx`) with the starry sky on the companion CD!

Create a Sequential Timeline

Although PowerPoint's shapes can be combined to make effective visuals, they tend to look very uninspiring without the proper fills and animations. In this section, I show you how you can create a timeline using shapes. To add pizzazz to the visual, I add gradient fills to all the shapes.

A timeline is something that's not available as part of PowerPoint's SmartArt feature. If you want to create a specialized diagram that's not part of the SmartArt repertoire, you can use the same principle of combining PowerPoint shapes to create any type of diagram.

Sequential timelines are perfect for representing

- ✔ Product development
- ✔ History timelines
- ✔ Legal processes

A product development timeline typically illustrates the stage progression of a product from idea to release — with all types of research, tests, and prototypes represented in between. Using PowerPoint's shapes, you can represent most of the tasks involved:

- ✔ Concept
- ✔ Research
- ✔ Licensing
- ✔ Testing
- ✔ Prototype
- ✔ Release

To see a finished timeline, open the sample presentation (`timeline.pptx`) on the CD.

The presentation was created for a fictitious pharmaceutical company that's working on a new, fictitious drug. In the presentation, you find three slides:

- ✔ The first slide shows you how the timeline has been constructed.
- ✔ The second slide is merely the first slide with gradient fills applied, as shown in Figure 16-5.
- ✔ The third slide is again the same timeline but with an animation build applied. (See Chapter 12 for more about animation.)

Follow these steps to create your own timeline on a slide:

1. **Draw a small rectangle and then resize it so that it that covers the top part of your slide to create a time bar (see Figure 16-6).**

2. **Draw several small rectangles in a row below the top strip that span the slide from edge to edge, as shown in Figure 16-6, to create a time divider.**

Timelines need a way to represent time. This can be done by creating the time bar and time divider on the top portion of the slide.

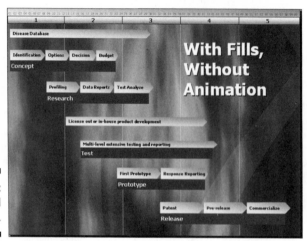

Figure 16-5:
A sequential timeline.

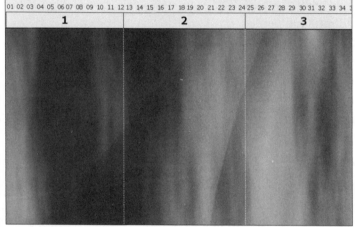

Figure 16-6:
Draw several small rectangles and create a time bar.

3. **Put numbers in the rectangles to represent a period of time. Add fills as required to the rectangles.**

4. **Position all the rectangles in a row and select them.**

5. **The Ribbon should now show the Drawing Tools Format tab — on this tab, choose Group⇨Group to group all the rectangles.**

Now you have to draw shapes that represent the actual tasks within the timeline.

6. On the Insert or Home tab on the Ribbon, choose Shapes to bring up the Shapes gallery. Within this gallery, you find the Pentagon shape within the Block Arrows section — select this and draw one of them on the slide.

7. Resize the pentagon as required and drag the yellow diamond handle on the pentagon slightly to taper the edge of the arrow end.

8. Copy the pentagon multiple times by pressing the Ctrl key as you drag the selected shape.

9. Position and resize all pentagons as required, as shown in Figure 16-7.

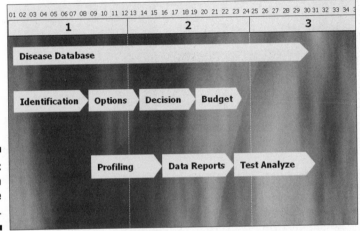

Figure 16-7:
Position all the pentagons.

10. To add text within a pentagon, right-click one and choose Edit Text. Then just type the text.

   After you add the text, some of the pentagons might require resizing. Scale them width-wise (never height-wise).

11. Because all pentagons have been placed in clusters, you might want to identify each cluster of tasks. Draw a long, thin rectangle below a cluster of tasks and add text as required, as shown in Figure 16-8.

   At this point, you might want to arrange all your shapes to achieve the relative position under the time bar. Your timeline will now looks similar to what you see in Figure 16-5.

If you follow the entire step-by-step procedure, you create a product development timeline. The best part is that you aren't restricted to creating such timelines for product development — feel free to adapt the process for your situation. Examples of use include historical timelines, progressive project status, event planning, training, and any other concept that evolves within a timeline frame.

Task 1

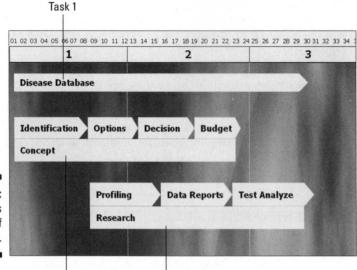

Figure 16-8:
Every task is
a cluster of
shapes.

Task 2 cluster of shapes   Task 3 cluster of shapes

Follow these guidelines to make your timelines travel that extra mile:

✔ Tasks can often be repetitive and overlapping with other tasks. Your timeline design has to accommodate such requirements.

✔ Because the timeline visual often takes an entire slide, use a clean background. Abstract backgrounds also work very well. For the same reason, use a blank or title-only slide layout for this slide.

✔ Leave out the details. Just mention the tasks along with a representative period to show their duration.

✔ If you need to add more detail, create an individual slide for each task and link it from the main timeline slide. Linking is discussed in Chapter 13.

Add Star Wars–Style Credits

In PowerPoint, you can create a *Star Wars*–style credit screen, with your text moving up against a starry background and then tapering and fading into oblivion.

The CD includes a single-slide PowerPoint presentation (starwarsempty. pptx) with a starry slide background that you can use for this presentation. I also include a finished presentation (starwarsstylecredits.pptx) based on this tutorial so that you can see how it looks.

Follow these steps to create your own *Star Wars*–style credits:

1. **Open the `starwarsempty.pptx` single-slide presentation from the CD that contains the starry background.**

2. **Click the Home tab on the Ribbon and click the arrow below the New Slide button to summon the Layout gallery. Choose the Blank Layout option to insert a new slide with no text placeholders.**

3. **Click the Insert tab on the Ribbon, click the Text Box button, and then click anywhere on the slide to place a text box.**

4. **Type a single or two-line credit text in the text box.**

   For example, I typed this:

   ```
   Concept And Creation
   Geetesh Bajaj
   ```

5. **Make sure the text box is selected, and format the text as desired.**

   If you want to closely mimic the *Star Wars* credit style, center justify the text by clicking the Center button in the Paragraph group on the Home tab. You can also change the font to Arial, change the color of your text to yellow, make the text bold, and increase the size of the font. (For all the details about formatting text, see Chapter 8.)

6. **To start adding the animation, select, drag, and move the text box to the bottom center of the slide.**

7. **Click the Animations tab on the Ribbon, and click the Custom Animation button to activate the Custom Animation pane.**

8. **In the task pane, click the Add Effect button and choose Motion Paths to open a flyout menu. From this flyout menu, choose the Up option.**

   If the Up option isn't available, choose the More Motion Paths option to open the Add Motion Path dialog box. Now choose the Up option within the Lines & Curves section and click OK.

9. **Change your settings for the motion path in the Custom Animation pane to match the following, as shown in Figure 16-9:**

   • *Start:* After Previous

   • *Path:* Unlocked

   • *Speed:* Slow

   With your text box and the motion path still selected on the slide, you see green-arrow (play) and red-arrow (play until) indicators on either side of the motion path, as shown in Figure 16-10.

Figure 16-9:
Match
these
custom
animation
settings.

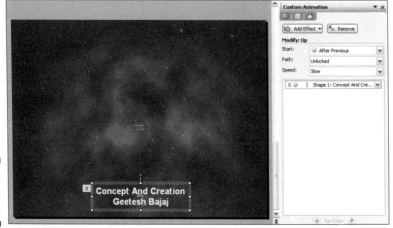

Figure 16-10:
Editing the
motion path.

10. **Click the red arrow to select the path.**

    If you see two white handles on either side of the motion path, you know that the path is selected.

11. **Drag and pull the white handle on the peak of the path (above the red arrow) to the top of the slide to extend the motion path to the entire height of the slide.**

    If you hold the Shift key while pulling the white handle, you ensure that your path is extended in a straight line.

12. **Drag the bottom of the path by pulling the bottom white handle somewhere close to the bottom of your slide.**

    You might want to preview the animation to fine-tune it by clicking the Play button on the Custom Animation pane.

13. **With the text box still selected, add another animation by clicking the Custom Animation button on the Animation tab of the Ribbon to activate the Custom Animation pane (if it is not already visible).**

14. **In the task pane, click the Add Effect button and choose Emphasis to open a flyout menu. From this flyout menu, choose the Grow/Shrink option.**

    If the Grow/Shrink option isn't available, choose the More Effects option to open the Add Emphasis Effect dialog box. Now choose the Grow/Shrink option within the Basic section and click OK.

15. **Change the animation settings.**

    Match your settings for the Grow/Shrink options with the following in the Custom Animation pane:

    - *Start:* With Previous
    - *Size:* Smaller (50%)
    - *Speed:* Slow

    Preview and fine-tune as required.

    At this point, this is what you've done:

    - The first motion path animation moved the text from the bottom of the slide to the top.
    - The second emphasis animation reduced the size of the text as it moved from bottom to top.

    Now, you ensure that the text fades into oblivion as it exits from the slide. This means you add a third animation to the same text box.

16. **With the text box still selected, click the Custom Animation button on the Animation tab of the Ribbon to activate the Custom Animation pane (if it is not already visible).**

17. **In the task pane, click the Add Effect button and choose Exit to open a flyout menu. From this flyout menu, choose the Fade option.**

    If the Fade option isn't available, choose the More Effects option to open the Add Exit Effect dialog box. Now choose the Fade option within the Subtle category and click OK.

18. **Fine-tune the Fade settings.**

    Match your settings for the Fade options with these in the Custom Animation pane:

    - *Start:* With Previous
    - *Speed:* Slow

Because all three animations happen simultaneously, you choose the Slow speed option for all three. If you want to choose a different speed (such as Very Slow), you change the speed of all three animation types — the Motion Path, the Emphasis, and the Exit.

19. Drag the text box off the bottom of the slide.

Select the text box and keep pressing the down-arrow key on your keyboard until the text box is just outside the slide area.

Preview and fine-tune again. You might want to extend the motion path upward (by dragging and pulling the top handle) to compensate for the added downward distance of the text box.

20. If you want more credits, duplicate the text box by copying and pasting — change the text credits as required and place the text box immediately over the earlier text box.

Repeat to create as many text boxes as required. Because all the text boxes overlap each other, it might be a little difficult to edit the text within them later. Use the Tab key to select each of these text boxes one at a time so that you don't make inadvertent changes to the wrong text box.

You can also use the Selection and Visibility task pane to select the text boxes. This task pane is discussed in Chapter 5.

21. Preview your slide by clicking the Play button on the Custom Animation pane.

22. Save your presentation.

You might want to check the sample presentation on the CD to check the settings I've used or to compare the presentations.

You just duplicated an animated text box within the same slide. You can carry this concept forward and duplicate text boxes across slides and even across presentations, thus making short work of an otherwise tedious job.

Experiment with adding a *Star Wars*–style soundtrack to the credits slide — you can search the Internet for a *Star Wars* theme sound in WAV or MP3 format. Whatever you do, make sure you respect copyrights.

Make a Countdown Timer

Creating a countdown timer in PowerPoint is so much fun — and countdown slides can be used to add impact to an announcement in an upcoming slide or just to give you another way to start a presentation.

Follow these steps to create your own countdown timer:

1. Choose the Home tab on the Ribbon and click the arrow below the New Slide to summon the Layout gallery. Choose the Blank Layout option to insert a new slide with no text placeholders.

2. Select the Insert tab on the Ribbon, click Text Box option, and click anywhere on the slide to place a text box.

3. Type the 1 or 01 or 001 (depending on how many digits you want your counter to display), as shown in Figure 16-11.

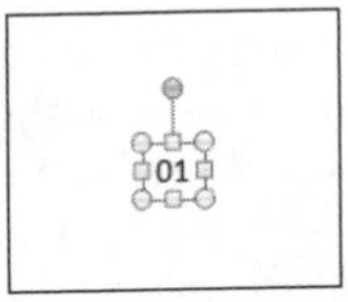

Figure 16-11:
Your first
countdown
digit!

4. With the text box still selected, access the Home tab of the Ribbon and click the Center button in the Paragraph group to center align the text.

5. Change the font size to something large, like 200 points, and resize the text box so that all digits are placed and visible on the same line.

6. Change the font style as required and position the text box right in the center of the slide.

7. Click the Animations tab on the Ribbon and select a simple transition.

   For this example, I chose the Box Out transition effect. You can also choose the No Transition option if you prefer. I've also set the Transition Speed to Fast and opted to automatically advance the slide after ten seconds. You might want to choose a shorter or longer time delay for the transition. (See Chapter 12 for all the details on transitions.)

8. Click the View tab on the Ribbon, and then click the Slide Sorter option. In the resultant Slide Sorter view, click the formatted timer slide to select the slide.

9. Click the Copy button on the Home tab of the Ribbon (or press Ctrl+C), and then click Paste (or press Ctrl+V) to paste an identical slide.

   Keep pasting that slide until you end up with the number of slides you want your countdown to contain. I used ten slides in this example. At this point, your Slide Sorter View might look like the left side of Figure 16-12.

10. Within each of the slides, change the countdown number so that all numbers appear in reverse order; the first slide contains 10 (or whatever the highest number is), and the last slide contains the 1.

Because my example presentation contains ten slides, it looks like the right side of Figure 16-12 after the number values have been edited.

11. **Click the Slide Show button (found on the View tab of the Ribbon) to run the presentation and see the countdown.**

A sample presentation with a countdown timer (`countdown.pptx`) can be found on the CD.

If you just finished creating your own countdown timer, you might want to experiment with slide backgrounds, transitions, animations, font color, and style to create a unique look. You might even want to experiment with calculator style digits (search online for a calculator font) or include seconds within the slides (for example 01:00).

Also consider adding some text, such as *minutes/seconds remaining*, to each countdown slide.

Figure 16-12: All your countdown slides (left); the slides in sequence (right).

Find Outside Sources for Elements that You Add to PowerPoint Presentations

Here's my favorite PowerPoint tip — and this doesn't even include a tutorial! Think of PowerPoint as the glue that binds all elements of a presentation together — these elements often include pictures, sounds, movies, charts, diagrams, and more.

Many times, you'll find that you can create these elements by using PowerPoint's editing options. But if you're serious about creating cutting-edge PowerPoint presentations, you'll soon realize that you want that out-of-the-ordinary look that sets your style apart from what everyone else is doing.

To attain this objective, you'll want to create your own presentation paraphernalia box that contains much more than just PowerPoint. The CD included with this book can give you a start — it includes hundreds of free elements you can use in your own presentations.

The Internet is a great place to look for custom elements to include in your presentations. Try using your favorite search engine to search for royalty-free archives of photos, clip art, music, sound effects, backgrounds, templates, and videos. Also, remember that royalty-free doesn't necessarily mean free!

Create and Edit Art Using an Image Editor

You can create some nice gradient fills and use preset textures for backgrounds within PowerPoint. You can use shapes to create all sorts of diagrams. But at some point, you're going to get bored with those options. That's where you need to move beyond PowerPoint and use an image editor. In fact, all images that you insert in PowerPoint should first be cleaned up and edited in an image-editing application such as Adobe Photoshop.

The possibilities are endless when you're using a program such as Photoshop to alter a photograph or to draw your own image. Some typical tasks you can do with Photoshop include

- ✔ Resizing an image so that it will fit the exact dimensions you need, whether it's 20 x 20 pixels or full-screen (usually 1024 x 768 pixels)

- ✔ Editing a photograph to remove red eyes from subjects, to correct for poor lighting, or to crop out unnecessary parts of the picture

✔ Applying a filter to an image to soften it, make it look like a watercolor painting, or turn it into a black light poster

✔ Creating your own texture fills

✔ Saving an image that uses a large, uncompressed format in a smaller, compressed format (for example, saving a huge .tif file as a much littler .jpg)

Photoshop is an expensive program, but Adobe also creates the less-expensive Photoshop Elements, which contains a surprisingly large number of Photoshop's capabilities. Other alternatives include Microsoft's Digital Image Pro and Corel's Paint Shop Pro.

Edit Sound Clips with a Sound Editor

You can add sound clips to a PowerPoint presentation, but you can't edit the sound clips with it. What program you choose for sound editing depends upon how you intend to use the sound clips:

✔ If you need musical background scores for presentations, you can get one of the sound libraries created for use with PowerPoint. These include CrystalGraphics' PowerPlugs: Music and Indigo Rose's Liquid Cabaret collection. Opuzz.com also provides coordinated music clips that work very well within PowerPoint.

✔ If you would rather create all the music on your own, look at something like Sony's ACID program. This lets you create music scores using sound loops and is surprisingly easy to use. You could end up creating your first background score within an hour.

✔ If all you need to do is polish your narrations and remove some hiss or noise artifacts, look at Bias SoundSoap — this is an intuitive application that intelligently cleans up your narrations. A more capable Pro version is also available.

✔ If you need more advanced sound editing, use high-end professional programs like Adobe Audition or Sony Sound Forge.

Chapter 17

Ten Solutions to PowerPoint Problems

· ·

In This Chapter

▶ Finding PowerPoint on your computer

▶ Coexisting with older PowerPoint versions

▶ Getting those links right

▶ Implementing simple PowerPoint solutions

▶ Making PowerPoint accessible

▶ Using Internet resources

· ·

*L*et me start by saying that PowerPoint has no problems at all. All those linking problems and the presentation perils are just figments of your overworked imagination. And that problem you faced last week was just a bad dream — if you had pinched yourself, it would have gone away.

It's also so easy to send a PowerPoint slide to prepress. What's Section 508 anyway? And certainly nobody needs to know about more PowerPoint resources after reading this book!

Well, the opening paragraphs are wishful thinking. Now let me welcome you to the real world, where problems happen. Fortunately, many problems have solutions and workarounds that make things simpler for you. That's precisely the reason for this chapter!

In this chapter, I offer hard-to-come-by information on overcoming sound and video issues in PowerPoint and help if you cannot locate PowerPoint on the computer! You also find out how to make various versions of PowerPoint co-exist. And yes, the chapter ends with a listing of must-see PowerPoint resource sites.

Where Is PowerPoint?

Yes, you read that right! This question has been asked so many times before that I knew it had to be the first thing in this chapter!

If you can't find PowerPoint, here's where you should start looking:

✔ Just because you have Microsoft Office installed doesn't mean you have PowerPoint as well. Some editions of Office, especially the ones that might have been pre-installed on your computer, do not include PowerPoint.

Yes, you can upgrade by adding PowerPoint to a version of Office that does not include it, but you need to make sure that you have a qualifying product for the upgrade to a new version of PowerPoint. Get more information at:

www.cuttingedgeppt.com/ppupgrade

✔ Maybe you have PowerPoint installed, but the shortcut that used to launch the program got deleted. To find out if you really have PowerPoint, follow these steps:

1. **If you're using Windows XP, choose Start⇨Run. If you're using Windows Vista, choose Start⇨All Programs⇨Accessories⇨Run.**

    This brings up the Run dialog box.

2. **Type** powerpnt.exe **in this dialog box and click OK.**

    If you have PowerPoint installed, the program's splash screen appears. If that doesn't happen, Windows might complain that it can't find powerpnt.exe, which means you don't have PowerPoint.

If you're using a computer at work, you might want to ask your system administrator whether PowerPoint is installed.

The technique above works with any version of PowerPoint, not just PowerPoint 2007.

Coexisting with Older PowerPoint Versions

So how many versions of PowerPoint are out there? Actually, way too many PowerPoint versions exist out there in the wild — in fact, Microsoft wishes existing PowerPoint users would upgrade because its older versions are the biggest competitor for the new versions!

So why don't people upgrade? After all, you are reading this book on PowerPoint 2007 — shouldn't everyone else follow your example and upgrade? Wow! Microsoft loves you, but others using older versions of PowerPoint have their excuses:

- Many users work in large organizations, and an upgrade to the latest version of PowerPoint (and Microsoft Office) is a big decision that involves upgrading hundreds or thousands of licenses.

- A very large number of users work for governments, and they think it's better to use the older version and save the upgrade costs for other, more pressing requirements.

- Many users are so happy with their versions of PowerPoint that they just don't want to upgrade! They also like to hold on to their dolls and toy cars from their toddler days!

- Upgrading can also entail an upgrade of your Windows version. For instance, PowerPoint 2007 runs only on Windows XP and Windows Vista.

- And yes, many users just find it too expensive to upgrade.

Whatever the reasons might be, the result is at least five other versions of PowerPoint are in use out there:

- PowerPoint 2000, 2002, and 2003 for Windows
- PowerPoint X and 2004 for Macintosh

And I'm not counting the really old versions here — I know one person who refuses to upgrade from PowerPoint 95!

These guidelines can help you coexist with users of older versions:

- You can save your PPTX presentations to the older PPT format. You will lose some editing capabilities, but most of the time, the PPT files work just fine in older versions of PowerPoint.

  Choose Office➪Save As and choose PPT as the file type to save your PowerPoint 2007 files for use with older versions.

- Microsoft has created an update for older versions of PowerPoint that enables them to open the new PPTX presentations.

  At least, this update works for PowerPoint 2000, 2002, and 2003 at the time of this writing. Updates for PowerPoint for Mac versions are also coming.

Heading Off Linking Problems

Nothing is as frustrating as when PowerPoint refuses to locate that linked narration or video, especially if this debacle happens in full view of an audience.

You can avoid link problems altogether by doing some housekeeping. The secret is to stop thinking of your presentations as mere .pptx files. Instead, start thinking of them as folders. Before you start to create a new presentation, just follow these steps:

1. **Create an empty folder.**

2. **Create a single-slide presentation and save it to this folder.**

3. **Copy all the sound and video files you want to insert in the presentation to this folder.**

   Copy all the other documents you want to hyperlink from the presentation, such as other PowerPoint presentations, Word and PDF documents, and Excel spreadsheets.

4. **After you finish copying these files into the same folder as the presentation, create your presentation and start inserting or linking to the files within the presentation.**

5. **If you want to link another sound, video, or document, copy it to the folder first and then insert it.**

6. **If you want to move the presentation to another computer, copy the entire folder (not just the presentation), and PowerPoint will have no problems finding those linked files!**

Fixing Broken Links

You might be saying, "Thank you for the nice folder idea, but my presentations are already created! What do I do with all those gazillion missing links in existing presentations? Surely you don't expect me to recreate each of them again!"

No, I don't expect you to recreate those links again — I suggest you download a copy of Steve Rindsberg's FixLinks Pro product from

www.cuttingedgeppt.com/fixlinkspro

FixLinks Pro isn't free, but a demo version is available. The demo version doesn't fix the links, but it does let you know which links are missing, which is more than PowerPoint will tell you.

The full version restores missing links for you and also copies linked files to the same folder as the presentation.

Common PowerPoint Problems and Solutions

The perils of PowerPoint stem (ironically) from how easy it is to use PowerPoint. Microsoft made PowerPoint work so much like Word and Excel (as far as the logical interface and look are concerned) that more people than Microsoft ever imagined are using PowerPoint!

To accommodate the growing number of novice users, Microsoft created the concept of content templates. These enable you to create everything from a science fair presentation to a tent card and everything in between. As a result, you end up with a presentation that looks and feels strikingly similar in appearance and content to millions of other presentations! And that's PowerPoint's biggest problem.

Here are some guidelines to combat this problem and help you create a truly cutting-edge presentation:

- ✔ **Start with an outline.** Create your presentation on paper first — or maybe Notepad or Microsoft Word. When you are not distracted by backgrounds and multimedia, you might end up with a stronger focus on the subject of your presentation. Then you can move the outline to PowerPoint and work with all the fancy stuff.

- ✔ **Look at the background.** Avoid shocking and fluorescent backgrounds. Stay away from bright photographs as backdrops. Whichever color or image you use as a background, make sure that all text is readable and other content on the slides is visible over it.

- ✔ **Color combinations are another important playing field.** Although this is too detailed a subject to discuss here, you should choose combinations that are both appealing and utilitarian. Also, use company-specific colors to further the corporate identity of your client or end user. For a sophisticated effect, try using black and white as your color combination!

✔ **Keep font sizes readable.** I've seen many great presentations marred by a 20-line paragraph that no one in the audience could read. Also, if you have to use a lot of text, make it a point to incorporate white text on a dark background, rather than the other way around.

✔ **Avoid long sentences.** Break your sentences into small points.

Try different line-spacing options in your text boxes. (See Chapter 8 for the skinny on text formatting and line spacing.)

✔ **Avoid using ALL-UPPERCASE characters in a sentence unless it is indispensable.** Unless you're typing in a company or product name that you want to highlight, all-uppercase letters give the impression that you're yelling.

✔ **Always cross-check any factual references in your presentation.** Nothing is more annoying for your audience than a blatant factual mistake.

Don't point out mistakes for which you can't offer any solutions.

✔ **Don't get carried away by the multitude of clip art available with PowerPoint.** Many excellent presentations have been made without using any clip art. In fact, the general professional trend nowadays is to use specific collages and subdued pictures instead of comic-style clip art.

✔ **Optimize and resize your images in an image editor such as Photoshop.** Don't insert a full-screen picture into PowerPoint and then resize it to a quarter of the screen.

Prepress Printing and PowerPoint

This could be one of your worst nightmares! Your boss loved the flowchart you created so much that he or she expects it to be used in the company's annual report, and you have the privilege of exporting that flowchart to a format that can be sent straight to prepress.

First, let me congratulate you for the flowchart. Now, as you must already be aware, there's no straightforward way to export the graphic to a professional graphic format like EPS so that your prepress folks can use it. PowerPoint just declared a dead end — all roads ahead are closed!

However, if you have Adobe Acrobat and Adobe Illustrator available on your system, you're in luck. Follow these steps to get the flowchart to prepress:

1. **Print the PowerPoint slide that contains your flowchart to an Acrobat PDF file using Adobe Acrobat's printer driver.**

   You can also use the free PDF add-in that Microsoft provides — check out more about installing this add-in in the Bonus Chapter on the CD.

2. **Open the PDF in Adobe Illustrator and delete everything but the flowchart.**

3. **Save (export) the flowchart as an EPS file by choosing File⇨Export or File⇨Save As in Illustrator.**

Section 508 and PowerPoint

Section 508 of the Rehabilitation Act was enacted by the U.S. Congress in 1998 so that people with disabilities could access information without barriers.

Under this Act, people with disabilities are guaranteed access to the same information as everyone else. That's easier said than done when it comes to PowerPoint. But you can still go a long way toward making your PowerPoint presentations more accessible to those with disabilities:

✔ **Keep all the text content within PowerPoint's default text placeholders.** Don't use any text boxes in your presentation, just the text placeholders. All text in the default placeholders becomes part of the presentation's outline. This allows specialized screen-reading applications to access all the content from the PowerPoint presentation.

✔ **Download the Web Publishing Accessibility Wizard for Microsoft Office and read Glenna Shaw's amazing report on PowerPoint accessibility at**

    www.cuttingedgeppt.com/accessibility

Remember, this report isn't yet updated for PowerPoint 2007, but most of the concepts still apply and most of the techniques will work.

PowerPoint Resources

Discovering more about PowerPoint is a continuous process, and the Internet is a treasure trove of information related to this program. Here is a list of my favorite PowerPoint sites:

✔ I unashamedly lead you first to my own site, Indezine, which discusses almost every aspect of PowerPoint. There are tutorials, reviews, interviews, templates, backgrounds, add-ins, books, blogs, tips — and even a biweekly e-zine that gives away freebies all the time.

`www.cuttingedgeppt.com/indezine`

✔ Top of the heap is Microsoft MVP Steve Rindsberg's celebrated PowerPoint FAQ. The site is bare of graphics, yet a mine of information. You'll find no tutorials, but when you are stuck with a problem, Steve's FAQ is the best place to go. The best way to use the FAQ is to enter your keywords into the search box on the site's home page.

`www.cuttingedgeppt.com/pptfaq`

✔ Microsoft's own PowerPoint home page is definitely a must-see resource, with info on program updates and downloads. You can also order a 30-day trial CD of Microsoft Office (which includes PowerPoint) here. It has links to several tutorial pages on Microsoft's site and the PowerPoint knowledge base.

`www.cuttingedgeppt.com/ppthome`

✔ If you have a problem that remains unsolved, visit the PowerPoint newsgroup archives at Google Groups. This is your window to an almost unlimited store of info on any aspect of PowerPoint.

`www.cuttingedgeppt.com/pptgoogle`

✔ Echo'sVoice is the site of Echo Swinford, a PowerPoint MVP and the technical editor of this book, whose site has detailed info on using Bézier curves, animation, masters, and color schemes in PowerPoint.

`www.cuttingedgeppt.com/echo`

✔ Shyam Pillai runs the OfficeTips site, where you can download tons of free add-ins for PowerPoint, in addition to some commercial ones. The PowerPoint section of the site also has a small FAQ section.

`www.cuttingedgeppt.com/shyam`

✔ You can find a wealth of PowerPoint information at Kathy Jacobs' site. A search facility is available onsite so you can quickly locate what you need.

`www.cuttingedgeppt.com/kathy`

✔ Glen Millar's site has some nice tutorials on using PowerPoint's AutoShapes imaginatively — and on animation.

`www.cuttingedgeppt.com/glen`

Appendix

About the CD

• •

In This Appendix

▶ Checking out system requirements

▶ Using the CD with Windows

▶ Finding out what you'll find on the CD

▶ Troubleshooting

• •

This book includes a CD-ROM that's packed with programs, demos, samples, a bonus chapter, and lots of other goodies! You're sure to find lots of great content that will help you create cutting-edge presentations.

System Requirements

You need a working copy of Microsoft Office PowerPoint 2007 on a Windows PC with a CD-ROM drive. Although this CD will work on most Windows systems, PowerPoint 2007 can be installed only on Windows XP and Windows Vista versions.

Using the CD

To install the items from the CD to your hard drive, follow these steps:

1. **Insert the CD into your computer's CD-ROM drive.**

   The license agreement appears.

   Note: The interface won't launch if you have autorun disabled. In that case, click Start➪Run (or Start➪All Programs➪Accessories➪Run). In the dialog box that appears, type **D:\start.exe**. (Replace D with the proper letter if your CD-ROM drive uses a different letter. If you don't know the letter, see how your CD-ROM drive is listed under My Computer.) Click OK.

2. **Read through the license agreement and then click the Accept button if you want to use the CD.**

   The CD interface appears. The interface allows you to install the programs and run the demos with just a click of a button (or two).

What You'll Find on the CD

The following sections are arranged by category and provide a summary of the software and other goodies you'll find on the CD. If you need help with installing the items provided on the CD, refer to the installation instructions in the preceding section.

Shareware programs are fully functional, free, trial versions of copyrighted programs. If you like particular programs, register with their authors for a nominal fee and receive licenses, enhanced versions, and technical support. *Freeware programs* are free, copyrighted games, applications, and utilities. You can copy them to as many PCs as you like — for free — but they offer no technical support. *GNU software* is governed by its own license, which is included inside the folder of the GNU software. There are no restrictions on distribution of GNU software. See the GNU license at the root of the CD for more details. *Trial, demo,* or *evaluation* versions of software are usually limited either by time or functionality (such as not letting you save a project after you create it).

Author-created material

All the examples provided in this book are located in the Author directory on the CD. The folders contain files for Chapters 3, 6, 7, 8, 9, 12, 13, and 16, plus hundreds of backgrounds, templates, and Flash samples.

Bonus chapter

The CD also includes a bonus chapter that covers exchanging information between PowerPoint and other programs such as Word and Excel. You find out how to create PDF files from your presentations, use Flash movies in your presentations, and put your presentation on the Web.

Software

The *Cutting Edge PowerPoint 2007 For Dummies* CD-ROM contains these powerful software programs:

- **TechSmith SnagIt 7:** A commercial product that captures still screen-shots with many options.

  `www.techsmith.com`

- **Neuxpower NXPowerLite:** This program compresses your presentation files as much as 90 percent.

  `www.neuxpower.com`

- **TechSmith Camtasia 3:** A commercial product that records your presentation to video.

  `www.techsmith.com`

- **Business Objects CX Now!:** A fully working lite version that enables you to transform data from Excel spreadsheets into animated and dynamic charts that can be embedded within PowerPoint presentations.

  `www.cx-now.com`

- **Sony Sound Forge:** This program is a demonstration version of professional-quality audio editing software.

  `www.sonymediasoftware.com`

- **Wildform WildPresenter Sampler:** This is a sampler of demo files that will work with the WildPresenter program that you can download from this site:

  `www.wildform.com`

- **Xara 3D 3:** This program is the full version of robust software for creating and editing 3D graphics.

  `www.xara.com`

Media

The *Cutting Edge PowerPoint 2007 For Dummies* CD-ROM contains these third-party resources to improve your presentations:

- **Liquid Cabaret Music Samples:** Free music samples for your presentations from the royalty-free Liquid Cabaret music library.

  `www.liquidcabaret.com`

- ✔ **Opuzz:** Free music samples for your presentations from Opuzz.

  `www.opuzz.com`

- ✔ **PowerFinish Templates:** Free background and document templates from the PowerFinish library of designs.

  `www.powerfinish.com`

- ✔ **Style Workshop Sampler:** Sample of "Drag'n'Drop Ready" graphics from Indigo Rose's Style Workshop.

  `www.styleworkshop.com`

- ✔ **Cartoons from Ron Leishman:** Samples from Toon-A-Day to brighten up your presentations and your day.

  `www.toonaday.com`

- ✔ **Movieclip.biz Video Clips:** A powerful sample of the broad range of Movieclip video samples available for your presentations.

  `www.movieclip.biz`

Troubleshooting

I tried my best to compile programs that work on most computers with the minimum system requirements. Alas, your computer may differ, and some programs may not work properly for some reason.

The two likeliest problems are that you don't have enough memory (RAM) for the programs you want to use, or you have other programs running that are affecting installation or running of a program. If you get an error message such as Not enough memory or Setup cannot continue, try one or more of the following suggestions and then try using the software again:

- ✔ **Turn off any antivirus software running on your computer.** Installation programs sometimes mimic virus activity and may make your computer incorrectly believe that it's being infected by a virus.

- ✔ **Close all running programs.** The more programs you have running, the less memory is available. Installation programs typically update files and programs, so if you keep other programs running, installation might not work properly. This might include closing the CD interface and running a product's installation program from Windows Explorer.

- ✔ **Have your local computer store add more RAM to your computer.** This is, admittedly, a drastic and somewhat expensive step. However, adding more memory can really help speed up your computer and allow more programs to run at the same time.

Customer Care

If you have trouble with the CD-ROM, please call the Wiley Product Technical Support phone number at (800) 762-2974. Outside the United States, call 1(317) 572-3994. You can also contact Wiley Product Technical Support at http://support.wiley.com. John Wiley & Sons will provide technical support only for installation and other general quality control items. For technical support on the applications themselves, consult the program's vendor or author.

Index

• G •

• O •

BUSINESS, CAREERS & PERSONAL FINANCE

Fundraising FOR DUMMIES
0-7645-9847-3

Investing FOR DUMMIES
0-7645-2431-3

Also available:
- Business Plans Kit For Dummies
  0-7645-9794-9
- Economics For Dummies
  0-7645-5726-2
- Grant Writing For Dummies
  0-7645-8416-2
- Home Buying For Dummies
  0-7645-5331-3
- Managing For Dummies
  0-7645-1771-6
- Marketing For Dummies
  0-7645-5600-2

- Personal Finance For Dummies
  0-7645-2590-5*
- Resumes For Dummies
  0-7645-5471-9
- Selling For Dummies
  0-7645-5363-1
- Six Sigma For Dummies
  0-7645-6798-5
- Small Business Kit For Dummies
  0-7645-5984-2
- Starting an eBay Business For Dummie
  0-7645-6924-4
- Your Dream Career For Dummies
  0-7645-9795-7

HOME & BUSINESS COMPUTER BASICS

Laptops FOR DUMMIES
0-470-05432-8

Windows Vista FOR DUMMIES
0-471-75421-8

Also available:
- Cleaning Windows Vista For Dummies
  0-471-78293-9
- Excel 2007 For Dummies
  0-470-03737-7
- Mac OS X Tiger For Dummies
  0-7645-7675-5
- MacBook For Dummies
  0-470-04859-X
- Macs For Dummies
  0-470-04849-2
- Office 2007 For Dummies
  0-470-00923-3

- Outlook 2007 For Dummies
  0-470-03830-6
- PCs For Dummies
  0-7645-8958-X
- Salesforce.com For Dummies
  0-470-04893-X
- Upgrading & Fixing Laptops For
  Dummies
  0-7645-8959-8
- Word 2007 For Dummies
  0-470-03658-3
- Quicken 2007 For Dummies
  0-470-04600-7

FOOD, HOME, GARDEN, HOBBIES, MUSIC & PETS

Chess FOR DUMMIES
0-7645-8404-9

Guitar FOR DUMMIES
0-7645-9904-6

Also available:
- Candy Making For Dummies
  0-7645-9734-5
- Card Games For Dummies
  0-7645-9910-0
- Crocheting For Dummies
  0-7645-4151-X
- Dog Training For Dummies
  0-7645-8418-9
- Healthy Carb Cookbook For Dummies
  0-7645-8476-6
- Home Maintenance For Dummies
  0-7645-5215-5

- Horses For Dummies
  0-7645-9797-3
- Jewelry Making & Beading
  For Dummies
  0-7645-2571-9
- Orchids For Dummies
  0-7645-6759-4
- Puppies For Dummies
  0-7645-5255-4
- Rock Guitar For Dummies
  0-7645-5356-9
- Sewing For Dummies
  0-7645-6847-7
- Singing For Dummies
  0-7645-2475-5

INTERNET & DIGITAL MEDIA

eBay FOR DUMMIES
0-470-04529-9

iPod & iTunes FOR DUMMIES
0-470-04894-8

Also available:
- Blogging For Dummies
  0-471-77084-1
- Digital Photography For Dummies
  0-7645-9802-3
- Digital Photography All-in-One Desk
  Reference For Dummies
  0-470-03743-1
- Digital SLR Cameras and Photography
  For Dummies
  0-7645-9803-1
- eBay Business All-in-One Desk
  Reference For Dummies
  0-7645-8438-3
- HDTV For Dummies
  0-470-09673-X

- Home Entertainment PCs For Dummie
  0-470-05523-5
- MySpace For Dummies
  0-470-09529-6
- Search Engine Optimization For
  Dummies
  0-471-97998-8
- Skype For Dummies
  0-470-04891-3
- The Internet For Dummies
  0-7645-8996-2
- Wiring Your Digital Home For Dummie
  0-471-91830-X

* Separate Canadian edition also available
† Separate U.K. edition also available

Available wherever books are sold. For more information or to order direct: U.S. customers visit www.dummies.com or call 1-877-762-2974.
U.K. customers visit www.wileyeurope.com or call 0800 243407. Canadian customers visit www.wiley.ca or call 1-800-567-4797.

 WILEY

SPORTS, FITNESS, PARENTING, RELIGION & SPIRITUALITY

0-471-76871-5

0-7645-7841-3

Also available:
- Catholicism For Dummies
  0-7645-5391-7
- Exercise Balls For Dummies
  0-7645-5623-1
- Fitness For Dummies
  0-7645-7851-0
- Football For Dummies
  0-7645-3936-1
- Judaism For Dummies
  0-7645-5299-6
- Potty Training For Dummies
  0-7645-5417-4
- Buddhism For Dummies
  0-7645-5359-3

- Pregnancy For Dummies
  0-7645-4483-7 †
- Ten Minute Tone-Ups For Dummies
  0-7645-7207-5
- NASCAR For Dummies
  0-7645-7681-X
- Religion For Dummies
  0-7645-5264-3
- Soccer For Dummies
  0-7645-5229-5
- Women in the Bible For Dummies
  0-7645-8475-8

TRAVEL

0-7645-7749-2

0-7645-6945-7

Also available:
- Alaska For Dummies
  0-7645-7746-8
- Cruise Vacations For Dummies
  0-7645-6941-4
- England For Dummies
  0-7645-4276-1
- Europe For Dummies
  0-7645-7529-5
- Germany For Dummies
  0-7645-7823-5
- Hawaii For Dummies
  0-7645-7402-7

- Italy For Dummies
  0-7645-7386-1
- Las Vegas For Dummies
  0-7645-7382-9
- London For Dummies
  0-7645-4277-X
- Paris For Dummies
  0-7645-7630-5
- RV Vacations For Dummies
  0-7645-4442-X
- Walt Disney World & Orlando
  For Dummies
  0-7645-9660-8

GRAPHICS, DESIGN & WEB DEVELOPMENT

0-7645-8815-X

0-7645-9571-7

Also available:
- 3D Game Animation For Dummies
  0-7645-8789-7
- AutoCAD 2006 For Dummies
  0-7645-8925-3
- Building a Web Site For Dummies
  0-7645-7144-3
- Creating Web Pages For Dummies
  0-470-08030-2
- Creating Web Pages All-in-One Desk
  Reference For Dummies
  0-7645-4345-8
- Dreamweaver 8 For Dummies
  0-7645-9649-7

- InDesign CS2 For Dummies
  0-7645-9572-5
- Macromedia Flash 8 For Dummies
  0-7645-9691-8
- Photoshop CS2 and Digital
  Photography For Dummies
  0-7645-9580-6
- Photoshop Elements 4 For Dummies
  0-471-77483-9
- Syndicating Web Sites with RSS Feeds
  For Dummies
  0-7645-8848-6
- Yahoo! SiteBuilder For Dummies
  0-7645-9800-7

NETWORKING, SECURITY, PROGRAMMING & DATABASES

0-7645-7728-X

0-471-74940-0

Also available:
- Access 2007 For Dummies
  0-470-04612-0
- ASP.NET 2 For Dummies
  0-7645-7907-X
- C# 2005 For Dummies
  0-7645-9704-3
- Hacking For Dummies
  0-470-05235-X
- Hacking Wireless Networks
  For Dummies
  0-7645-9730-2
- Java For Dummies
  0-470-08716-1

- Microsoft SQL Server 2005 For Dummies
  0-7645-7755-7
- Networking All-in-One Desk Reference
  For Dummies
  0-7645-9939-9
- Preventing Identity Theft For Dummies
  0-7645-7336-5
- Telecom For Dummies
  0-471-77085-X
- Visual Studio 2005 All-in-One Desk
  Reference For Dummies
  0-7645-9775-2
- XML For Dummies
  0-7645-8845-1

HEALTH & SELF-HELP

0-7645-8450-2

0-7645-4149-8

Also available:
- Bipolar Disorder For Dummies
  0-7645-8451-0
- Chemotherapy and Radiation
  For Dummies
  0-7645-7832-4
- Controlling Cholesterol For Dummies
  0-7645-5440-9
- Diabetes For Dummies
  0-7645-6820-5* †
- Divorce For Dummies
  0-7645-8417-0 †

- Fibromyalgia For Dummies
  0-7645-5441-7
- Low-Calorie Dieting For Dummies
  0-7645-9905-4
- Meditation For Dummies
  0-471-77774-9
- Osteoporosis For Dummies
  0-7645-7621-6
- Overcoming Anxiety For Dummies
  0-7645-5447-6
- Reiki For Dummies
  0-7645-9907-0
- Stress Management For Dummies
  0-7645-5144-2

EDUCATION, HISTORY, REFERENCE & TEST PREPARATION

0-7645-8381-6

0-7645-9554-7

Also available:
- The ACT For Dummies
  0-7645-9652-7
- Algebra For Dummies
  0-7645-5325-9
- Algebra Workbook For Dummies
  0-7645-8467-7
- Astronomy For Dummies
  0-7645-8465-0
- Calculus For Dummies
  0-7645-2498-4
- Chemistry For Dummies
  0-7645-5430-1
- Forensics For Dummies
  0-7645-5580-4

- Freemasons For Dummies
  0-7645-9796-5
- French For Dummies
  0-7645-5193-0
- Geometry For Dummies
  0-7645-5324-0
- Organic Chemistry I For Dummies
  0-7645-6902-3
- The SAT I For Dummies
  0-7645-7193-1
- Spanish For Dummies
  0-7645-5194-9
- Statistics For Dummies
  0-7645-5423-9

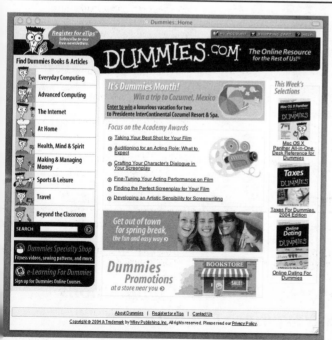

Get smart @ dummies.com®

- **Find a full list of Dummies titles**
- **Look into loads of FREE on-site articles**
- **Sign up for FREE eTips e-mailed to you weekly**
- **See what other products carry the Dummies name**
- **Shop directly from the Dummies bookstore**
- **Enter to win new prizes every month!**

* Separate Canadian edition also available
† Separate U.K. edition also available

Available wherever books are sold. For more information or to order direct: U.S. customers visit www.dummies.com or call 1-877-762-2974.
U.K. customers visit www.wileyeurope.com or call 0800 243407. Canadian customers visit www.wiley.ca or call 1-800-567-4797.

Do More with Dummies

**Instructional DVDs • Music Compilations
Games & Novelties • Culinary Kits
Crafts & Sewing Patterns
Home Improvement/DIY Kits • and more!**

Check out the Dummies Specialty Shop at www.dummies.com for more information!

WILEY

Wiley Publishing, Inc.
End-User License Agreement

READ THIS. You should carefully read these terms and conditions before opening the software packet(s) included with this book "Book". This is a license agreement "Agreement" between you and Wiley Publishing, Inc. "WPI". By opening the accompanying software packet(s), you acknowledge that you have read and accept the following terms and conditions. If you do not agree and do not want to be bound by such terms and conditions, promptly return the Book and the unopened software packet(s) to the place you obtained them for a full refund.

1. **License Grant.** WPI grants to you (either an individual or entity) a nonexclusive license to use one copy of the enclosed software program(s) (collectively, the "Software") solely for your own personal or business purposes on a single computer (whether a standard computer or a workstation component of a multi-user network). The Software is in use on a computer when it is loaded into temporary memory (RAM) or installed into permanent memory (hard disk, CD-ROM, or other storage device). WPI reserves all rights not expressly granted herein.

2. **Ownership.** WPI is the owner of all right, title, and interest, including copyright, in and to the compilation of the Software recorded on the physical packet included with this Book "Software Media". Copyright to the individual programs recorded on the Software Media is owned by the author or other authorized copyright owner of each program. Ownership of the Software and all proprietary rights relating thereto remain with WPI and its licensers.

3. **Restrictions on Use and Transfer.**

   (a) You may only (i) make one copy of the Software for backup or archival purposes, or (ii) transfer the Software to a single hard disk, provided that you keep the original for backup or archival purposes. You may not (i) rent or lease the Software, (ii) copy or reproduce the Software through a LAN or other network system or through any computer subscriber system or bulletin-board system, or (iii) modify, adapt, or create derivative works based on the Software.

   (b) You may not reverse engineer, decompile, or disassemble the Software. You may transfer the Software and user documentation on a permanent basis, provided that the transferee agrees to accept the terms and conditions of this Agreement and you retain no copies. If the Software is an update or has been updated, any transfer must include the most recent update and all prior versions.

4. **Restrictions on Use of Individual Programs.** You must follow the individual requirements and restrictions detailed for each individual program in the "About the CD" appendix of this Book or on the Software Media. These limitations are also contained in the individual license agreements recorded on the Software Media. These limitations may include a requirement that after using the program for a specified period of time, the user must pay a registration fee or discontinue use. By opening the Software packet(s), you agree to abide by the licenses and restrictions for these individual programs that are detailed in the "About the CD" appendix and/or on the Software Media. None of the material on this Software Media or listed in this Book may ever be redistributed, in original or modified form, for commercial purposes.

5. **Limited Warranty.**

   (a) WPI warrants that the Software and Software Media are free from defects in materials and workmanship under normal use for a period of sixty (60) days from the date of purchase of this Book. If WPI receives notification within the warranty period of defects in materials or workmanship, WPI will replace the defective Software Media.

   (b) WPI AND THE AUTHOR(S) OF THE BOOK DISCLAIM ALL OTHER WARRANTIES, EXPRESS OR IMPLIED, INCLUDING WITHOUT LIMITATION IMPLIED WARRANTIES OF MERCHANTABILITY AND FITNESS FOR A PARTICULAR PURPOSE, WITH RESPECT TO THE SOFTWARE, THE PROGRAMS, THE SOURCE CODE CONTAINED THEREIN, AND/OR THE TECHNIQUES DESCRIBED IN THIS BOOK. WPI DOES NOT WARRANT THAT THE FUNCTIONS CONTAINED IN THE SOFTWARE WILL MEET YOUR REQUIREMENTS OR THAT THE OPERATION OF THE SOFTWARE WILL BE ERROR FREE.

   (c) This limited warranty gives you specific legal rights, and you may have other rights that vary from jurisdiction to jurisdiction.

6. **Remedies.**

   (a) WPI's entire liability and your exclusive remedy for defects in materials and workmanship shall be limited to replacement of the Software Media, which may be returned to WPI with a copy of your receipt at the following address: Software Media Fulfillment Department, Attn.: *Cutting Edge PowerPoint 2007 For Dummies*, Wiley Publishing, Inc., 10475 Crosspoint Blvd., Indianapolis, IN 46256, or call 1-800-762-2974. Please allow four to six weeks for delivery. This Limited Warranty is void if failure of the Software Media has resulted from accident, abuse, or misapplication. Any replacement Software Media will be warranted for the remainder of the original warranty period or thirty (30) days, whichever is longer.

   (b) In no event shall WPI or the author be liable for any damages whatsoever (including without limitation damages for loss of business profits, business interruption, loss of business information, or any other pecuniary loss) arising from the use of or inability to use the Book or the Software, even if WPI has been advised of the possibility of such damages.

   (c) Because some jurisdictions do not allow the exclusion or limitation of liability for consequential or incidental damages, the above limitation or exclusion may not apply to you.

7. **U.S. Government Restricted Rights.** Use, duplication, or disclosure of the Software for or on behalf of the United States of America, its agencies and/or instrumentalities "U.S. Government" is subject to restrictions as stated in paragraph (c)(1)(ii) of the Rights in Technical Data and Computer Software clause of DFARS 252.227-7013, or subparagraphs (c) (1) and (2) of the Commercial Computer Software - Restricted Rights clause at FAR 52.227-19, and in similar clauses in the NASA FAR supplement, as applicable.

8. **General.** This Agreement constitutes the entire understanding of the parties and revokes and supersedes all prior agreements, oral or written, between them and may not be modified or amended except in a writing signed by both parties hereto that specifically refers to this Agreement. This Agreement shall take precedence over any other documents that may be in conflict herewith. If any one or more provisions contained in this Agreement are held by any court or tribunal to be invalid, illegal, or otherwise unenforceable, each and every other provision shall remain in full force and effect.